PEARSON

my World GEOGRAPHY

Africa

D1360009

PEARSON

Boston, Massachusetts • Chandler, Arizona • Glenview, Illinois • Upper Saddle River, New Jersey

Acknowledgments appear on page T93, which constitutes an extension of this copyright page.

ISBN-13 978-0-13-369586-1
ISBN-10 0-13-369586-7

14 16

Master Teachers and Contributing Authors

George Sabato
Past President, California Council
for the Social Studies
Placerville Union School District
Placerville, California

Michael Yell
Past President, National Council
for the Social Studies
Hudson Middle School
Hudson, Wisconsin

Program Authors

Gregory H. Chu
Professor and Chair of Department
of Geography
University of Wisconsin-La Crosse
La Crosse, Wisconsin

Don Holtgrieve
Department of Planning, Public
Policy, and Management
University of Oregon
Eugene, Oregon

Susan Hardwick
Department of Geography
University of Oregon
Eugene, Oregon

Program Consultant

Grant Wiggins
President of Authentic Education
Hopewell, New Jersey

Teacher Consultants

James F. Dowd IV
Pasadena, California

Susan M. Keane
Rochester Memorial School
Rochester, Massachusetts

Timothy T. Sprain
Lincoln Middle School
La Crosse, Wisconsin

Marilyn Weiser
North Dakota Geographic
Alliance Coordinator
Minot State University
Minot, North Dakota

CONTENTS

Africa

How to Read the Table of Contents

- T page numbers refer to teacher resource pages.
- Other page numbers refer to Student Edition pages.
- Follow the first number if your students use the Eastern Hemisphere edition. Follow the second number if your students use the World Geography edition.

Note: Case Study and Primary Source Student Edition pages appear only in the Eastern Hemisphere edition. Survey users can access these pages online at myworldgeography.com.

	Eastern Hemisphere	World Geography
Africa Regional Overview	322	494
West and Central Africa Chapter Resource Guide	T2	T2
myStory: A String of Dreams	329	501
Section 1 Chapter Atlas	T8	T8
Section 2 History of West and Central Africa	T14	T14
Case Study: Famous Cities and Kingdoms of West Africa	T20	T20
Section 3 West and Central Africa Today	T22	T22
Primary Source: *Things Fall Apart*	T28	T28
West and Central Africa **Chapter Assessment**	358	524
Southern and Eastern Africa Chapter Resource Guide	T30	T30
myStory: A Hopeful Song	361	527
Section 1 Chapter Atlas	T36	T36
Section 2 History of Southern and Eastern Africa	T42	T42

Evelyn, from Ghana, in West Africa ▲

Primary Source: Literature of
Southern and Eastern Africa ....T48 ....T48

Section 3 Southern and Eastern
Africa Today ....T50 ....T50

Case Study: The Effects of
Colonialism ....T56 ....T56

Southern and Eastern Africa
Chapter Assessment 390 550

North Africa Chapter Resource Guide ....T58 ....T58

myStory: Shaimaa's Neighborhood 393 553

Section 1 Chapter Atlas ....T64 ....T64

Section 2 History of North Africa ....T70 ....T70

Case Study: Ancient
Egyptian Culture ....T76 ....T76

Section 3 North Africa Today ....T78 ....T78

Primary Source: Reform in Morocco ....T84 ...... T84

North Africa **Chapter Assessment** 422 576

Unit Closer **21st Century Learning** 424 578

Answer Key ....T86 ....T86

Shaimaa, from Egypt, in North Africa ▼

Khulekani, from South Africa ▶

Africa

- Prepare to learn about Africa and activate prior knowledge by creating KWL (Know, Want to know, Learned) tables, filling out only the K and W columns. Correct any misconceptions or misinformation on the tables.

- Have students preview maps, photos, and other visuals and predict what they will learn about Africa.

GUIDE ON THE SIDE

What time is it there? Have students look at the time zone display to determine by how many hours the times in Washington, D.C., and Accra, Ghana, differ. (5 hours)

Analyze Maps Point out the political map and have students answer the following questions.

- What are the capitals of Algeria, the Republic of the Congo, and Namibia? (Algiers, Brazzaville, and Windhoek)

- What major bodies of water surround Africa? (Atlantic Ocean, Mediterranean Sea, Indian Ocean)

- Why might some people say northern Africa is part of Europe? (Many countries in northern Africa are just a short boat ride from southern Europe so they might share cultural features.)

Regional Overview

Africa

The continent of Africa is home to a wide range of climates and ecosystems, from rain forests to savannas and deserts. More than 900 million Africans live in 53 countries. They speak more than 2,000 different languages and belong to several thousand ethnic groups. Some of the countries with the largest populations are Nigeria, Democratic Republic of the Congo, South Africa, Ethiopia, Morocco, and Egypt.

What time is it there?

Washington, D.C.	Accra, Ghana
9 A.M. Monday	2 P.M. Monday

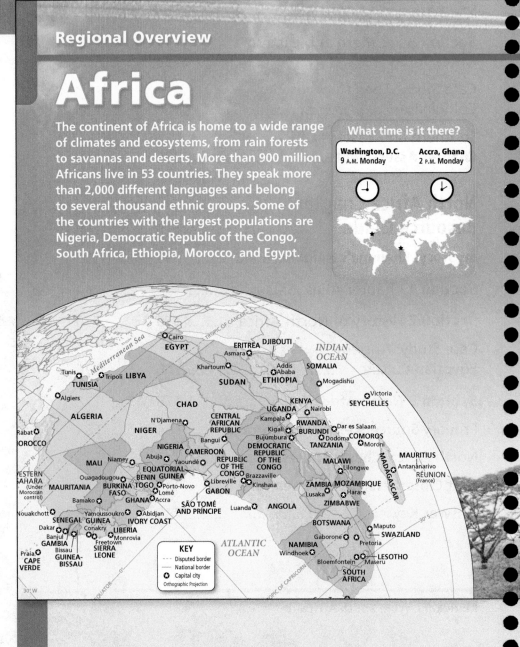

NOTES

THE UNIT AHEAD

In this unit, students will

- study the geography of Africa.
- get to know teenagers from Ghana, South Africa, and Egypt.
- go On Assignment in West, Central, Northern, Eastern, and Southern Africa.
- make connections between the physical geography, history, politics, and culture of Africa.

✈ **The Unit Ahead**	⇨ **Chapter 6** West and Central Africa
	⇨ **Chapter 7** Southern and Eastern Africa
	⇨ **Chapter 8** North Africa

my worldgeography.com

Plan your trip online by doing a Data Discovery Activity and watching the myStory Videos of the region's teens.

my Story

Evelyn
Age: 15
Home: Kpong, Ghana
Chapter 6

my Story

Khulekani
Age: 19
Home: Port St. Johns, South Africa
Chapter 7

my Story

Shaimaa
Age: 18
Home: Cairo, Egypt
Chapter 8

Giraffes on the savanna in Tanzania

GUIDE ON THE SIDE

my Story

Make Predictions Make predictions about the teens you will get to know in this unit.

- What do the photos suggest about ethnicity in Africa? (It is diverse.)

- Find the communities in which Khulekani and Shaimaa live. Given the distance between South Africa and Egypt, how might the teens' lives be different? How might they be the same? (Sample: The cultures and geographies of the two cities are probably very different, but teenagers everywhere have overlapping experiences as they become adults.)

NOTES

GEOGRAPHY

Sahara The Sahara stretches 3,000 miles (4,830 km) across the African continent and covers 3,500,000 square miles (9,065,000 sq km) total. Still, the Sahara is not all the same. Some parts are the sand dunes often associated with desert. Most of the Sahara, however, is rocky plateaus or rough gravel. The land covers two very different, but equally important, treasures. First, there is water at the surface of oases and two rivers, and under the surface in seasonal streams and deep aquifers. Second, there are huge deposits of mineral wealth, such as copper and iron, and fossil fuels, such as oil and gas.

GUIDE ON THE SIDE

Analyze Visuals Ask students to look at the labeled satellite photo, which shows key physical patterns in the region.

- Which parts of the region are mostly desert? (northern Africa and southern Africa)

- How is the Kalahari Desert different from the Sahara? (It is smaller. It has more semi-desert areas while the Sahara is mostly true desert.)

- Which parts of Africa have no desert? (Central Africa and much of western Africa have no desert.)

- What role might water as a natural resource play in the different parts of Africa? (In the desert parts, access to water is probably crucially important for survival. In the center of Africa, there is probably more than enough water for all needs.)

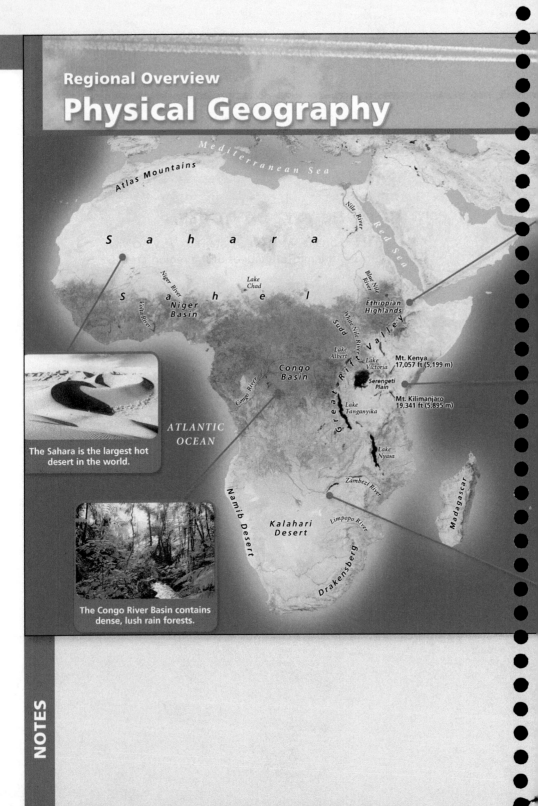

Regional Overview
Physical Geography

The Sahara is the largest hot desert in the world.

The Congo River Basin contains dense, lush rain forests.

QUICK FACTS

Serengeti Many of the animals on the Serengeti plain live in Tanzania's Serengeti National Park. The Park provides protected land for more than 1,000,000 wildebeests and gazelle, 200,000 zebras, and 3,000 lions, elephants, and rhinoceros. Visitors can sometimes see massive herds moving across the treeless plain, migrating in and out of nearby Maasai Mara Game Reserve in neighboring Kenya.

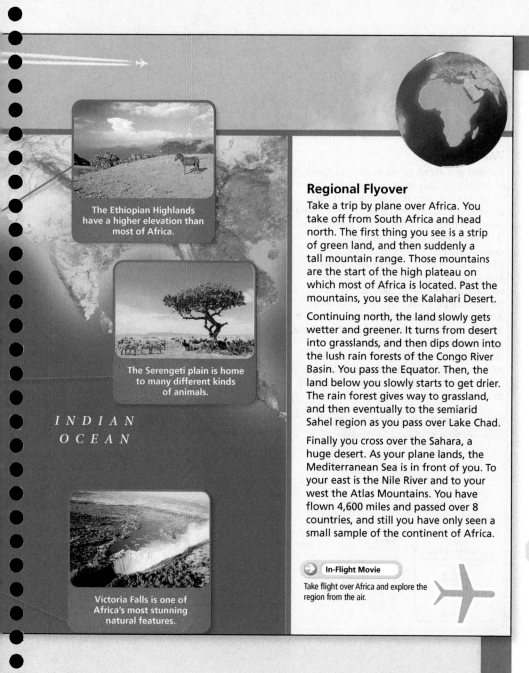

The Ethiopian Highlands have a higher elevation than most of Africa.

The Serengeti plain is home to many different kinds of animals.

INDIAN OCEAN

Victoria Falls is one of Africa's most stunning natural features.

Regional Flyover

Take a trip by plane over Africa. You take off from South Africa and head north. The first thing you see is a strip of green land, and then suddenly a tall mountain range. Those mountains are the start of the high plateau on which most of Africa is located. Past the mountains, you see the Kalahari Desert.

Continuing north, the land slowly gets wetter and greener. It turns from desert into grasslands, and then dips down into the lush rain forests of the Congo River Basin. You pass the Equator. Then, the land below you slowly starts to get drier. The rain forest gives way to grassland, and then eventually to the semiarid Sahel region as you pass over Lake Chad.

Finally you cross over the Sahara, a huge desert. As your plane lands, the Mediterranean Sea is in front of you. To your east is the Nile River and to your west the Atlas Mountains. You have flown 4,600 miles and passed over 8 countries, and still you have only seen a small sample of the continent of Africa.

 In-Flight Movie

Take flight over Africa and explore the region from the air.

Regional Flyover

Analyze Visuals Read Regional Flyover and ask the following questions about the labeled satellite photo.

- Which parts of Africa get the most rainfall? (areas near the Equator and on coasts)

- Why might people live in areas with rainfall? (Water is essential to life.)

- What are some ways that natural features might help Africans make a living? (Sample: taking visitors to natural features, fishing, hunting animals, growing crops)

- What features of Africa might be interesting to visitors? (natural wonders such as Victoria Falls, the Serengeti, or the rainforest)

◯ **Inflight Movie**

Before playing the Inflight Movie, ask students these questions:
- What have you seen or would you expect to see while looking out the window of a plane?
- What can you find out about a place by flying overhead?
- How is this information important to understanding the geography of a place?

CORE CONCEPTS: WATER AND CLIMATE

Review Core Concepts 3.3 before discussing the importance of water to Africa's human geography. Discuss the water cycle and the difference between fresh and salt water. Then remind students that the human body contains about 50–75 percent water and that people in some places use as much as 100 gallons (380 liters) each day. Have students conclude why water is so important to human life and suggest what life would be like with very little water. Help them connect the discussion to population patterns in Africa.

Water

Analyze Visuals Indicate the population density and precipitation maps. Have students use these visuals with the text to better understand the human geography of Africa.

- What parts of Africa are most densely populated? (the central band and eastern coast)

- What parts of Africa get the most rain? (the central band)

- Find Cairo in the population density map. Then find it on the precipitation map. How can you explain the city's population density? Check the physical map from this Unit Opener for a hint. (There must be another source of water besides rainfall, such as the Nile River.)

Regional Overview
Human Geography

Water

Rainfall and access to water are so important in Africa that they largely determine where its people live. Few people live in the dry deserts, but huge cities can spring up where rivers cut through them. Dense populations thrive in wetter areas. In between the deserts and rain forests, smaller groups of people live on grasslands and semiarid plains. Some countries in Africa are packed with natural resources such as gold or oil, while others are less fortunate. Although Africa contains 22 percent of Earth's land, it is home to only 14 percent of Earth's people. Each region of the continent presents a different set of challenges to its people. Africans have adapted to these challenges in different ways, giving rise to a wide variety of cultures and ways of living.

Population Density in Africa

Mediterranean Sea
Cairo
EGYPT
NIGERIA
Lagos
Addis
Ababa
ETHIOPIA
ATLANTIC
OCEAN
Nairobi
Kinshasa
INDIAN
OCEAN
Johannesburg
SOUTH
AFRICA

KEY
Population Density

Persons per sq. mile	Persons per sq. kilometer
500	195
300	115
150	60
25	10
1	1

○ Large city

Precipitation in Africa

Mediterranean Sea
ATLANTIC
OCEAN
INDIAN
OCEAN

KEY
Precipitation

cm per year	in. per year
300	120
100	40
60	25
40	15
20	10
10	5

0   1,000 mi
0   1,000 km
Lambert Azimuthal Equal-Area Projection

ECONOMICS

The Costs of AIDS Another key factor affecting Africa is disease, in particular HIV/AIDS. Some fifteen million Africans have died from the virus that attacks immune systems. Their illness and subsequent deaths greatly affected the region's economy. Hospitals and healthcare workers lose money as they try to meet the needs of sick patients. Families lose the wages of ill or deceased family members and the opportunity to work if they are caring for the ill. They also sell possessions to pay for treatment and may use up savings on funerals. Communities lose food supplies as people are unable to tend to crops.

"Our fields are idle because there is nobody to work them. . . . If we are sick, or spend our time looking after family members who are sick, we have no time to spend working in the fields."

—Toby Solomon, commissioner for the Nsanje district, Malawi; "Malawi village underscores impact of AIDS", The Associated Press, October 20, 2005

myWorld IN NUMBERS

	Egypt	Ethiopia	South Africa	Nigeria	United States
Food per day per person (kcal)*	3,320	1,810	2,900	2,600	3,830
Oil production per day (barrels)	664,000	0	199,100	2,352,000	8,457,000
Gross domestic product per capita	$5,000	$700	$9,700	$2,100	$45,800
Population	82 million	83 million	49 million	146 million	304 million

SOURCE: CIA World Factbook Online, 2009
* SOURCE: UN Food and Agriculture Organization (2003)

Put It Together
1. What physical feature covers most of northern Africa?
2. Is Nigeria densely or sparsely populated?
3. How are rainfall and population density related? Why do you think this is the case?

Data Discovery
Find your own data to make a regional data table.

Size Comparison
Africa is much larger than the continental United States.

PUT IT TOGETHER 1. Sahara
2. densely populated 3. Population is greater in areas with more rainfall, probably because water is essential to people and businesses.

GUIDE ON THE SIDE

myWorld in Numbers

Analyze Visuals Point out the table and use the questions below to help students analyze the data and draw conclusions.

- Which two African countries produce the most oil? (Nigeria, Egypt)

- Does this help their economies? Explain. (Sometimes; Egypt has high oil production and high per capita GDP. Nigeria has high oil production but lower per capita GDP.)

- How do the statistics of the United States compare with those in Africa? (Its statistics are greater in every category.)

Data Discovery

Students can practice chart and graph skills online with the Data Discovery features on living in Africa. Students can use their trackers to save data for their On Assignment stories later in the unit.

Plan With Understanding by Design*

Chapter Objectives
Begin With the End in Mind

Students will demonstrate the following enduring understandings:
- The environment affects people's lives, and in turn, people affect the environment.

- Conflict affects people's safety and access to opportunities.
- People struggle to form stable economies that allow everyone to have a good quality of life.

Connect
Make Learning Meaningful

Student Edition
- **Essential Question** Who should benefit from a country's resources?
- **myStory** Evelyn both plans a future that involves her family's bead factory in Ghana and studying.

my worldgeography.com
myStory Online Get to know Evelyn and her family's business of making beads.

Student Journal
Essential Question Preview

Experience
Teach Knowledge and Skills

Student Edition
- Read Sections 1, 2, and 3.
- Answer Reading Checks and Section Assessment questions.

my worldgeography.com
On Assignment Visual Glossary, Active Atlas, Data Discovery, Timeline, Culture Close-up, and Language Lesson.

Student Journal
- Sections 1, 2, and 3 Word Wise
- Sections 1, 2, and 3 Take Notes

Teacher's Edition
myWorld Activities
- Section 1: **Compare Climates** T10
- Section 2: **The Promise of Independence** T16
- Section 3: **Two Economies** T24

21st Century Learning Online Tutor
- Read Special-Purpose Maps
- Categorize
- Sequence
- Give an Effective Presentation
- Identify Main Ideas and Details
- Draw Conclusions

Understand
Assess Understanding

Assessment Booklet
- Chapter Tests
- Benchmark Tests

Teacher's Edition
myWorld Chapter Activity
Students study oil's effect on other countries in order to advise a fictional African leader on how to take advantage of newly discovered oil.

Student Journal
Essential Question Writer's Workshop

my worldgeography.com
On Assignment Students will write an article or create a multimedia slideshow about their virtual travels in the region.

Success Tracker™
Online at myworldgeography.com
Administer chapter tests and remediate understanding.

Student Edition
Chapter Assessment

* "Understanding by Design" is registered as a trademark with the Patent and Trademark Office by the Association for Supervision of Curriculum Development (ASCD). ASCD has not authorized, approved or sponsored this work and is in no way affiliated with Pearson or its products.

Connect to the Essential Question

 Essential Question

Who should benefit from a country's resources?

Use the Essential Question poster and follow these steps to help students understand the Essential Question.

Connect to Their Lives

1. Have students discuss the way they might divide up a pizza pie they were sharing with friends. (If students have already studied the Essential Question, encourage them to note changes in the way they think people should share things now.) As students respond, note the different they share among groups. In some groups, everyone might get the same number of slices. In others, most might go to the person with the biggest appetite. Or the pie might might be divided according to how much each person paid. Ask, What is the fairest way to share?

2. Have students consider advantages and disadvantages of different ways of sharing. Post the following table for them to complete

Different Ways to Share				
Sharing Strategy	Equal portions for all	Biggest appetite gets more	More for those who pay more	Other
Pros				
Cons				

3. Discuss student's responses. Ask, Why do different people think different ways of sharing are best?

Connect to the Content

4. Now have the students brainstorm ways that countries can divide up the benefits from their natural resources. They might point out that resources seem to go to the wealthiest, or argue that benefits should be divided up equally between all people.

5. Ask students to identify how the places in the chapter have shared resources. Post the following chart for them to complete.

Ways to Divide Resources in the Real World			
Sharing Strategy	Shares are based on need.	Wealthy and powerful people take more than others.	Everybody fights.
Used here?			
Example (if used)			

Explore   worldgeography.com

Welcome to myWorldGeography

http://www.myworldgeography.com

ON ASSIGNMENT: West and Central Africa

For this chapter's assignment, students will
- take a digital trip to West and Central Africa.
- take on the role of a journalist.
- gather notes, images, and data throughout their journey.
- write an article or create a multimedia slideshow connecting the information and images gathered during their trip and this chapter's Essential Question, *Who should benefit from a country's resources?*

ITINERARY

During their trip, students will make the following stops:

 myStory Video

Learn more about daily life in Ghana by visiting Evelyn.

 Active Atlas

Read physical, climate, and natural resources maps on West and Central Africa.

Timeline

Explore a timeline about early trading kingdoms in West Africa.

 Culture Close-up

Check out a griot's performance.

 Data Discovery

Gather data about literacy rates in West and Central Africa.

Self-Test

Assess their own knowledge of chapter content.

While on their trip, students will practice the following skills:

- **Analyze timelines** to learn more about the region's past.
- **Draw conclusions** about how natural resources are used.

TIGed
TakingITGlobal for Educators

Extend the reach of every lesson by helping students connect to a global community of young people with common interests and concerns. Visit myworldgeography.com to
- explore Country Pages relating to West and Central Africa.
- delve deeper into this chapter's Essential Question, *Who should benefit from a country's resources?*
- find online alternatives to and solutions for the Unit Closer 21st Century Learning Activity.

 worldgeography.com

TEACHER CENTER

Preview and assign student materials, enrich your teaching, and track student progress with the following resources:
- Online Lesson Planning and Resource Library
- Presentations for Projection
- Online Teacher's Edition and Ancillaries
- Google Earth Links

Assess Enduring Understandings

myWorld Chapter Activity **Step-by-Step Instructions** 1 hour

To Drill or Not To Drill?

Teach this activity at the end of the chapter to assess enduring understandings.

OBJECTIVES

Students will demonstrate the following enduring understandings:
- The environment affects people's lives, and in turn, people affect the environment.
- Conflict affects people's safety and their access to opportunities.
- People struggle to form stable economies that allow everyone to have a good quality of life.

Students will provide the following evidence of understanding:
- Report on Oil Development

LEARNING STYLES
- Verbal
- Logical

MATERIALS
- Activity Support: Student Instructions and Rubric, p. T6
- Activity Support: Evaluation Report, p. T7
- Paper and pens/pencils
- Activity Cards: #73–78
  73. Harming the Environment
  74. Bringing in Money
  75. Fighting over New Wealth
  76. Sharing the Wealth
  77. Surviving a One-Resource Economy
  78. Creating Jobs

Activity Steps

1. **Set Expectations:** Tell students that they will be playing the role of advisors to the president of a fictional nation in West and Central Africa. This nation has recently discovered a large oil deposit within its borders, and the president has asked her ministers to look at evidence to help her decide what to do about the discovery. Students will use information from the activity cards, Sections 1 through 3, and myWorldGeography.com to write an argument to support drilling or not drilling.

2. **Organize Groups:** Split the class into six groups. Give each group an activity card. Each group reads the card given to it and fills in the Evaluation Report.

   ELL Intermediate Review academic vocabulary specific to this activity before handing out the cards: *positive, negative, mixed, development, extraction, hazards, profits,* and so forth.

3. **Present to the Class and Compile Data:** Groups present their findings to the class, identifying

positive, negative, or mixed outcomes of oil development. Students listen and make careful notes tracking effects of oil development and classifying them as positive, negative, or mixed.

   L3 On-Level Allow auditory learners to use a tape recorder during the presentations.

4. **Report:** Each student writes a report recommending for or against oil drilling. Reports should respond to the questions on the next page.

   L2 Extra Support Have students first write the positive, negative, or mixed effects from their notes in complete sentences. Students can use the sentences as the basis for their report.

   ELL Early Intermediate Provide fill-in-the-blank sentences for students to complete with the effects of oil development, and have students use those sentences as the basis for their report.

Name _____ Class _____ Date _____

myWorld Chapter Activity Support **Student Instructions and Rubric**

To Drill or Not to Drill?

Activity Instructions Read the following summary of your myWorld Chapter Activity. Follow your teacher's directions for more information.

1. Read the activity card that is assigned to your group. Pay attention to the effects of oil development you see on the card.

2. Based on the information on the card, complete the Evaluation Report with your group.

3. With your group, present your findings to the class. As other groups present their data, take notes on the different effects of oil development and classify them as positive, negative, or mixed.

4. Write a report answering this question: Should your country develop the oil it has recently found? Consider these questions:
   a. What are some positive outcomes that could be caused by oil development?
   b. What are some negative outcomes that could be caused by oil development?
   c. What are some mixed outcomes that could be caused by oil development?
   d. What do you recommend should be done? Are the potential benefits more important then the serious risks?

myWorld Chapter Activity Rubric		3 Exceeds Understanding	2 Reaches Understanding	1 Approaches Understanding
Gathering Information	**Presentation**	Participates fully in preparing for and giving the presentation	Helps analyze data and prepare for presentation	Is able to describe the data collected by the group and the group's presentation plan
	Data	Divides data into "positive," "negative," and "mixed"	Divides data into "positive," and "negative"	Does not divide or group data
Report	**Clarity**	States a clear position and supports it with substantial facts	Supports an opinion with facts	Gives some of the reasons for his or her position
	Spelling and Grammar	Makes no more than one grammatical or spelling mistake	Makes some spelling and grammatical mistakes, but they do not interrupt understanding	Makes spelling and grammatical mistakes that interrupt understanding

Name _____ Class _____ Date _____

myWorld Chapter Activity Support Evaluation Report

To Drill or Not to Drill?

Directions Using the information on the Activity Card assigned to your group, identify effects of oil drilling on your country. List the effects in the table below, state whether you think they are positive, negative, or mixed, and then explain why.

Name of Your Card _____

Effects of oil drilling	Positive, negative, or mixed?	Your reasons

Based on the information on your card, how does oil development affect a country:

1 Bad for a country   **3** Good and bad   **5** Good for a country

T7

West and Central Africa

- Introduce the Essential Question so that students will be able to understand the big ideas of this chapter (see earlier page, **Connect to the Essential Question**).
- Help students prepare to learn about West and Central Africa by looking at the chapter's maps, charts, and photos.

- Have students make and record chapter predictions with the *Essential Question Preview* in the **Student Journal.**
- Ask them to analyze maps on this page.

GUIDE ON THE SIDE

Explore the Essential Question . . .

Have students complete the Essential Question Writer's Workshop in their **Student Journal** to demonstrate in-depth understanding of the question in the context of this chapter.

Analyze Maps Point out the political map.

- Which is the largest country? (the Democratic Republic of the Congo)
- What do the capitals of Senegal, Sierra Leone, Liberia, and Ghana all have in common? (They are all on the coast.)
- Both the Democratic Republic of the Congo and the Republic of the Congo are named after what natural feature? (the Congo River)

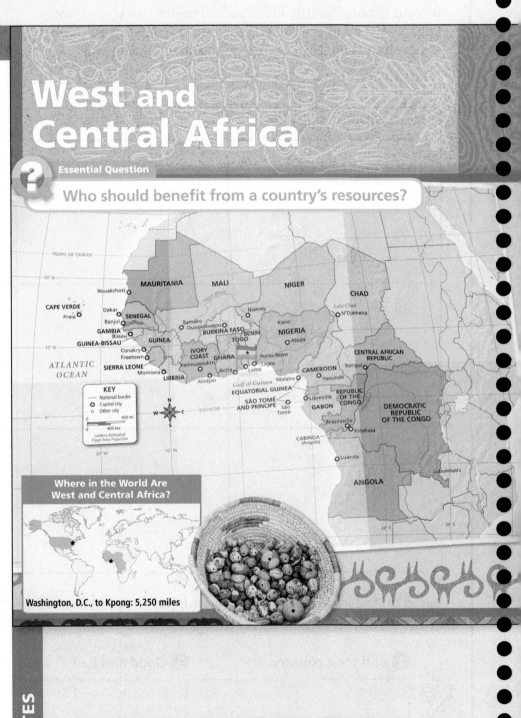

West and Central Africa

? Essential Question

Who should benefit from a country's resources?

KEY
- National border
- ⊕ Capital city
- ○ Other city

400 mi
400 km
Lambert Azimuthal
Equal-Area Projection

Where in the World Are West and Central Africa?

Washington, D.C., to Kpong: 5,250 miles

NOTES

INTRODUCE my Story

Get students excited to learn about West and Central Africa by first experiencing the region through the eyes of Evelyn, who helps her grandmother in the family's bead-making business in Ghana.

- Read myStory and watch the myStory Video about her life.
- Have students complete *A String of Dreams* in the **Student Journal** to prepare to learn about commerce and women's lives in West and Central Africa.

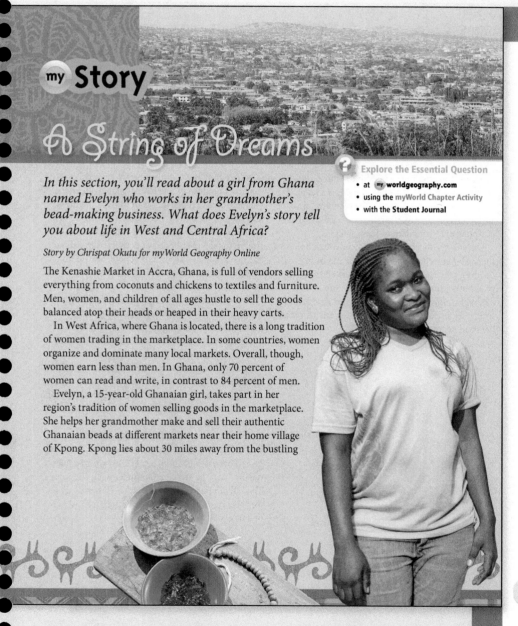

my Story

A String of Dreams

In this section, you'll read about a girl from Ghana named Evelyn who works in her grandmother's bead-making business. What does Evelyn's story tell you about life in West and Central Africa?

? Explore the Essential Question
- at **my worldgeography.com**
- using the **myWorld Chapter Activity**
- with the **Student Journal**

Story by Chrispat Okutu for myWorld Geography Online

The Kenashie Market in Accra, Ghana, is full of vendors selling everything from coconuts and chickens to textiles and furniture. Men, women, and children of all ages hustle to sell the goods balanced atop their heads or heaped in their heavy carts.

In West Africa, where Ghana is located, there is a long tradition of women trading in the marketplace. In some countries, women organize and dominate many local markets. Overall, though, women earn less than men. In Ghana, only 70 percent of women can read and write, in contrast to 84 percent of men.

Evelyn, a 15-year-old Ghanaian girl, takes part in her region's tradition of women selling goods in the marketplace. She helps her grandmother make and sell their authentic Ghanaian beads at different markets near their home village of Kpong. Kpong lies about 30 miles away from the bustling

GUIDE ON THE SIDE

my Story

A String of Dreams

- **Summarize** How do the women in Evelyn's family make their living? (They have a business making and selling beads.)

- **Compare and Contrast** What pattern will Evelyn break to make her different from other women in her family? (the pattern in which women cannot read or write, and earn less money than men)

⊙ **On Assignment**

Have students go to myworldgeography.com to receive their assignments from a virtual newspaper editor. Students will explore Ghana and beyond in order to better understand Evelyn's story and the key ideas of the chapter.

CULTURE

Ghanaian Beads Historians believe that Ghanaian bead-making began when Europeans traded beads to Africans in exchange for gold. As a result, early Ghanaian beads were copies of European-style beads. Over time, local beadmakers developed their own style. The valuable *bodom* beads that Evelyn's family makes are an early Ghanaian bead style. These beads are often the size of a golf ball. The transparent beads that Evelyn makes reflect a more recent style from the 1990s. The designs are painted onto the beads. Ghanaians consider beads to be important, perhaps having the power to heal.

GUIDE ON THE SIDE

- **Identify Details** How long has Adede been running her bead business? (over 31 years)
- **Summarize** How has Adede shared her experience with her family? (She has taught her daughters and grandchildren about bead-making.)
- **Identify Details** What role does Evelyn play in bead making? (She crushes the glass.)
- **Infer** Do you think Evelyn is strong? Explain. (Yes; crushing glass is hard work so Evelyn must be strong to do it.)

Bottles are crushed on a stone. The glass is poured into molds that are baked in a kiln.

Members of Evelyn's family string finished beads.

markets of Accra. Kpong is Evelyn's home and where her grandmother's bead business, Adede Beads Enterprises, is located. The plantain farms and thick greenery that surround the small village of Kpong are very different from Accra.

Evelyn's grandmother, Madam Adede, is a successful entrepreneur herself. She has been running the bead business she inherited from her grandfather for more than 31 years. Adede owns a humble home where she and her family live and work. The small building in the backyard serves as her bead factory.

Evelyn crushes bottle glass to make beads. The pail blocks the glass from flying up into her eyes or spilling onto the ground.

Adede specializes in the ancient craft of bead making practiced by the Krobo people of eastern Ghana. Adede taught this craft to two daughters and six grandchildren. She expects the business to continue for many generations. Adede has chosen Evelyn to take over her business someday. Evelyn has just graduated from high school. She hopes to study accounting at a university. But the cost won't be easy for her family to afford.

Evelyn already plays an important role in the family business. It is her job to crush glass in preparation for making the beads. Today she is making transparent glass beads, which are formed from a very fine glass powder. Evelyn begins by breaking glass bottles they have collected. It is hard work, but Evelyn is accustomed to the heavy labor and stifling heat that comes with everyday life at the bead factory in Kpong.

Crushing the glass is the first of many steps necessary to produce a finished piece of clear beaded jewelry. Adede explains that they also make glazed beads and *bodom* beads. The word *bodom* means "dog" in Twi, a common language in Ghana. The bodom beads are very large, bold beads, named for their resemblance to the attention-getting bark of a dog.

NOTES

QUICK FACTS

Krobo Odumase Market The market where Evelyn and her family sell beads is one of the largest in the country for beadmakers. Every Saturday, people come from miles around to sell and shop for beads.

The busy marketplace features many kinds of goods.

The sign for the family business

The family beads on sale at the Krobo Odumase Market

Beads, such as those made by Evelyn, are worn not only for adornment, but also to identify the various ethnic cultures of Ghana. Beads are often worn at parties, weddings, and church services.

Today the family is taking its beads to sell at the Krobo Odumase Market a few miles from Kpong. Adede's bead stand in the marketplace displays their colorful jewelry to the buyers in the market. Everyone works hard to sell as much as possible. They need money not only to support the family but also to send Evelyn to university.

For her part, Evelyn plans to pay back this kindness. Evelyn says, "After university, I'll get a job outside and help my grandma, too, because I have my siblings to take care of. It's important to have two jobs. So if one fails, you have the other one." The road ahead of Evelyn is difficult, but her family's bead business has paved the way.

Meet the Journalist

Name Travis Hamilton
Favorite Moment Seeing children play and laugh

myStory Video

Join Evelyn as she explores the Krobo Odumase Market.

GUIDE ON THE SIDE

- **Cause and Effect** Why does Evelyn's family work so hard? (to support themselves and to send Evelyn to university)

- **Compare and Contrast** How will Evelyn's experience be different from Adede's? How will it be the same? (She will go to university. She will work hard to take care of her family.)

 myStory Video

Have students watch the video at myworldgeography.com about Evelyn's life working in her family's bead-making business.

NOTES

SECTION 1 LESSON PLAN

Chapter Atlas

OBJECTIVES

Students will know

- physical features and climate patterns in the region.
- ways people have adapted to and changed the region's environment.

Students will be able to

- contrast regional climate zones.
- respond to regional environmental problems.

SET EXPECTATIONS

In this section, students will

- read West and Central Africa Today.
- fill in a table about different environments, their plants and animals, and the ways people have adapted to them.
- go On Assignment in West and Central Africa and study locations in the region.

CORE CONCEPTS

You may wish to teach or reteach the following lessons from the Core Concepts Handbook:

- Types of Climate, pp. 40–41
- Ecosystems, pp. 42–43
- Population Distribution, pp. 76–77

KEY

Differentiated Instruction

L1 Special Needs   **L2** Extra Support

L3 On-Level   **L4** Challenge

English Language Instruction

ELL Beginner   **ELL** Early Intermediate   **ELL** Intermediate

ELL Early Advanced   **ELL** Advanced

1 Connect
Make learning meaningful

Make Connections Ask students to think about the climate they live in. Have them list several adjectives that describe their climate, such as *warm, snowy,* or *wet.* Write some of the words on the board. Tell them they will learn about several different types of climate that exist in this region.

ELL **Beginner** Have students draw a picture of an environment they are familiar with and label it with descriptive words. Provide students with a word bank of adjectives.

Activate Prior Knowledge Remind students about the type of environment they saw in the **myStory Video.** Ask them to discuss how an environment might help determine the lifestyle of people who live in it, and how other environments might cause people to live different lifestyles.

L1 **Special Needs** Have students watch the **myStory Video** again with this question in mind: What words describe the environment Evelyn lives in?

Prepare Follow the steps in the section **Preview.** Preteach the Key Terms. Then have students complete *Word Wise* in their journals using in-text clues and the glossary for help.

2 Experience
Teach knowledge and skills

Read Use **Background** notes and **Guide on the Side** questions to model active reading. Have students use *Take Notes* in their **Student Journal** to record important places to know in West and Central Africa on an outline map. Students should use the maps in the Chapter Atlas and the Active Atlas at myworldgeography.com for assistance.

ELL **Intermediate/Early Advanced** Tell students that the suffix *-ation* can mean "the act of becoming." Have them apply this meaning to the key terms *desertification* and *deforestation*.

ELL **Advanced** Explain the colloquialism that uses the word *belt* to describe an area, comparing *tsetse belt* from the section with other uses of the word *belt*.

L4 **Challenge** Have students read *Enrichment: Rainforests of Central Africa.*

Practice: myWorld Activity Students will review and compare the different environments of West and Central Africa. Turn to pages T10–T11 for **Step-by-Step Instructions** and **More Activities.** Have students complete **21st Century Online Tutor** *Categorize* and apply this skill to the activity.

T8

SECTION 1 RESOURCE GUIDE

FOR THE STUDENT

my worldgeography.com Student Center
- Active Atlas

Student Edition (print and online)
- Chapter Atlas

Student Journal (print and online)
- Section 1 Word Wise
- Section 1 Take Notes

21st Century Learning Online Tutor
- Read Special-Purpose Maps
- Categorize

FOR THE TEACHER

my worldgeography.com Teacher Center
- Online Lesson Planner
- Presentations for Projection
- SuccessTracker

ProGuide: Africa
- Lesson Plan, pp. T8–T9
- 🏃 myWorld Activity Step-by-Step Instructions, p. T10
- Activity Support: Pick an Environment, p. T11
- myWorld Geography Enrichment, p. T12
- Section Quiz, p. T13

Accelerating the Progress of ELLs
- Organizing Information Strategies, p. 48

3 Understand
Assess understanding

Review Review *Word Wise* and *Take Notes* in the **Student Journal.**

Assess Knowledge and Skills Use the Section Assessment and Section Quiz to check students' progress.

Assess Understanding Review students' responses to the Section Assessment Essential Question prompt.

Remediate Use these strategies to review and remediate.

If students struggle to . . .	Try these strategies.
Understand the concept of climate belts.	Review the climate map, pointing out how the climate gets drier the farther one goes from the equator.
Read the special-purpose maps in the section.	Assign additional practice with the **21st Century Online Tutor.**
Understand how people use the land.	Make a 2-column table on the board showing economic activities in one column and natural resources/land required in the other.

ELL Support

ELL Objective Students will be able to use comparative and superlative forms of words to discuss climate.

Cultural Connections Ask students to share how they would say one climate is colder than another climate or is the coldest climate in their home language. Ask them to assign places that are colder than others or the coldest from their home country or their family's home country.

ELL Intermediate Content Tip Use the climate map in Section 1 and the pictures that accompany it to help students understand what different climates might look and feel like in this region.

ELL Activity Ask students to draw a line and guide them to label it as a continuum from driest to wettest. Then have them place the climate zones from the region on this continuum. **(Logical)**

my worldgeography.com Lesson Planner

myWorld Activity   **Step-by-Step Instructions**

 15 min

Compare Climates

OBJECTIVES
Students will
- distinguish between the different climate zones of West and Central Africa.
- explain how people adapt to these different climate zones.

Activity Steps

1. Tell students they will be asked to categorize which plants and animals live in which West and Central African climate regions, and how people have adapted their lifestyles to fit the different environments. They will then draw a picture of one of the environments.

2. Have students complete *Activity Support: Pick an Environment*. They will write the names of plants and animals in the correct boxes and write a sentence about how people might adapt to life in each climate.

   ELL Beginner Show students a picture of each of

LEARNING STYLE
- Visual
- Logical

21st Century Learning
- Categorize

MATERIALS
- Blank paper
- Colored pencils
- Activity Support: Pick an Environment, p. T11

the plants and animals listed on the Activity Support to make the activity more concrete and visual.

3. Assign students to draw a picture of one of the four climate regions. Make sure that they include plants and animals and people who have adapted to that environment.

   L1 Special Needs Allow students who have trouble concentrating to choose which environment they will draw.

4. Post students' pictures on the wall. Have students discuss the differences between the climate regions as a class.

More Activities From myWorld Teachers

Local Connections Have students look at a climate map of the United States and determine what climate zone they live in. Ask them to create a Venn diagram, comparing and contrasting their climate with the tropical wet climate in the Democratic Republic of the Congo. **(Visual)**

Pack Your Bags Tell students that they are taking a trip to one of the climate zones of West and Central Africa. They are to "pack their bag" so that they have the appropriate clothing and other supplies to

live in that environment for a week. Make sure students consider the time of year for certain climate zones. **(Logical)**

Where to Go? Have students meet in groups and discuss what they consider to be the most desirable conditions in which to live. After they establish what they consider their ideal conditions, have them try to locate places in West and Central Africa that best meet those conditions, and note what type of human settlements appear there. **(Verbal)**

 my worldgeography.com **Teacher Center** ➔ Find additional resources in the online Teacher Center.

Name _____ Class _____ Date _____

myWorld Activity Support   **Pick an Environment**

Compare Climates

Directions Match each animal and plant with the climate it lives in by writing one plant and one animal name in each box in the table. Then complete the list below.

Plants

Date palm trees grow well in hot, dry places.

Baobab trees can survive long droughts.

Grass grows during the rainy season and dies in the dry season.

Ferns live in wet, shady places.

Animals

Scorpions like very hot temperatures and spend time burrowed under sand dunes.

Senegal gerbils live off vegetation but prefer dry places.

Gazelles eat grass and can migrate to where grazing is best.

Bonobo chimpanzees eat fruit and sleep in trees.

	Desert (arid)	Sahel (semiarid)	Savanna (tropical wet and dry)	Rainforest (tropical wet)
Animals				
Plants				

List one way that humans might change their lifestyle to survive in each climate zone.

1. Desert _____

2. Sahel _____

3. Savanna _____

4. Rainforest _____

T11

Name _____ Class _____ Date _____

Enrichment: Rain Forests of Central Africa

Directions Read the selection below. Then answer the questions
that follow and complete the activity.

Rain forests cover hundreds of thousands of square
miles of the Congo River Basin in Central Africa.
Equatorial rain forests are one of the most unusual
ecosystems on Earth. Rain forests are divided into
layers stacked one on top of another. Each is home
to different plants and animals.

Heavy rains allow trees to grow very tall and
dense. The highest layer of the forest is the
canopy, made of the tops of the tallest trees.
Animals who live in this layer need to be able to
fly or jump expertly to move from tree to tree.
Parrots and different species of monkeys thrive in
the canopy.

Below the canopy is the understory. The canopy blocks most light
before it reaches this layer, yet smaller trees, beautiful orchids, and
many animals live there. At the lowest level, even less light reaches
the plants and animals. Because of this, few plants grow on the forest
floor. Larger animals like mountain gorillas live there.

Surprisingly, rain forest soil is often not very fertile. Heat and humidity
cause plant matter to break down too quickly. Thick layers of rich soil
cannot build up. When people clear the forest to plant crops, the soil
wears out quickly. People then clear a new patch of forest. In this way,
the soil's lack of fertility contributes to deforestation.

1. Why do different plants and animals live in different layers of
the rain forest?

_____

_____

2. How do the rain forest's poor soils contribute to deforestation?

_____

3. Activity Draw a diagram of the three main layers of the rain forest.
Research more plants and animals that live in each layer and
include them in your diagram.

Name _____ Class _____ Date _____

Section Quiz

Directions Answer the following questions using what you learned
in Section 1.

1. _____ In which climate zone is the Sahel
located?
  a. arid
  b. semiarid
  c. tropical wet
  d. tropical wet and dry

2. _____ What is the expansion of deserts
called?
  a. deforestation
  b. desertification
  c. evaporation
  d. decimation

3. _____ What spreads malaria?
  a. tsetse flies
  b. giraffes
  c. mosquitoes
  d. air pollution

4. _____ Which of the follow is <u>not</u> located in
Western and Central Africa?
  a. Nile Basin
  b. Niger Basin
  c. Chad Basin
  d. Congo Basin

5. _____ What does it mean for land to be
arable?
  a. It is rich in mineral resources.
  b. It is covered with forests.
  c. It is swarming with insects.
  d. It is able to be farmed.

6. Complete the chart to demonstrate your understanding of West
and Central Africa's different climate zones.

Climate Zone	Description
Arid	Dry year-round, desert
Semiarid	
Tropical wet and dry	
Tropical wet	

Chapter Atlas

- Model preparing to read by previewing the Key Ideas, Key Terms, headings, visuals, and captions. Have students make predictions about what they will learn. For ELL support, post the prompt, "I predict I will read about . . ."
- Preview and practice reading special-purpose maps by discussing the population density map on page 338. Help students make predictions about

the population patterns the map might show. Ask, What contrasts does the map show? (great population density and low population density)

- Preteach this section's high-use Academic Vocabulary and Key Terms using the table on the next page and in-text definitions. Have students practice Key Terms by completing the *Word Wise* page in their journals.

GUIDE ON THE SIDE

Physical Features

- **Identify Details** What large desert is partly in West and Central Africa? (the Sahara)
- **Compare and Contrast** How do the Sahara and the tropical rainforest differ? (One is very dry, and the other has plentiful rainfall.)
- **Predict** Why would you guess that West and Central Africa is dry in the north, wet in the center, and dry again in the south? (sample: because of its location near the Equator, different patterns of rainfall)

 Reading Skill

Label an Outline Map While they read, have students identify the Places to Know! on the outline map of the region in the **Student Journal.**

Section 1
Chapter Atlas

Key Ideas
- Location together with wind and rainfall patterns creates a wide variety of environments in West and Central Africa.
- Climate zones vary from very dry to wet and tropical.
- Climate zones influence where and how people live in West and Central Africa.
- People have both adapted to and changed the environments of this region.

Key Terms • Sahel • savanna • arable land • desertification • deforestation • malaria

⟶ Visual Glossary

🌐 **Reading Skill: Label an Outline Map** Take notes using the outline map in your journal.

A group of people travels by boat on the Niger River in Niger. ▼

Physical Features
The physical features of West and Central Africa are rich and varied. They range from vast deserts to dense rain forests. The world's largest hot desert, the Sahara, reaches down into West and Central Africa from the north. Other dry areas also occur in the far south. Between the dry areas, grasslands blend into the lush tropical rainforest at the region's center.

In contrast, the region's landforms do not have great variety. Much of the continent of Africa as a whole is a plateau. Although highland areas exist, no major mountain chains interrupt the plateau.

ACADEMIC VOCABULARY

High-Use Word	Definition and Sample Sentence
strategy	*n.* a plan for reaching a goal *Sam had a thorough strategy for balancing school and sports.*
decade	*n.* a period of ten years *On your tenth birthday, you had been alive for a decade.*

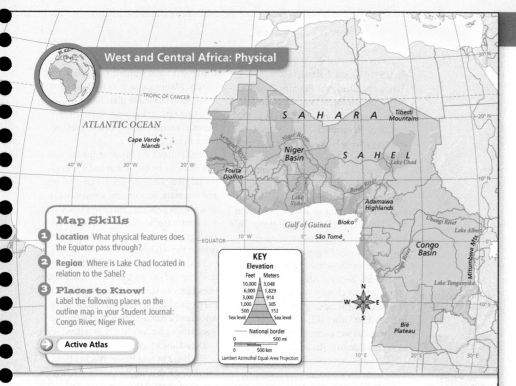

West and Central Africa: Physical

Map Skills

1. **Location** What physical features does the Equator pass through?
2. **Region** Where is Lake Chad located in relation to the Sahel?
3. **Places to Know!** Label the following places on the outline map in your Student Journal: Congo River, Niger River.

➤ **Active Atlas**

KEY
Elevation
Feet	Meters
10,000	3,048
6,000	1,829
3,000	914
1,000	305
500	152
Sea level	Sea level

—— National border

0   500 mi
0   500 km
Lambert Azimuthal Equal-Area Projection

GUIDE ON THE SIDE

- **Identify Details** What is a drainage basin? (the entire area of land that drains into a river or lake)
- **Compare and Contrast** How is Lake Chad similar to the Congo River? (Both drain large areas of land of water.)
- **Draw Conclusions** If most of the Niger River is navigable, how might this affect the people who live along it? (They will be able to more easily trade and communicate with one another.)

Map Skills Ask students to look at the physical map and answer the following questions:

- Which has a lower elevation, the Niger Basin or the Congo Basin? (the Niger Basin)
- How can you use elevation to see that the Bié Plateau is a plateau? (It is a large area with a constant, high elevation.)

➤ **Active Atlas**

- Have students go to myworldgeography.com to see more data about the physical geography of West and Central Africa.

The plateau has been ground down by millions of years of weathering and erosion. Low elevations in the northwest build to higher elevations in the southeast.

West and Central Africa boasts some of the largest drainage basins in the world. A drainage basin is the entire area of land from which rainfall flows into a river or lake. The Chad basin drains a huge area. At its center lies the large but shallow Lake Chad. Lake Chad is the largest body of water in the Sahel. The **Sahel** is a semiarid, fairly dry area that lies between the Sahara and regions to the south that receive more rainfall.

The Niger River basin is the largest in western Africa. More rain falls in some parts of the basin than in others. Heavy rain causes flooding at times in parts of the basin.

The huge Congo River drains most of central Africa. Heavy rainfall feeds the Congo through most of the year. In fact, the Congo basin hosts Africa's largest network of navigable rivers, or rivers that ships can pass through. However, waterfalls and rapids can make passage difficult and dangerous.

Reading Check **What are two important rivers in the region?**

READING CHECK Niger River, Congo River.

MAP SKILLS 1. The Equator passes through the Congo Basin and Congo River. **2.** Lake Chad is in the Sahel region. **3.** Students should correctly locate and label each place on the outline map in their Student Journal.

ANSWERS

GEOGRAPHY

Hurricanes The same wind patterns that cause the intertropical convergence zone (ITCZ) also cause hurricanes in the United States and the Caribbean Sea. Thunderstorms occur frequently along the ITCZ. Under the right conditions, several of these thunderstorms can join together to form larger storm systems that become hurricanes.

GUIDE ON THE SIDE

A Variety of Climates

- **Identify Details** What is the ITCZ? (a belt of rising air responsible for climate patterns in the region)

- **Summarize** How do climate patterns mirror each other on both sides of the equator? (They gradually get drier farther from the Equator.)

- **Compare and Contrast** How are the Sahel and the savanna different? How are they similar? (The Sahel is drier than the savanna and is not covered with grass. Both are relatively dry.)

Analyze Visuals Have students consider the photo of the herder and his cattle.

- What climate region is this man from? (the Sahel)

- Why might he herd cattle instead of working farmland? (Agriculture is difficult in such a dry region.)

 myWorld Activity

Compare Climates Find Step-by-Step Instructions and an Activity Support on pp. T10–T11. **(Visual/Logical)**

A Variety of Climates

Africa sits astride the Equator. Roughly half of the continent is in the Northern Hemisphere, and the other half is in the Southern Hemisphere. This location strongly affects West and Central Africa's climate zones.

As you read in the Core Concepts, a belt of rising air called the intertropical convergence zone, or ITCZ, circles the Equator. The rising air causes heavy rain to fall in the ITCZ around the globe. This band of rain moves north around July and south around February. The movement creates the wet and dry seasons of the tropics. Because Africa is so flat, each of the region's climate zones gradually changes into the next. These zones are mirrored on either side of the Equator.

A tropical wet climate can be found along the Equator. Rain falls plentifully all year long, especially in spring and fall. Temperatures are warm year-round.

In West and Central Africa, dense rain forests grow in the tropical wet zone.

A man herds cattle in the semiarid Sahel.▼

The forests teem with birds, reptiles, and insects. Mammals such as monkeys and flying squirrels make their home in the forest canopy, or topmost layer. Large animals, such as elephants and gorillas, roam the forest floor.

Farther from the Equator, the climate gets drier bit by bit. North and south of the tropical wet zone lies the tropical wet and dry zone. As its name suggests, this area always gets less rain than the warmer and wetter tropical areas. Temperatures are high all year, but vary more from summer to winter.

This climate supports the **savanna**, a landscape of flat grasslands with scattered trees that can survive dry spells. Near the tropical forests, the savanna has tall woodlands. Farther from the forest, the woodlands give way to dry grassland with scattered low shrubs.

The band of rain barely reaches the Sahel. The Sahel has only a short rainy season of at most three months. Less rain falls than on the savanna. Daily temperatures are high. As in a desert, evening temperatures can dip very low.

Beyond the bands of precipitation lie the arid zones. These desert regions get little rainfall. Brutally hot days contrast with very cold nights. Not surprisingly, fewer animal species live in the drier regions, especially in the desert, where vegetation is sparse. Small mammals, such as rats and hares, are found along with gazelles, hyenas, and ostriches.

Reading Check **How is a tropical wet climate different from a tropical wet and dry climate?**

myWorld Activity
Compare Climates

READING CHECK In a tropical wet climate zone, rain falls consistently all year round. In a tropical wet and dry climate zone, rain falls heavily in some seasons while other seasons are drier.

334 Eastern Hemisphere
506 World Geography

COMMON MISCONCEPTIONS

African Jungles When many people think of Africa and especially West and Central Africa, they think of lush rainforests full of exotic animals. West and Central Africa do in fact contain large rainforests, especially in the Congo Basin. However, much of the region is very dry. The Sahara in the north is so dry that it is almost uninhabitable. In the Sahel, water scarcity is a major issue, even causing conflict as people compete over limited resources.

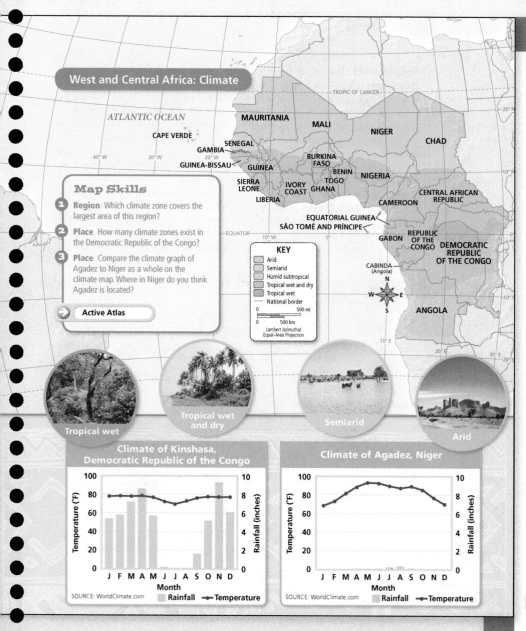

West and Central Africa: Climate

Map Skills

1. **Region** Which climate zone covers the largest area of this region?
2. **Place** How many climate zones exist in the Democratic Republic of the Congo?
3. **Place** Compare the climate graph of Agadez to Niger as a whole on the climate map. Where in Niger do you think Agadez is located?

Active Atlas

KEY
- Arid
- Semiarid
- Humid subtropical
- Tropical wet and dry
- Tropical wet
- National border

Tropical wet

Tropical wet and dry

Semiarid

Arid

Climate of Kinshasa, Democratic Republic of the Congo

SOURCE: WorldClimate.com   Rainfall — Temperature

Climate of Agadez, Niger

SOURCE: WorldClimate.com   Rainfall — Temperature

MAP SKILLS 1. tropical wet and dry **2.** three: humid subtropical, tropical wet, and tropical wet and dry **3.** Agadez is located in the northern, arid part of Niger.

GUIDE ON THE SIDE

Map Skills Point out and discuss the map.

- Name four countries that are mostly arid. (Mauritania, Mali, Niger, Chad)
- What natural feature does the tropical wet area in the Democratic Republic of the Congo fall within? (the Congo Basin)

Analyze Graphs Point out and discuss the climate graphs of Kinshasa and Agadez.

- Which city gets more rainfall? (Kinshasa)
- Comparing rainfall for April and June, which climate zone is Kinshasa in? (tropical wet and dry)

Active Atlas

- Have students go to myworldgeography.com to see more data about climates in West and Central Africa.

ANSWERS

HISTORY

Congo's Riches The natural wealth of the Democratic Republic of the Congo was one of the major reasons for Belgian colonization of the area. King Leopold II and other wealthy Belgians carved out a vast empire along the Congo River. The Belgians used forced labor and brutality to extract rubber, palm oil, and minerals from the land and treated the country's resources as their private possessions. More than a century later, the people of Central Africa are still fighting over DRC's resources.

GUIDE ON THE SIDE

People and the Land

- **Identify Details** How much of Chad's land is arable? (less than 3%)
- **Summarize** Why do more people live in the South of Chad than in the North? (because the wetter climate makes more land arable)
- **Compare and Contrast** How are the lives of desert nomads different from those of farmers in wet climates? (Sample: Nomads move from place to place and herd animals. They live in movable dwellings. Farmers live in one place and grow crops. They live in permanent homes.)

Map Skills Point out and discuss the Natural Resources map.

- What are the major natural resources of the Democratic Republic of the Congo? (hydroelectricity, diamonds, gold, oil, copper)
- Where is most of the region's oil? (on the coast)

 Active Atlas

Have students go to myworldgeography.com to see more data about the natural resources of West and Central Africa.

People and the Land

The environment of West and Central Africa affects where and how people live. Over time, the region's people have developed <u>strategies</u> to get the most out of their challenging environment. What the land and climate will support often affects how people make a living.

Take Chad as an example. Less than three percent of Chad is **arable land,** or land fit for farming. The desert areas of northern Chad support only a few groups of people. They are nomads, or people who move from place to place without a permanent home. The nomads who live in Chad raise camels and a few crops in oases. They live in easily movable dwellings, such as tents or mats attached to frames of tree branches. In central Chad, people raise cattle on the savanna. In the wetter south, people grow cotton on land that was once rain forest. Nearly half of Chad's people live in the south.

In contrast to Chad, nearly 33 percent of Nigeria's land is arable. Cacao is the biggest cash crop. Nigeria's land is rich in minerals, too. Among all of its resources, Nigeria's huge oil reserves stand out.

strategy, *n.,* a plan for reaching a goal

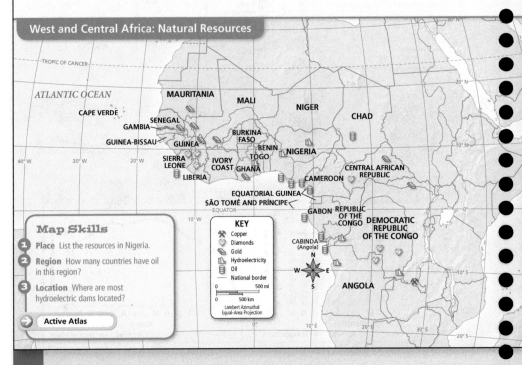

West and Central Africa: Natural Resources

Map Skills
1. **Place** List the resources in Nigeria.
2. **Region** How many countries have oil in this region?
3. **Location** Where are most hydroelectric dams located?

Active Atlas

MAP SKILLS 1. hydroelectricity, oil **2.** seven **3.** on rivers

QUICK FACTS

Deforestation Deforestation is a major environmental issue in West and Central Africa. In the wetter areas forests cover much of the land. Trees must be cut down where people want to build farms or houses. As populations rise, forests are being rapidly destroyed.

For example, 59.6 percent of the Democratic Republic of the Congo is covered in forests. From 1990 to 2000, as population grew by more than 15,000,000, more than 2,000 additional square miles of forest were lost.

Tapping this resource, however, hurts Nigeria's environment. An estimated 1.5 million tons of oil have dripped from leaky pipelines into the Niger Delta over the past 50 years. Oil seeps into wetlands, forests, and farmlands. It pollutes air and water and causes fires.

Many countries in this region have rich natural resources. Like Nigeria, Angola, Cameroon, Chad, and other countries also have oil reserves. The Democratic Republic of the Congo has deposits of copper, diamonds, uranium, and other minerals. Liberia and Sierra Leone have diamond fields. These natural resources have the potential to bring great wealth to the region. As you will read, they have also often caused conflict.

Many people in the region use land to farm and graze animals. Although not always harmful, this use of land can hurt the environment. During dry periods in the Sahel, herders allow too many of their animals to graze. In addition, people also chop down trees for firewood or to sell.

These uses, combined with drought, have caused parts of the Sahel to dry out and become desert. This change from arable land to desert is called **desertification.** Chad and other Sahel nations are working on ways to stop desertification.

The Ivory Coast (also called Côte d'Ivoire) gets plentiful rain. Even so, desertification threatens this nation as well. The main culprit is deforestation. **Deforestation** is the loss of forest cover that occurs when the trees in a forest are removed faster than they can grow back. The soil dries out without the shade of trees to protect it from the hot sun.

The Ivory Coast has a very high rate of deforestation. More than 90 percent of its forests have been cleared by the timber industry in the past few <u>decades.</u> Foreign-owned companies have done much of the harvesting of this raw material for their industries. Deforestation is also a problem in the Democratic Republic of the Congo.

decade, *n.,* a period of ten years

Reading Check **What causes desertification?**

- **Identify Details** What is Nigeria's most important resource? (oil)
- **Predict** Why might abundant natural resources cause conflict? (Sample: because people fight over who should benefit from them)
- **Analyze Text** What does *desertification* mean? (the process of lands drying out and becoming desert)

Analyze Visuals Point out the photograph of the man cutting down a tree.

- How does deforestation lead to desertification? (When trees are cut down, soil becomes loose and blown or washed away.)

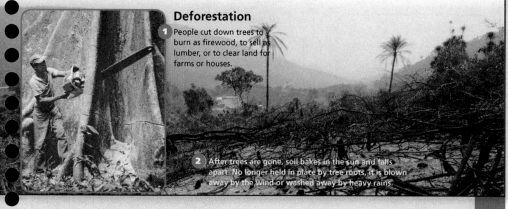

Deforestation

1 People cut down trees to burn as firewood, to sell as lumber, or to clear land for farms or houses.

2 After trees are gone, soil bakes in the sun and falls apart. No longer held in place by tree roots, it is blown away by the wind or washed away by heavy rains.

READING CHECK Too much grazing, chopping down trees, and drought all contribute to desertification.

CORE CONCEPTS: POPULATION GROWTH

Review Core Concept 6.1 before discussing West and Central Africa's growing population. Review the reasons why populations have grown rapidly in the past two centuries. Have students discuss how increasing populations can pose difficulties for poorer nations.

GUIDE ON THE SIDE

Population

- **Draw Conclusions** Why is Nigeria so populous? (It has arable land.)
- **Cause and Effect** What are three reasons why West and Central Africans move from rural areas to cities? (crop failures, desertification, and conflict)

Map Skills Point out and discuss the population map.

- Which of the region's cities have 5 million or more residents? (Lagos, Abidjan, Kinshasa)

Population

Just as the environment affects what people do for a living, it also affects where they live. As you have read, Nigeria has plenty of land that is good for farming. Not surprisingly, it also has the largest population in the region. In fact, it is the most populous nation in all of Africa, with 148 million people. In contrast, fewer people live in countries that are in desert regions. For instance, Mauritania is home to only about 3.3 million people.

People often think of Africans as rural farmers. In this region of Africa, many people do still farm or raise livestock. However, more and more people are moving to cities such as Lagos in Nigeria or Accra in Ghana.

People may move to cities to look for work because a season's crops have failed. Conflict forces others from their homes. Some move away from the Sahel because of desertification. The desert spreads to where they raise animals or crops.

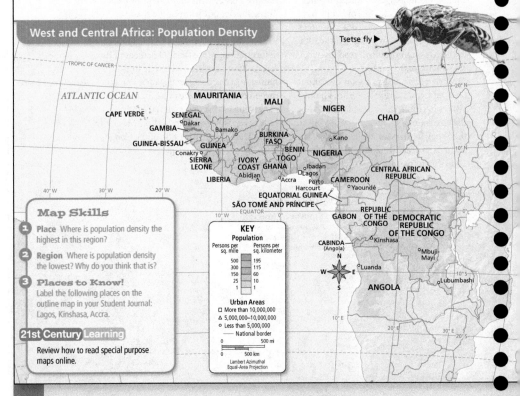

West and Central Africa: Population Density

Map Skills

1. **Place** Where is population density the highest in this region?

2. **Region** Where is population density the lowest? Why do you think that is?

3. **Places to Know!** Label the following places on the outline map in your Student Journal: Lagos, Kinshasa, Accra.

21st Century Learning
Review how to read special purpose maps online.

KEY
Population

Persons per sq. mile	Persons per sq. kilometer
500	195
300	115
150	60
25	10
1	1

Urban Areas
□ More than 10,000,000
△ 5,000,000–10,000,000
○ Less than 5,000,000
— National border

0 ___ 500 mi
0 ___ 500 km
Lambert Azimuthal
Equal-Area Projection

MAP SKILLS 1. Along the coast from Ghana to Nigeria, in northern Nigeria, and on the coast in Senegal **2.** In the north, from Mauritania to Chad, because of the Sahara Desert **3.** Students should correctly locate and label each place on the outline map in their **Student Journal**.

READING CHECK They are becoming more urban.

READING CHECK Malaria is spread by mosquitoes.

GEOGRAPHY

Malaria Malaria is a serious challenge for West and Central African countries, but it can be overcome. Although it was once endemic to the hot, humid southeastern United States, it was eradicated there by 1951. State, local, and federal governments drained places where mosquitoes bred, and sprayed DDT, an insecticide, where people lived. Although attempts were made to repeat this success in Africa, problems such as the warmer climate and lack of central organization made this impossible. Today, efforts to fight malaria concentrate on providing those at risk with anti-malarial drugs and bed-nets.

Unfortunately, the city doesn't always hold a better life for them. Because the cities are growing so quickly, they are overcrowded. There are shortages of good housing and good jobs.

Reading Check How are West and Central Africa's populations changing?

The Problem of Disease

Some big environmental challenges in West and Central Africa come in very small packages: insects. Insects carry parasites, or small organisms that live off of a larger organism. The tsetse (TEE tsee) fly spreads a parasite that causes a disease known as sleeping sickness. It is fatal to both humans and cattle. The disease is widespread. The presence of the tsetse fly limits where cattle can be raised, and where people can live.

Mosquitoes spread **malaria**, another life-threatening disease caused by parasites. Mosquitoes thrive in environments that are hot and wet. Therefore, malaria is common throughout the tropical and subtropical regions of Africa. Ninety percent of deaths from malaria occur in these regions.

Some diseases are both treatable and preventable. Sadly, many people in this region cannot afford to take even the simplest measures to protect themselves.

Nigerian doctor Emmanuel Miri visits rural villages to educate communities on disease prevention and treatment.

66 Most people in rural areas are farmers, and when you have a disease like Guinea worm [a parasite], you are incapacitated, unable to continue with your work. By preventing the hundreds of thousands of cases that we do each year, we are freeing up that many more people to farm so that they will have food and be able to take care of their families. 99

—Emmanuel Miri

Local education programs like Miri's are helping to combat many diseases.

Reading Check How does malaria spread?

my World IN NUMBERS

Mosquito nets treated with insecticide help prevent malaria. Yet, in 2007, only **6%** of households in the Ivory Coast owned one.

GUIDE ON THE SIDE

The Problem of Disease

- **Express Opinions** Do you think the challenges of city life are more difficult than the challenges of rural life? (Sample: City life is more difficult because of overcrowding.)

- **Compare and Contrast** How are malaria and sleeping sickness similar? (Both are carried by insects.)

- **Draw Conclusions** Why are so many of the world's malaria cases found in Africa? (because mosquitoes thrive in many African climate zones, and because African countries lack the resources to fight the disease)

- **Identify Details** How do tsetse flies affect where people live? (People avoid living near tsetse flies because the insects carry illness.)

Section 1 Assessment

Key Terms

1. Use the following terms to describe the challenging environment of West and Central Africa: deforestation, desertification, malaria.

Key Ideas

2. What are some ways in which the Sahel is different from the tropical wet zone?

3. Why do so few of Chad's people live in the north of the country and so many in the south?

4. What is one problem oil production causes in Nigeria?

Think Critically

5. **Summarize** Why are people in West and Central Africa moving from the countryside to the city?

6. **Draw Inferences** Use what you have learned in this section to explain why Ghana has a higher percentage of arable land than Mali.

Essential Question

Who should benefit from a country's resources?

7. How might not having abundant farmland or natural resources affect a country? Go to your Student Journal to record your answer.

SECTION 1 ASSESSMENT 1. Deforestation occurs when people cut down trees for farmland. Without trees to hold soil, desertification occurs. Malaria, a disease spread by mosquitoes, slows population growth. 2. The Sahel is dryer than the tropical wet zone, and has wet/dry seasons instead of rain all year. 3. Northern Chad is drier and less fit for agriculture than southern Chad. 4. Oil production causes environmental problems. 5. Sample: People often move to cities for work. 6. Ghana gets more rain, which creates arable land. 7. Lack of farmland or natural resources may make a country poor and less able to meet its citizens' needs.

ANSWERS

Eastern Hemisphere   **339**
World Geography   **511**

History of West and Central Africa

OBJECTIVES

Students will know

- ways that physical geography has shaped West and Central African history.
- how European colonialism and independence affected West and Central Africans.

Students will be able to

- sequence events in regional history.
- trace effects of colonialism and independence on regional societies.

SET EXPECTATIONS

In this section, students will

- read History of West and Central Africa.
- perform a skit relating to the independence of West and Central African countries.
- go On Assignment in West and Central Africa and learn about the Songhai Empire.

CORE CONCEPTS

You may wish to teach or reteach the following lessons from the Core Concepts Handbook:

- Economic Development, pp. 64–65
- Trade, pp. 66–67
- Cultural Diffusion and Change, pp. 96–97

KEY

Differentiated Instruction	English Language Instruction
L1 Special Needs **L2** Extra Support	**ELL** Beginner **ELL** Early Intermediate **ELL** Intermediate
L3 On-Level **L4** Challenge	**ELL** Early Advanced **ELL** Advanced

1 Connect
Make learning meaningful

Make Connections Ask students to think about a time when they felt as if they were treated unfairly. Ask the class to think about how West and Central Africans felt about Europeans trying to take over their region.

L3 On-Level Have students consider other ways in which people are treated unfairly today and what could be done to change the situation.

Activate Prior Knowledge Remind students that in the previous section they read about West and Central Africa's different river basins and climate zones. Ask them to consider how these different environments might affect where and how people in the past lived.

L2 Extra Support Review the physical map and the map of climate zones in the previous section.

Prepare Follow the steps in the section **Preview.** Preteach the Key Terms. Then have students complete *Word Wise* in their journals using in-text clues and the glossary for help.

2 Experience
Teach knowledge and skills

Read Use **Background** notes and **Guide on the Side** questions to model active reading. Have students use *Take Notes* in their **Student Journal** to complete a timeline of West and Central African history. Have students complete **21st Century Online Tutor** *Sequence*, and apply this skill to reading the section.

L1 Special Needs Allow students with reading difficulties to choose their own seats or reading environment. Let them use a new note card to take notes on the content under each red heading.

ELL Beginner Use gestures and an act-it-out activity to tell a story about West and Central African history, perhaps Mansa Musa's journey to Mecca.

L4 Challenge Have students read *Enrichment: Kwame Nkrumah* to learn about one of West and Central Africa's most important independence leaders.

 Practice: myWorld Activity Students will trade colored pieces of paper to simulate the gold-salt trade. **Step-by-Step Instructions** and **More Activities** follow on pp. T16–T17.

SECTION 2 RESOURCE GUIDE

FOR THE STUDENT

my worldgeography.com Student Center
- Timeline

Student Edition (print and online)
- History of West and Central Africa

Student Journal (print and online)
- Section 2 Word Wise
- Section 2 Take Notes

21st Century Learning Online Tutor
- Sequence
- Give an Effective Presentation

FOR THE TEACHER

my worldgeography.com Teacher Center
- Online Lesson Planner
- Presentations for Projection
- SuccessTracker

ProGuide: Africa
- Lesson Plan, pp. T14–T15
- myWorld Activity Step-by-Step Instructions, p. T16
- Activity Support: Hopes and Challenges Skit, p. T17
- myWorld Geography Enrichment, p. T18
- Section Quiz, p. T19

Accelerating the Progress of ELLs
- Peer Learning Strategies, p. 46

3 Understand
Assess understanding

Review Review *Word Wise* and *Take Notes* in the **Student Journal.**

Assess Knowledge and Skills Use the Section Assessment and the Section Quiz to check students' progress.

Assess Understanding Review students' responses to the Section Assessment Essential Question prompt.

Remediate Use these strategies to review and remediate.

If students struggle to . . .	Try these strategies.
Sequence historical events	Extend practice with the **21st Century Online Tutor.**
Describe the impact of trade in the region	Have students simulate effects of trade, such as the movement of people.
Trace causes and effects of European colonialism	Review the Closer Look at European Colonization in Africa.

ELL Support

ELL Obective Students will be able to use prefixes to understand new words.

Cultural Connections Remind students that many people from West and Central Africa were forced against their will to move to the Americas during the trans-Atlantic slave trade. Being forced to move is one among many reasons why people leave their homes and move to a new place. If appropriate, explore why people might emigrate to the United States.

ELL Intermediate/Early Advanced Content Tip Tell students that the prefix *pan-* means "all or every." Use this definition to teach the term *Pan-Africanism.* Give examples of other words that use that prefix, such as *pandemic* or *panorama.*

ELL Activity Post a large timeline similar to the one that appears in the **Student Journal.** Discuss each Key Term with the class and decide together where on the timeline it belongs. As you do so, discuss the meaning of each term. **(Logical/Verbal)**

 **myWorld Activity**   **Step-by-Step Instructions**

 60 min

The Promise of Independence

OBJECTIVES
Students will
- write and perform a skit about the promises and challenges of independence for West and Central African countries.
- understand the effects of colonialism, and particularly colonial borders, on West and Central Africans.

LEARNING STYLE
- Kinesthetic
- Verbal

21st Century Learning
- Give an Effective Presentation

MATERIALS
- Pens or pencils
- Paper
- Activity Support: Hopes and Challenges Skit, p. T17

Activity Steps

1. Tell students that they will be writing and performing a skit in groups. The skits will depict hopes and challenges that West and Central African countries faced after independence. For example, a skit might show two independence leaders debating, one talking about positive expected changes and the other warning of likely problems.

2. Organize groups of roughly five students, and have each name a director to assign roles and a secretary to record the script.

   ELL **Intermediate** Define *director* and *secretary*.

3. Allow students 10 minutes to choose their director and secretary, and to start writing their script. Then interrupt the activity and reorganize the groups. Explain that this is to mimic the effects of colonialism on West and Central Africans, in which

Europeans divided the region without regard to preexisting ethnic and linguistic groupings.

   L2 **Extra Support** Explain that this reorganization will make the activity more difficult, and offer help.

4. Move students into random new groups, but leave each director and secretary together. Instruct directors and secretaries to continue with the skit in progress, but with the new group members. Note the confusion and difficulty that results.

5. Have groups act out their skits, then complete *Activity Support: Hopes and Challenges Skit* to consider effects of independence and the difficulties of dealing with people in random groupings.

   L1 **Special Needs** Allow students to complete the Activity Support on a computer.

 More Activities From myWorld Teachers

 Local Connections Ask students to consider the borders of their town, city, or county. Ask them if they think those borders make sense. Have students redraw a map of their town to include an outside resource or group of people. **(Logical)**

Take a Trip Draw a map of Africa and Southwest Asia on a large piece of paper or project one onto a screen. Have students finger-walk the

route of Mansa Musa's pilgrimage to Mecca, noting distance and places he would have seen along the way. **(Kinesthetic)**

Role Play Have students pretend they are the president of a newly independent West or Central African country. Have them make a list of the changes they would make to improve life in their country. **(Verbal)**

my worldgeography.com (**Teacher Center** →)   Find additional resources in the online Teacher Center.

Name _____ Class _____ Date _____

myWorld Activity Support   **Hopes and Challenges Skit**

The Promise of Independence

Directions Write and perform a skit with your group depicting the hopes and challenges that came with independence for West and Central African countries. While you are working, your teacher will give you further instructions that will help you understand the impact of colonialism on West and Central Africans.

What are three things that will improve about West and Central Africa after independence?	What are three challenges that West and Central Africa will face after independence?
1.	1.
2.	2.
3.	3.

What did your teacher do while you were working on your skit?

_____

What did this represent?

_____

How did it affect your work?

_____

_____

How might borders imposed by Europeans have made life difficult for West and Central Africans?

_____

_____

T17

Name _____ Class _____ Date _____

Enrichment: Kwame Nkrumah

Directions Read the selection below. Then answer the questions
that follow and complete the activity.

Kwame Nkrumah's political career had a very
promising start. Educated in the United States and
Britain, Nkrumah was committed to independence for
his country of Ghana. Although the British colonial
government imprisoned him for leading protests and
strikes, Nkrumah won the colony's first free election
from his jail cell. He guided Ghana to independence
through a democratic and mostly nonviolent process.
In 1957, Nkrumah became the first prime minister of
independent Ghana.

Nkrumah's ambitions were bigger than just
independence for Ghana. He fought to free all Africans
from colonial rule and then unite them under a single
government. As prime minister, he held conferences
with other African independence leaders and even tried
to unify Ghana with neighboring countries. He was an
icon of Pan-Africanism.

However, Nkrumah began to lead Ghana down the
wrong path. He became oppressive, throwing his
opponents in prison and making himself a dictator. At
first he worked to encourage trade and improve Ghana's
infrastructure, but later he concentrated power in the
central government. This led to economic collapse. The military,
fed up with Nkrumah, overthrew him in 1966. He died in exile in
Romania. Still, people in the region respect Nkrumah for the role
in played in freeing the continent from colonial rule.

1. What was Kwame Nkrumah's greatest accomplishment?

_____

_____

2. Why was Kwame Nkrumah overthrown despite his service to his
country?

_____

3. Activity Write a paragraph explaining what you think Kwame
Nkrumah meant when he said: "Our independence is meaningless
unless it is linked with the total liberation of the African continent."

Name _____ Class _____ Date _____

Section Quiz

Directions Answer the following questions using what you learned
in Section 2.

1. _____ What did West Africans trade to
North Africans in exchange for salt?
   a. camels
   b. gold
   c. silver
   d. masks

2. _____ Why did Mansa Musa go to Mecca?
   a. to go on a military campaign
   b. to go on a religious pilgrimage
   c. to trade masks for ivory
   d. to escape his enemies

3. _____ Which of the following was an effect
of the trans-Atlantic slave trade on West
and Central Africa?
   a. It increased the population.
   b. It led to an increase in wars.
   c. More manufactured goods were
produced.
   d. Agriculture became more profitable.

4. _____ What do colonialism and imperialism
both require?
   a. one country giving money to another
   b. two countries sharing resources
   c. two countries working together
   d. one country ruling another country

5. _____ What idea does Pan-Africanism
refer to?
   a. All African ethnic groups should have
their own country.
   b. All Africans should be united, regardless
of ethnicity.
   c. All Africans should speak a European
language like French or English.
   d. Nigeria should be the dominant country
in Africa.

6. List the main reasons why Europeans colonized West and Central
Africa. State which reason you think is the most important, and
explain why.

   _____

   _____

   _____

History of West and Central Africa

- Model preparing to read by previewing the Key Ideas, Key Terms, headings, visuals, and captions. Have students make predictions about what they will learn. For ELL support, post the prompt, "I predict I will read about . . ."
- Preview and practice the reading skill, sequence, by reviewing the schedule of the school day.

- Preteach this section's high-use Academic Vocabulary and Key Terms using the table on the next page and in-text definitions. Have students practice Key Terms by completing the *Word Wise* page in their journals.

GUIDE ON THE SIDE

Trade in Early West and Central Africa

- **Draw Conclusions** Why did the difficult environment of West and Central Africa cause people to trade? (because trade allowed people to exchange scarce resources)

- **Express Opinions** What do you think are some benefits of trade? What are some of the drawbacks? (Sample: A benefit is that trade can help you get things you cannot make for yourself. A drawback is that sometimes people take advantage of one another in trading.)

┼┼┼┼┼┼ **Reading Skill**

Sequence While they read, have students practice this skill by completing the *Take Notes* graphic organizer in the **Student Journal**.

Section 2

History of West and Central Africa

Key Ideas
- The people of West Africa traded with each other from an early date, leading to well-developed trading kingdoms.
- The Atlantic slave trade, beginning in the 1500s, followed by European colonization in the 1800s, disrupted life in the region.
- Most West and Central African countries gained independence in the 1960s, but deeply rooted problems remain.

Visual Glossary

Key Terms • salt trade • Atlantic slave trade • middle passage • colonialism • imperialism • Pan-Africanism

┼┼┼┼┼┼ **Reading Skill: Sequence** Take notes using the graphic organizer in your journal.

Geography shaped life in early West and Central Africa in many ways. The people turned to trade to cope with a challenging environment. The natural resources and location of the area encouraged trade.

Trade in Early West and Central Africa

During ancient times in the savannas and forests of West Africa, people grew crops and raised animals. Sometimes, a community produced more food than it needed. In this case, the farmers or herders eagerly traded their products at local markets. In time, small kingdoms arose to guide and direct this local trade.

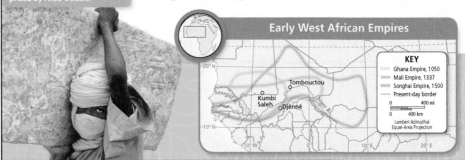

Empire of Ghana
Arab traders traded salt like this for gold. Gold had little value south of the Sahara but was prized by Arab traders.

Early West African Empires

KEY
Ghana Empire, 1050
Mali Empire, 1337
Songhai Empire, 1500
Present-day border

Tombouctou
Senegal
Kumbi Saleh
Djénné
Niger R.

0   400 mi
0   400 km
Lambert Azimuthal
Equal-Area Projection

-20° N
-10° N
20° W   10° W   0°   10° E   20° E

ANSWERS

ACADEMIC VOCABULARY

High-Use Word	Definition and Sample Sentence
decline	*v.* to get weaker *As people get older, their health may decline.*
transition	*n.* movement from one condition to another *Young teens are in a transition from childhood to adulthood.*

GUIDE ON THE SIDE

Salt for Gold Beginning around A.D. 750, these kingdoms began to develop a long-distance trade with Arab traders who lived in North Africa. They exchanged all sorts of goods with their neighbors. The bestsellers were gold and salt. Unlike today, salt was rare and expensive. West Africans traded gold for the Arabs' salt in what was called the **salt trade.**

Arab trading partners brought more than salt to the region. They also carried scholarship, law, and the religion of Islam to West Africa. The trade networks gave birth to new cities. Rulers gained power by collecting taxes and tribute.

Three great trading empires arose in West Africa between 600 and the mid-1600s. Each had its days of glory. Each fell due to a combination of factors.

Ghana Leads the Way Ghana, the first of the great empires, flourished between 600 and 1200. The modern country of Ghana took its name from this empire. However, the empire of Ghana ruled over much of present-day Mali and Mauritania. It did not include present-day Ghana.

Success led to a larger population, which strained resources. Then, around 1050, power struggles with peoples to the north weakened Ghana. In 1240, the leader of a newer empire called Mali attacked Ghana's last strongholds. Soon Mali swallowed up the old empire.

Mali Makes an Impression Mali's greatest emperor, Mansa Musa, ruled from about 1312 to 1337. He practiced Islam. He made a spectacular pilgrimage, or religious journey, to the Arabian city of Mecca in 1324. The trip strengthened Mali's ties with North Africa. It drew the world's attention to the empire. However, Mali, too, weakened and <u>declined.</u>

decline, *v.,* to get weaker

Songhai's Glory In the mid-1400s, the empire of Songhai took over from Mali. It became the largest empire in African history. Songhai took over the great trading cities of Tombouctou (also spelled Timbuktu) and Djenné. Tombouctou flourished as the center of the salt trade and of Islamic learning and culture in West Africa. But by the early 1600s, the empire had split into smaller states.

Reading Check **What was the effect of Mansa Musa's pilgrimage to Mecca?**

- **Summarize** Along with salt, what did Arab traders bring to West Africa? (Islam, Islamic scholarship, and Islamic law)
- **Infer** Why might the modern country of Ghana have taken its name from the Ghana Empire, even though it is not located in the same place? (Sample: The people of modern Ghana admired the prosperity and power of the Ghana Empire.)
- **Identify Details** What made Tombouctou important? (It was a center of Islamic culture and the gold-salt trade.)

Empire of Mali
A Spanish map from the late 1300s shows Mansa Musa. Mansa Musa's pilgrimage to Mecca in 1324 drew the world's attention.

Songhai Empire
At its height, Songhai controlled a region roughly the size of the United States. The Great Mosque at Djenné (right) was rebuilt in the 1900s.

Timeline

Timeline

Have students go to myworldgeography.com to learn more about the history of the Songhai Empire.

READING CHECK The pilgrimage strengthened Mali's ties to North Africa and drew the world's attention to the empire.

ANSWERS

HISTORY

The Middle Passage "The closeness of the place, and the heat of the climate, added to the number in the ship, which was so crowded that each had scarcely room to turn himself, almost suffocated us. . . . The air soon became unfit for respiration, from a variety of loathsome smells, and brought on a sickness among the slaves, of which many died. . . . The shrieks of the women, and the groans of the dying, rendered the whole a scene of horror almost inconceivable."

—Olaudah Equiano, *The Interesting Narrative of the Life of Olaudah Equiano, or Gustavus Vassa, the African*

GUIDE ON THE SIDE

Europeans in the Region

- **Identify Details** Why did Europeans seek out African slave labor? (to work on colonial plantations in the Americas)

- **Cause and Effect** What were two effects of the Atlantic Slave Trade? (Wars between African states increased. African culture influenced the Americas.)

- **Summarize** What is colonialism? (Colonialism is a policy by which a country seeks to rule territory outside of its borders.)

Analyze Visuals Point out and discuss the model of the slave ship.

- Why were conditions on board slave ships so crowded? (because slave traders wanted to pack as many slaves onto the boats as possible)

Europeans in the Region

In the late 1400s, West and Central Africans began trading with new partners, Europeans. Like Arab traders, gold drew Europeans to West and Central Africa. Soon, they became involved in the slave trade.

Trading in enslaved people was not new in Africa. Various forms of slavery existed before European contact. Slaves were part of the trans-Saharan trade. However, the Europeans' slave trade affected many more people. It had more serious effects on African society.

The Atlantic Slave Trade Begins In the 1500s, Europeans began to colonize the Americas. They brought enslaved Africans across the Atlantic Ocean to work on colonial plantations. This trade is called the **Atlantic slave trade**. It was part of the triangular trade between Europe, its American colonies, and Africa. African traders sold slaves for manufactured goods from Europe, such as cloth and guns. Thousands of the captives died during the grueling **middle passage,** the voyage across the Atlantic that formed the middle leg of the triangle.

This model of a slave ship from 1790 shows the cruel way slave traders packed their ships with as much human cargo as possible. The captives were locked in these positions for six weeks or more. ▼

Effects of the Trade The Atlantic slave trade was the largest forced migration in history. Perhaps 13 million people left Africa in slave ships. This migration had several effects.

Some scholars believe that the slave trade changed the relationship between African states in the region. Stronger states attacked weaker ones to get slaves to trade. These wars hurt governance and economies in the region.

Africans who went to North America, the Caribbean, and South America brought their cultures with them. Their traditions influenced religion, music, and other ways of life in the Americas.

Colonialism Slavery was outlawed in the United States and Europe in the early 1800s. But European interference was far from over. In the late 1800s, European countries looked to Africa for more colonies. **Colonialism** is a policy by which one country seeks to rule other areas. The policy of creating an empire by taking over other areas is also often called **imperialism**. European countries had colonized nearly all of Africa by 1900.

Reading Check **What was the triangular trade?**

READING CHECK The triangular trade was the trade between Europe, Africa, and the American colonies.

HISTORY

America in West Africa The colonial map of West and Central Africa from 1914 shows that in the whole region only Liberia was independent. Liberia has a unique history, closely connected to the United States. In the early 1800s, some white Americans disagreed with slavery but did not want to allow slaves to be part of American society. They believed the slaves should be sent to Africa, where their ancestors had been taken from. These Americans founded the American Colonization Society in 1816, and purchased land along the coast in West Africa. Eventually 10,000 former slaves and free black Americans were sent to the colony which became known as Liberia. It declared independence in 1847. The United States still maintained close relations with Liberia afterwards.

Closer Look

EUROPEAN COLONIZATION IN AFRICA

In the 1880s, European powers made a mad dash for territory in Africa. This rush is known as the "Scramble for Africa." Africans resisted the start of European rule. But they couldn't stand against the Europeans' powerful new weapons, such as the Maxim machine gun. From the 1880s until the 1960s, European powers ruled almost every part of Africa. Some of colonization's damaging effects are still being felt today.

THINK CRITICALLY What did European powers want from the colonies?

Poster showing Africa as a market for British goods ▲

CAUSES European nations wanted colonies
- to win prestige.
- to get natural resources needed to produce industrial goods in Europe.
- as markets for goods made in factories.

EVENT Europeans got colonies
In 1884, European leaders met and divided up Africa among themselves. No African leaders took part. Before long, Europe controlled nearly the entire continent.

EFFECTS Colonial powers hurt Africa
- by ignoring the location of ethnic groups when drawing borders.
- by not developing colonial economies beyond their own aims.
- by forcing Africans to extract resources or grow cash crops.

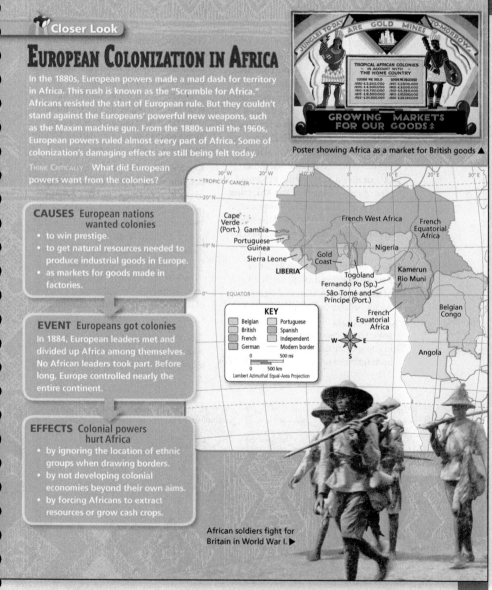
African soldiers fight for Britain in World War I. ▶

THINK CRITICALLY European powers wanted the colonies to provide natural resources for their factories, markets for their manufactured goods, and prestige among other European nations.

Closer Look

European Colonization in Africa

- **Analyze Text** What was the "Scramble for Africa"? (the rush of European powers trying to seize territory in Africa)
- **Identify Details** What important group of people met in 1884? (European leaders)
- **Cause and Effect** What were some effects of European colonization? (Europeans imposed borders that split or combined ethnic groups, held back African economic development, and forced Africans to work for them.)

Analyze Maps Point out and discuss the map.
- Which country is independent? (Liberia)
- Which colonial power ruled most of West Africa? (France)

CULTURE

Pan-African Colors One of the first things a newly independent nation needs to do is to choose a flag. Many flags in West and Central Africa and across the continent contain the colors red, yellow, and green. These colors represent Pan-African unity and independence, and were chosen because they were the colors of the only African country never to be colonized—Ethiopia. Thirteen countries in the region use these colors on their flag, including Ghana and Mozambique.

GUIDE ON THE SIDE

Independence and Beyond

- **Identify Details** What is Pan-Africanism? (the idea that all African peoples should be united)

- **Identify Details** Why did Joseph Mobutu change the name of the Belgian Congo to Zaire? (to reclaim the nation's cultural identity)

- **Summarize** How can you tell that Joseph Mobutu was a corrupt leader? (because he ruled as a dictator and used violence to maintain power while the people of his country suffered)

 myWorld Activity

The Promise of Independence
Find Step-by-Step Instructions and an Activity Support on pp. T16–T17.
(Kinesthetic/Verbal)

---

myWorld Activity
The Promise of Independence

Independence and Beyond

Most Africans did not take part in colonial government. Some colonies, however, did ask a small number of Africans to help run their governments. As these Africans became educated, leaders emerged. They grew frustrated with the unfair rule of colonial powers. After World War II, a political leader in Ghana named Kwame Nkrumah (KWAH mee n KROO muh), promoted the idea of Pan-Africanism. **Pan-Africanism** was a political and social movement to unite black Africans around the world. Throughout Africa, Africans called for independence.

Early Dreams and Harsh Realities Between 1960 and 1975, nearly all of the colonies in West and Central Africa became independent nations. The <u>transition</u> of power to African governments was mostly peaceful. But in some countries, the people had not been involved in government for decades.

transition, *n.,* movement from one condition to another

Also, Europeans still controlled many economic structures. The borders of the countries were drawn without regard to ethnic and language groups.

Despite bright hopes, the new nations soon ran into problems. Groups within countries fought one another. Governments banned opposition parties. Military dictators often led these governments.

Trouble in the Congo For example, Belgium abruptly granted independence to the Belgian Congo in 1960. Within months, the new nation was in chaos. In 1965, army leader Joseph Mobutu seized power. Mobutu renamed the country Zaire (zah EER) after a traditional name for the Congo River. He claimed to want to restore the nation's cultural identity. Instead, he ruled as a dictator for 32 years of incredible corruption. Meanwhile, Congo's people suffered.

Civil War in Nigeria In the 1940s, Nigerian leaders united more than 40 ethnic groups to oppose British rule.

A happy crowd greets the news of independence in the Belgian Congo in 1960.

By 1965, the dictator Joseph Mobutu (middle left) controlled the Congo, using violence to maintain power.

ANSWERS

READING CHECK Civil war broke out over Biafra

SECTION 2 ASSESSMENT **1.** Salt trade brought wealth and Arab culture to the region. The Atlantic slave trade took Africans to the Americas through the middle passage, on which many died. Colonialism and imperialism imposed Europeans and their culture on Africa. Pan-Africanism tried to unite Africans against outside influences. **2.** West African kingdoms grew rich through salt and gold trade with

HISTORY

The Cold War in Africa Like other parts of the developing world, newly independent African nations were a Cold War battleground. The United States and its European allies supported some regimes and rebel movements while the Soviet Union and its allies supported others. For example, western powers aided Joseph Mobutu in Zaire (Democratic Republic of the Congo) while the Soviet Union supported a leftist government in Mozambique. During the Angolan Civil War, the United States, South Africa, and Zaire supported one faction while the Soviet Union, Cuba, and Mozambique supported the other.

Everyone from soldiers to market women joined the call for freedom. Nigeria became independent in 1960.

However, ethnic unity did not last long. In 1967, three eastern states that were controlled by the Igbo (ig boh, also called Ibo) ethnic group attempted to leave Nigeria. They wanted to secede, or formally break away, and form their own country. The new country would be called the Republic of Biafra. One reason behind the move was that Igbos had been the victims of ethnic fighting in northern Nigeria.

Another reason was that Biafra was rich in oil. A bloody civil war followed. An estimated 500,000 to several million people died before Biafra rejoined Nigeria.

Economic Dependence and Dictatorship The new nations often continued relationships with their former colonial rulers. They stayed loyal to their former rulers in return for technical advice and loans. This arrangement tended to keep their economies focused on exporting cash crops and natural resources that mainly benefited European nations. As a result, homegrown manufacturing and businesses grew slowly. Taking on foreign loans created huge debts.

From 1945 until 1989, the United States and the Soviet Union carried on a rivalry called the Cold War. African nations were caught in the middle. To further their ends, both sides often supported dictators that were friendly to their point of view.

When the Cold War ended, so too did some of the support from Cold War powers. This paved the way for a new push for democracy throughout the region. By the early 1990s, most nations in the region had reestablished some form of elected government. Some of these democracies have been successful. Others have remained unstable.

Reading Check **What happened after Nigeria gained independence?**

▲ In 1960, Nigeria's first president, Nnamdi Azikiwe (NUM dee ah ZEE kway) said, "The past is gone with all its bitterness." But soon Nigeria plunged into conflict.

Section 2 Assessment

Key Terms

1. Use the following words to explain how outsiders have affected West and Central Africa throughout history: salt trade, Atlantic slave trade, middle passage, colonialism, imperialism, Pan-Africanism.

Key Ideas

2. How were the West African trading empires able to grow and become wealthy?

3. Describe the effects of the Atlantic slave trade.

4. What are some reasons why European powers created African colonies?

Think Critically

5. **Compare Viewpoints** How might Nnamdi Azikiwe's view of the future in 1960 be different from that of someone who fought in Nigeria's civil war in later years?

6. **Summarize** How did Cold War rivalries affect West and Central Africa?

? Essential Question

Who should benefit from a country's resources?

7. What role did natural resources play in the history of West and Central Africa? Go to your Student Journal to record your answer.

Famous Cities and Kingdoms of West Africa

OBJECTIVES

Students will

- describe cultural contributions of important cities and kingdoms of West Africa.
- **21st Century Learning** synthesize information from the text with personal experiences.
- **ELL** use English words to compare and contrast West African cities and kingdoms.

SET EXPECTATIONS

In this case study, students will

- read Famous Cities and Kingdoms of West Africa.
- write a letter about travel to Tombouctou, Ife, Oyo, or Benin.

1 Connect

Point out that each member of a group has unique talents and skills, which are shared with others. For example, one student might teach another how to play a game. Explain that if groups lose members, they might also lose the skills of those members. For example, when a bilingual child leaves home for college, her parents might struggle to communicate in English. Tell students that West African cities and kingdoms all had unique talents and skills. These contributed to regional civilization, but as the talents and skills changed so did the region.

L1 Special Needs Have students make a concept web with My Skills in the center. Allow each student to share the one that they think makes them unique.

2 Learn

Preview Have students preview Key Ideas, Key Terms, visuals, and headings. Ask which West African cities they see represented. Have them predict the kinds of cultural contributions these cities might have made to West African civilization.

Read While students read Famous Cities and Kingdoms of West Africa, ask questions found in the **Guide in the Side** to build understanding of Key Ideas and lesson objectives.

ELL **Intermediate** Post compare-and-contrast terms and then help students link cities with compare-and-contrast statements.

myWorld Activity: Letter to Home Tell students that they will take the role of travelers visiting a West African city. Using *Activity Support: Travel Notes*

25 min

students will record details about that city. They will then write a letter about their visit to someone back home. Letters should contain sketches, found photos, and quotations from people met on the visit. **(Visual/Verbal)**

L2 Extra Support Review the informal letter format with students. Give students a variety of closings from which to choose.

ELL **Beginning** Hold up a sign with "A B C" and a piece of mail to show the difference between *letter* as a part of the alphabet and as a written communication.

L4 Challenge Students may wish to make oral travelogues or podcasts.

3 Understand

Review Have students list each African kingdom or city and the features for which it is known. Ask them how the region changed when Benin's trading skills were no longer needed.

Assess Check students' answers to the Assessment questions for completeness and accuracy. Evaluate students' letters for accuracy, details, and connections made between the West African city visited and their community at home.

Remediate If students are struggling to identify contributions of each city, have them create four-column tables with headings for each West African city, and use captions and visuals to gather information about each place's unique features.

Name _____ Class _____ Date _____

myWorld Activity Support **Travel Notes**

Letter to Home

Directions Pretend you are a traveler visiting one of the cities you read about in the Case Study. Along the way, you have been taking notes about what you have seen and learned about the city's culture and civilization. Now it's time to write a letter about your trip to someone back home. Use the steps below to plan your letter. Then write your letter on another piece of paper, and find or sketch images to include.

1. Choose a city from the Case Study as a stop on your journey. Answer the following questions about your chosen city:

   a. What is the city called? _____

   b. When in history is the city important? _____

   c. What is the city known for? _____

   d. Where is the city located? _____

   e. What interesting things did I see in the city? _____

   f. Why did I find these things interesting? _____

   g. What did I see or experience that relates to something
   I know from home? _____

2. Develop ideas for your letter by thinking about what would interest someone from home. Take notes in this table to compare and contrast the West African city with your community:

West African City	My Community

3. Based on your notes, and what you know about your community, why might someone want to visit this West African city?

   _____

   _____

4. Draft your letter on lined paper. Be sure to use correct letter format.

GEOGRAPHY

Tombouctou's Location What made Tombouctou's location important? Why did it become a major stop on the trade routes for salt and gold? One reason is the city's location near water. In fact, the first settlers of Tombouctou were nomads who used it as a seasonal camp because it has an oasis. The city's name comes from one of these nomads, a woman named Buktu. The city's name means "Buktu's well." In addition, Tombouctou is near the Niger River, which provided water and possibly a means of transportation.

Tombouctou: Center of Trade and Learning

- **Summarize** When and where was Tombouctou founded? (It was founded in 1100 A.D. in modern-day Mali.)

- **Cause and Effect** Why was the city important? (Its location made it important for trade.)

- **Draw Conclusions** Other than trading salt and gold, what other needs might traders have in Tombouctou? (Traders probably needed to collect supplies for their journeys.)

Case Study

Famous Cities and Kingdoms of West Africa

Key Ideas	• A variety of cities and kingdoms rose in West Africa before the arrival of Europeans in the region.	• Each city or kingdom contributed to the region's culture and history.

Key Terms • Tombouctou • Yoruba • oni • Benin

▲ A sign in Arabic and French points to Tombouctou.

As you have read, large, wealthy kingdoms such as Ghana, Mali, and Songhai flourished in West Africa before the colonial period. Tombouctou became an important city and cultural center during the Mali and Songhai eras. But these kingdoms were not the only kingdoms in the region. Many other states and cities also contributed to West and Central Africa's rich cultural legacy, including Ife, Oyo, and Benin.

Tombouctou: Center of Trade and Learning

You have already read about the city of **Tombouctou** (also spelled Timbuktu). It was founded around A.D. 1100 in modern-day Mali. For many centuries, it was one of the most important cities in West Africa.

Tombouctou was part of the Mali and Songhai empires. It became important because of its location at the edge of the Sahara. Caravans, or groups of traders, carrying gold came up from the south. Most did

A modern-day camel caravan makes its way across the Sahara. ▼

CORE CONCEPTS: CULTURAL DIFFUSION AND CHANGE

Review Core Concept 7.6 before discussing with your students trading patterns in West African cities and kingdoms. Recall that trade is one important way in which culture is spread. Tell them that every so often, traders would have to stop to replenish supplies and would interact with the people who lived along their route. Ask students to draw conclusions about the aspects of culture that traders might bring on their journeys. Then discuss how traders might be influenced by the cultures of cities such as Tombouctou, Ife, and Benin City.

not travel past Tombouctou across the dry Sahara. Desert caravans loaded with salt came from the north to Tombouctou. There they traded salt for gold. The city grew rich from the trade. Its wealth made it famous as far away as Europe.

But Tombouctou was more than just a marketplace. It was a college town—a center of Islamic learning and law. The University of Sankore (SAN kohr) was founded in a mosque in Tombouctou. It attracted the best minds from all over West Africa. Tombouctou was a large town, and one quarter of its people were scholars. They left behind thousands of manuscripts that help modern historians learn about African history.

Around 1600, the city began to decline. However, people around the world, and especially in West Africa, remembered its wealth and wisdom. A proverb from the region shows the city's fame:

> 66 Salt comes from the North, gold comes from the South, but the word of God and the treasures of wisdom come from Timbuktu [Tombouctou]. 99
>
> —Proverb from West Africa

Reading Check Which empires claimed Tombouctou?

The Yoruba Cities

The **Yoruba** ethnic group lives mainly in modern Nigeria, southeast of Tombouctou. Yorubas have a common language, culture, and history in western Nigeria. The traditional Yoruba homeland included both forests and savanna. This homeland was to the southeast of the empire of Ghana. It did not come under the control of the empires of Ghana, Mali, or even Songhai.

The various groups of Yoruba people of the region never united into one kingdom. They did found many city-states, ruled by kings. Sometimes one city was the most powerful, sometimes another. But as far back as historians can tell, every Yoruba state recognized Ife (EE fay) as the most important city of all.

According to Yoruba stories, Ife was the place where life itself was created. It was the oldest city in the area, dating back to around 1000. It was also the most important religious and cultural center of the Yoruba people.

A manuscript written in Sankore during Tombouctou's glory days ▼

READING CHECK Mali, Songhai

CULTURE

Yoruba Traditions According to Yoruba beliefs, life began in Ife because that is where the creator first made land. The Yoruba believe that the Creator, who they call Olodumare, covered Ife with water. Olodumare then sent messengers to Ife with a chicken, some soil, and five pieces of iron. The messengers set the iron down—presumably in a place where the water was shallow—put the soil on top of it and then left the chicken to spread it around with its feet. This spread land around the world.

- **Cause and Effect** How did the Oyo kingdom grow strong? (Its people used iron and cavalry to defeat neighboring peoples. It also traded with Europeans in the slave trade.)

- How did the Oyo kingdom lose strength? (Its land on the coast was conquered, so it could no longer trade there.)

Map Skills Point out and discuss the map of the Oyo and Benin Empires.

- How could the Oyo Empire affect people living to its north? (It could control direct access to the coast.)

Artists in Ife produced beautiful bronze statues. The rulers of the city were called **onis** (OH neez). They were the religious leaders of the Yoruba people. The Yoruba believed that the first oni of Ife was Oduduwa and that he was the first to bring iron to the area.

Ife did not build a large kingdom. The Yoruba city-state of Oyo did. The people of Oyo used iron and a strong cavalry, or soldiers fighting on horseback, to dominate the grassy savanna. In 1730, Oyo defeated the neighboring kingdom called Dahomey and began to expand to the south. Although Oyo became more powerful than its neighbor Ife, its kings always recognized Ife's special position.

Eventually the Oyo empire reached the coast. There Oyo traders acted as middlemen for traders from Europe.

The Oyo sold the European traders slaves from farther inland. The empire fell quickly after it lost control of trade routes on the coast. Outsiders conquered it.

Reading Check **Where did the Yoruba believe life was created?**

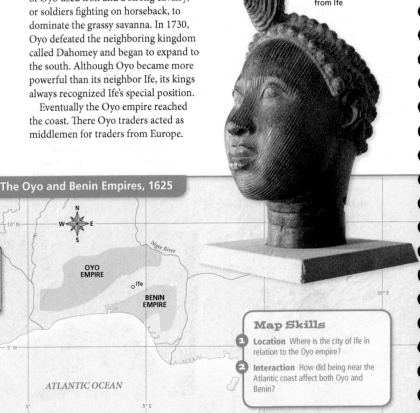

▼ A bronze sculpture from Ife

The Oyo and Benin Empires, 1625

KEY
- Benin empire
- Oyo empire
- ○ City

0 — 100 mi
0 — 100 km
Mercator Projection

OYO EMPIRE

○ Ife

BENIN EMPIRE

Niger River

ATLANTIC OCEAN

10° N

5° N

0°   5° E   15° E

Map Skills

1 **Location** Where is the city of Ife in relation to the Oyo empire?

2 **Interaction** How did being near the Atlantic coast affect both Oyo and Benin?

GOVERNMENT

Checks and Balances in Benin In the 1400s, Ewuare, the leader of Benin, made important changes in Benin's government. He created what we call checks and balances. The United States government also has checks and balances. This is when different parts of government have the power to oversee—or check—the actions of other parts of government. These actions help to balance power so that no one part of government has too much. For Ewuare, spreading out power allowed him to keep different chiefs busy fighting each other instead of banding together to fight him. On the positive side, the structure of Benin's government allowed individuals—even those not of royal class—to rise to great power and authority.

Benin, an Empire in the Forest

To the south of Oyo and Ife, the city of **Benin** began to expand in the rain forest along the coast in present-day southern Nigeria. By around 1300, Benin City was the most powerful city in its area. Its neighbors had to send it tribute, or regular payments sent to an overlord. Over time it grew into an empire.

Like the people of Oyo, the people of Benin recognized the spiritual and cultural importance of Ife. They asked a prince from Ife to be their king. Benin became an artistic center in its own right. Its artisans produced famous woodcarvings and brass work.

The Benin empire was well organized and strong before Europeans arrived on the scene. When the Europeans did come, Benin was one of the first and most important African states they had to deal with. Long before Oyo fought its way to the coast, the Benin empire was trading with Europeans.

Traders from Benin, like those from Oyo, served as middlemen for the slave trade. The empire came to depend on this trade. When the British abolished the slave trade in the 1800s, Benin became weak and politically unstable. The British were able to conquer it.

Reading Check **What geographic area was Benin's home?**

◄ Artisans in the forest kingdom of Benin produced beautiful bronze reliefs.

A forested area along the coast of West Africa today ▼

Assessment

1. How did Tombouctou's geography help make it rich?

2. What do Tombouctou's manuscripts show about the city?

3. Why was Ife so important even though it was not powerful?

4. Why was access to the coast so important for Oyo and Benin?

5. What was one factor that caused Benin to fall?

ASSESSMENT **1.** Tombouctou's geography made it a center for trade of salt and gold, which brought many traders and their money to the city. **2.** The manuscripts show the city's scholarly life. **3.** People in the surrounding cultures viewed Ife as a spiritual and cultural center because they believed that life was created there. **4.** Both Oyo and Benin needed access to the coast because their economies depended on trading slaves from inland to Europeans at the coast. **5.** Samples: loss of the slave trade, political instability

Benin, an Empire in the Forest

- **Compare and Contrast** How were the people of Benin like the people of Oyo? (Both recognized the spiritual and cultural importance of Ife.)

- **Identify Evidence** How can we see the influence of Ife on Benin? (Benin asked a prince from Ife to be its king.)

- **Sequence** Which empire traded with Europeans first, Oyo or Benin? (Benin)

- **Summarize** What was Benin like before Europeans arrived? (It was well organized and strong.)

- **Cause and Effect** How did the slave trade change Benin? (The empire came to depend on the slave trade.)

- What happened when Britain ended the slave trade? Explain. (Benin collapsed and Britain captured it. Without the slave trade, Benin had no economy. It became weak and unstable.)

West and Central Africa Today

OBJECTIVES

Students will know
- regional struggles with poverty, disease and violence.
- ways that regional cultures endure despite challenges.

Students will be able to
- identify main ideas about West and Central Africa today.
- draw conclusions about economic challenges for the region.

SET EXPECTATIONS

In this section, students will
- read West and Central Africa Today.
- compare and contrast development in two West and Central African countries.
- go On Assignment in West and Central Africa and learn about musicians and artists in the region.

CORE CONCEPTS

You may wish to teach or reteach the following lessons from the Core Concepts Handbook:
- Urbanization, pp. 80–81
- The Arts, pp. 94–95
- Conflict and Cooperation, pp. 110–111

KEY

Differentiated Instruction	English Language Instruction
L1 Special Needs **L2** Extra Support	**ELL** Beginner **ELL** Early Intermediate **ELL** Intermediate
L3 On-Level **L4** Challenge	**ELL** Early Advanced **ELL** Advanced

1 Connect
Make learning meaningful

Make Connections Ask students to share some of their impressions of Africa from the news and other sources. They may have seen many images of warfare and poverty. Remind students that there is more to the region than unfortunate circumstances and they should try to look beyond the negative images they may often see.

L4 Challenge Ask students to find a recent news article about an event in West and Central Africa and evaluate it for bias. Have students write letters to the editor of their region's newspaper asking questions about the paper's coverage of African news.

Activate Prior Knowledge Remind students that in the previous section they learned about African nations achieving independence. Ask them to consider how the problems the new countries faced might affect life in the region today.

L2 Extra Support Have students review the Closer Look in the previous section to understand the effects that colonialism had on the region.

Prepare Follow the steps in the section **Preview.** Preteach the Key Terms. Then have students complete *Word Wise* in their journals using in-text clues and the glossary for help.

2 Experience
Teach knowledge and skills

Read Use **Background** notes and **Guide on the Side** questions to model active reading. Have students use *Take Notes* in their **Student Journal** to take notes on the culture of West and Central Africa. Have students complete **21st Century Online Tutor** *Identify Main Ideas and Details* and apply this skill to reading the section.

ELL Early Intermediate Have students make vocabulary cards for key terms in the chapter.

L1 Special Needs Allow volunteers to read the section out loud before special needs students read independently.

L3 On-Level Have students explore alternative economic development by completing *Enrichment: Microcredit and Entrepreneurs.*

Practice: myWorld Activity Students will compare the development of the Democratic Republic of the Congo and Ghana side by side and consider how the two are different and why this might be so. **Step-by-Step Instructions** and **More Activities** follow on pp. T24–T25.

SECTION 3 RESOURCE GUIDE

FOR THE STUDENT

my worldgeography.com Student Center
- Culture Close-up
- Data Discovery

Student Edition (print and online)
- West and Central Africa Today

Student Journal (print and online)
- Section 3 Word Wise
- Section 3 Take Notes

21st Century Learning Online Tutor
- Identify Main Ideas and Details
- Draw Conclusions

FOR THE TEACHER

my worldgeography.com Teacher Center
- Online Lesson Planner
- Presentations for Projection
- SuccessTracker

ProGuide: Africa
- Lesson Plan, pp. T22–T23
- 🏃 myWorld Activity Step-by-Step Instructions, p. T24
- Activity Support: Comparison Table, p. T25
- myWorld Geography Enrichment, p. T26
- Section Quiz, p. T27

Accelerating the Progress of ELLs
- Reading Support Strategies, p. 42

---

3 Understand
Assess understanding

Review Review *Word Wise* and *Take Notes* in the **Student Journals.**

Assess Knowledge and Skills Use the Section Assessment and Section Quiz to check students' progress.

Assess Understanding Review students' responses to the Section Assessment Essential Question prompt.

Remediate Use these strategies to review and remediate.

If students struggle to . . .	Try these strategies.
Identify main ideas and details	Assign additional practice with the **21st Century Tutor.**
Connect instability and poverty.	Use flowcharts to describe instability and resulting poverty in the region.
Identify ways regional cultures are addressing their problems.	Review Hope for Change in the Future and have students list solutions.

ELL Support

ELL Objective Students will be able to discuss economic concepts in English.

Cultural Connections Ask students to compare your local economy with that of their home countries. Students should name the types of jobs and the types of products that are produced and exported, and then describe how easy or difficult they think it is to start a business or get a loan.

ELL Advanced Content Tip Discuss the Key Term *microcredit*. Explain that the prefix *micro* means "very small." Thus, *microcredit* means a very small amount of credit, whose Latin root *credere* means "to believe." A bank gives a small loan if they believe you can only pay back a small amount.

ELL Activity Post a T-chart labeled Before Independence and After Independence. Pass out index cards labeled with a trend or event from one period or the other. Have student groups identify the period for a card and explain why. (**Kinesthetic/ Linguistic**)

30 min

myWorld Activity **Step-by-Step Instructions**

Two Economies

OBJECTIVES

Students will

- compare the economic development of Ghana and the Democratic Republic of the Congo.
- draw conclusions about how a country could develop more successfully.

LEARNING STYLE

- Logical
- Interpersonal

21st Century Learning

- Draw Conclusions

MATERIALS

- Pen or pencil
- Activity Support: Comparison Table, p. T25

Activity Steps

1. Tell students they will compare the economic development of Ghana and the Democratic Republic of the Congo. Students will consider ways that the two countries are similar and ways that they are different, and try to explain these results. Finally, they will act out a skit to give advice to the Prime Minister of either country.

2. Organize groups of at least three. Have groups fill out *Activity Support: Comparison Table.*

    ELL **Beginner** Create mixed-English-proficiency groups. Provide photographs of structures or activities that imply economic development (such as highways, factories, people at computers.)

    L2 **Extra Support** Review the location and recent history of the two countries, focusing on stability. Differentiate Democratic Republic of the Congo from Republic of the Congo.

3. Have groups write a skit for two members to perform. One student plays a United Nations advisor while the other plays the Prime Minister of one of the two nations.

4. Have some students perform their skits. Have listeners take notes about the advice from each advisor.

    L3 **On-Level** Have visual learners take notes in the form of an outline or a table.

More Activities From myWorld Teachers

Local Connection Have students research aid organizations in West and Central Africa, such as those giving microcredit loans. Have the class make posters inviting community donations to support the group's work. **(Visual/Verbal)**

Award Microcredit Students will role-play awarding a micro-loan. What questions would they ask? How much money would they offer to small

business owners? What are some successful businesses? What business would they choose to support with their loan? **(Interpersonal)**

Culture Comparison Have students research the culture of a West or Central African nation. Have each student create a table showing which aspects of the culture are traditional and which are influenced by modern European or American culture. **(Logical)**

 my worldgeography.com (Teacher Center) → Find additional resources in the online Teacher Center.

Name _____ Class _____ Date _____

myWorld Activity Support   **Comparison Table**

Two Economies

Directions Read the statistics below about Ghana and the Democratic Republic of the Congo. Refer back to *West and Central Africa Today* for reminders about recent events in both of these countries. Answer the questions below.

	Ghana	**Democratic Republic of the Congo**
Average income per person	$1,400	$300
Average age at death	59.85 years	54.36 years
Cell phones per 100 people	35	10

Source: *CIA Factbook Online*

Which of these two countries is having the most economic success?

_____

Why do you think the people of one country are better off than the people of the other?

_____

_____

What could the poorer country do to improve its economic conditions?

_____

_____

Name _____ Class _____ Date _____

Enrichment: Microcredit and Entrepreneurs

Directions Read the selection below. Then answer the questions that follow and complete the activity.

Ending poverty is the biggest challenge facing West and Central Africa. One way that very poor people can help themselves is by starting small businesses or expanding ones they already own. But this can be very expensive. Loans help, but traditional lenders often charge high interest rates. Potential entrepreneurs, or new business owners, become trapped by debt they can never repay.

Microcredit is one solution to this problem. Microcredit banks lend poor people small amounts of money at a very low interest rate. Entrepreneurs use that money to start or expand a business. Microcredit programs have helped people in developing countries improve their standard of living.

One person who improved her life with a microcredit loan was Oumy Konte. She sells fish at a market in Dakar, Senegal. With a traditional loan, she used to have to pay back most of her profits in interest every day. After she got a microcredit loan, she was able to keep more of her profits, expand her business, and save money. Oumy improved her family's standard of living, giving her children more food and a good education.

1. How are microcredit loans different from traditional loans?

   _____

2. How did a microcredit loan help Oumy Konte?

   _____

   _____

3. **Activity** Imagine you are starting a business and need a loan. Write a proposal to a bank describing your business idea, detailing why you think it will succeed, and how much money you will need to start.

Name _____ Class _____ Date _____

Section Quiz

Directions Answer the following questions using what you learned
in Section 3.

1. _____ Which of the following is part of a
country's infrastructure?
a. swimming pools
b. movie theaters
c. roads
d. art museums

2. _____ What is the African Union?
a. an African workers' organization
created to fight for higher pay
b. an independent country located in West
and Central Africa
c. the leading soccer team in Liberia
d. an international organization created
to work toward African unity and
economic development

3. _____ Subsistence farmers grow
a. food to sell on the market.
b. cash crops on large tracts of land.
c. only enough food to feed their families.
d. nothing these days; most have sold their
farms and moved to the city.

4. _____ Compared to the Democratic
Republic of the Congo, Ghana is
a. extremely stable.
b. less stable.
c. about as stable.
d. somewhat more stable.

5. _____ Griots are similar to _____
a. painters, because they create images on
paper.
b. baseball stars, because they are strong
and athletic.
c. hip-hop artists, because they tell stories
using rhyme and rhythm.
d. carpenters, because they build useful
objects.

6. Do you think that oil development has been good or bad for
Nigeria? Support your answer with at least *two* reasons.

_____

_____

_____

West and Central Africa Today

- Model preparing to read by previewing the Key Ideas, Key Terms, headings, visuals, and captions. Have students make predictions about what they will learn. For ELL support, post the prompt, "I predict I will read about . . ."

- Preview and practice the reading skill, identify main ideas, by having students explain the main idea of a recent movie they have seen.

- Preteach this section's high-use Academic Vocabulary and Key Terms using the table on the next page and in-text definitions. Have students practice Key Terms by completing the *Word Wise* page in their journals.

Economic Challenges

- **Identify Details** What are some examples of infrastructure? (roads, bridges, hospitals)

- **Summarize** How can the roots of West and Central Africa's economic problems be traced back to colonialism? (European rulers destroyed the traditional economy without building anything to replace it.)

- **Synthesize** How have resource-export-based economies led to debt? (Nations that don't manufacture goods need to import them, and end up importing more than they export. To make up the difference and develop infrastructure they need to borrow money.)

 Reading Skill

Identify Main Ideas While they read, have students practice this skill by completing the *Take Notes* graphic organizer in the **Student Journal.**

Section 3

West and Central Africa Today

Key Ideas
- Many West and Central African countries have struggled to build their economies.
- Some of the nations in the region still experience violent upheaval.
- The people of the region enjoy rich, varied cultures.
- West and Central Africans search for solutions to economic problems, disease, and violence.

Key Terms • infrastructure • corruption • griot • African Union • microcredit

▶ Visual Glossary

 Reading Skill: Identify Main Ideas and Details Take notes using the graphic organizer in your journal.

Traffic moves slowly along a rough road in Lagos, Nigeria.

After independence, many countries in West and Central Africa struggled to establish strong economies and stable governments. Today, West and Central Africans still struggle with poverty and unrest. They seek ways to solve continuing problems.

Economic Challenges
The nations of West and Central Africa are among the poorest in the world. Even nations with rich natural resources have struggled to build and maintain healthy economies.

Legacies of Colonialism Colonial powers did little to foster the economies of their colonies. When they gained independence, the new nations of West and Central Africa did not have strong infrastructures. **Infrastructure** is the body of public works, such as roads, bridges, and hospitals, that a country needs to support a modern economy. To build infrastructure, nations borrowed money from other countries. Many now owe huge debts.

Some of the nations in this region still depend on exporting one or two products. This dependence is risky because the price of products can go up and down drastically. In return for raw materials, West and Central Africans import manufactured goods. They often spend more on imports than they earn with exports. This situation is called a negative balance of trade.

ACADEMIC VOCABULARY

High-Use Word	Definition and Sample Sentence
ceasefire	*n.* an agreement to stop fighting temporarily *During the ceasefire, people could travel safely again.*
innovative	*adj.* fresh, new, or original *The team replaced their old training with Henry's innovative new method.*

Corruption **Corruption,** or the use of power for personal gain, is common in this region. International observers consider Nigeria to be one of the most corrupt nations in the world. The country is in the top ten of the world's largest oil exporters. Yet, around 70 percent of Nigerians live on less than one dollar per day. Corruption and poor management of money by the government both play a role in keeping most Nigerians poor.

Oil is a very capital-intensive business. In other words, it requires a large investment of money to buy machinery. Often, businesses from other countries have made this investment and, in turn, gained huge profits. Nigerians living near the oil fields resent the fact that oil profits often benefit only foreigners and corrupt officials. This resentment has led to violence that has hurt the country as a whole.

Subsistence Farming Another challenge in this region is that the majority of people are subsistence farmers. For example, about 80 percent of people in Mali survive by growing food to eat. Many parts of West and Central Africa lack good farmland, so farming is a difficult way of life. Since they don't make money by selling goods, many farmers cannot afford equipment that would make their farms more profitable.

Children often work on the family farm. Sending them to school is a sacrifice for the family. Many parents make the sacrifice because they know education will improve the lives of their children.

Reading Check **How have many nations in the region paid for infrastructure?**

Political Challenges

When the colonies of West and Central Africa became independent, they faced many political problems. As you have read, the borders that new nations inherited cut across ethnic groups. Also, poverty and weak economies meant that vital goods were scarce, or hard to find. Competition over scarce necessities and rich natural resources caused tension.

In many nations, violence between ethnic groups raged in civil wars. Years of warfare damaged economies and hurt the formation of strong democratic governments. Some countries still struggle with poor economies and bad leadership, leading to more violence.

A Country in Turmoil: The Democratic Republic of the Congo As you have read, the greedy dictator Joseph Mobutu ruled the Democratic Republic of the Congo (which he called Zaire) for more than 30 years. In 1997, rebels led by Laurent Kabila caused Mobutu to fall from power.

myWorld Activity
Two Economies

A farmer in Nigeria uses a hand tool to tend to his field. ▼

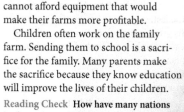

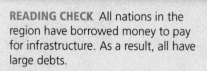

READING CHECK All nations in the region have borrowed money to pay for infrastructure. As a result, all have large debts.

- **Analyze Text** What does "capital-intensive business" mean? (needing a big investment in machinery)
- **Cause and Effect** How can subsistence farming lead to uneducated workers? How do some families change this result? (Children leave school to farm. Some families are willing to give up this labor so that children can go to school.)

Political Challenges

- **Cause and Effect** How did colonialism cause violence and instability in the region? (Colonial borders split ethnic groups or combined rival groups, which then fought for control.)

 myWorld Activity

Two Economies Find Step-by-Step Instructions and an Activity Support on pp. T24–T25. **(Logical/Interpersonal)**

GOVERNMENT

Coup in Mauritania One example of the kind of political instability that plagues West and Central Africa happened in Mauritania on August 6, 2008. Mauritania held its first democratic election in 2006, choosing Sidi Ould Cheikh Abdallahi as the nation's president. He had the support of Mauritania's former military rulers, but when Abdallahi tried to fire the generals in 2008, they arrested him and seized power. Most politicians supported the coup, accusing Abdallahi of corruption and incompetence.

GUIDE ON THE SIDE

- **Express Opinions** Why do you think the civil war in the Democratic Republic of the Congo was so destructive? (sample: because it involved so many countries and ethnic groups)

- **Draw Conclusions** What was Ghana's major problem after independence? (instability)

- **Identify Details** What are Ghana's biggest sources of wealth? (gold and cocao)

In the Democratic Republic of the Congo, rebel forces have recruited children in their teens, sometimes by force, to fight.

In Ghana, citizens vote to elect their president and legislative representatives, as do citizens in the United States.

ceasefire, *n.*, an agreement to stop fighting temporarily

Kabila renamed the country the Democratic Republic of the Congo. But he did little to restore democracy. Former Mobutu supporters, with the aid of Uganda and Rwanda, rebelled in 1998. Uganda and Rwanda supported the rebels to continue their own ethnic conflicts. Angola, Namibia, and Zimbabwe joined the war on the side of the Kabila government. The conflict continued despite a <u>ceasefire</u> in 1999.

In 2001, Joseph Kabila came to power when his father was assassinated. With help from the United Nations, his government and the rebels reached a peace agreement in 2002. However, real peace has been slow in coming. Rebel forces still fight in the eastern part of the country. The fighting goes on in part because various groups want to control the rich mineral resources of that area.

The fighting has left the nation in shambles. Since 1998, an estimated 5 million people have died because of the war or the poor conditions brought about by the war.

Ghana, Back From the Brink Compared to other nations in the region, Ghana, where Evelyn lives, was in good shape upon independence. Still, it has had its problems. Ghana's first president was the independence movement leader Kwame Nkrumah. As he worked to build Ghana's economy, he also became a dictator. He fell from power in a coup, or sudden overthrow, in 1966.

Ghana then suffered several coups until air force officer Jerry Rawlings seized power in 1981. He restored constitutional democracy and won election as Ghana's president in 1992. Since that time, Ghana has been fairly stable.

Rawlings introduced several economic reforms. By the 1990s, Ghana had one of the fastest-growing economies in Africa. Its greatest income comes from gold and cacao production. In the future, Ghana plans to diversify exports and improve the status of women. It also aims to promote good governance.

Reading Check **How did Ghana come to achieve stability?**

CULTURE

Religions West and Central African culture is a blend of the civilizations that helped to shape it. Indigenous religions are practiced in some areas, but the region is predominantly Christian and Muslim. Islam spread south from the Sahara, while Christianity came with the Europeans. Percentages of religious populations listed by country include:

Ghana: 68.8 percent Christian; 15.9 percent Muslim; 8.5 percent Traditional

Nigeria: 50 percent Muslim; 40 percent Christian; 10 percent Traditional

Democratic Republic of the Congo: 80 percent Christian; 10 percent Muslim; 10 percent Traditional

The Cultures of the Region

There are many rich and varied cultures in West and Central Africa. Traditional and modern ways exist side by side, often blending to form new traditions.

Religion Before contact with the outside world, ethnic groups throughout the region developed their own religions. Then new religions were introduced through trading networks. Islam spread south from the Sahara. Mali, for example, has an overwhelmingly Muslim population. Next, Europeans brought Christianity to the region. For example, in Angola, many ethnic groups practiced religions based on ancestor worship and local deities. After the arrival of the Portuguese in the 1400s, many people adopted Christianity.

The Arts In West and Central Africa today, people enjoy both traditional dance and modern ballet. Modern music reflects traditional rhythms and styles. Even when it comes to sports, fans flock to both traditional and newer games. In Senegal, for example, the two most popular sports are soccer and traditional wrestling.

Stories are told through both oral tradition and literature. In West Africa, musician-storytellers called **griots** use music to track their heritage and record history as well as to entertain. Many see hip-hop artists as modern griots. Writers and filmmakers use literature and the cinema to explore Africa's cultural heritage as well as issues facing Africa today.

Reading Check How do griots preserve traditions in West Africa?

▲ West and Central Africans have created ceremonial masks for centuries.

A Nigerian girl reads from the Quran. ▼

 Culture Close-up

In Senegal, a griot plays the kora, a traditional instrument. ▼

▲ A dancer wears a traditional mask and costume in Central Africa.

READING CHECK Griots combine storytelling and music to track cultural heritage and record tradition.

The Cultures of the Region

- **Identify Details** Which major religions were brought by traders from outside of the region? (Islam, Christianity)

- **Summarize** What are some ways in which West and Central Africans blend modern and traditional cultures? (Sample: Traditional dance and modern ballet are popular; modern music styles incorporate traditional rhythms.)

- **Compare and Contrast** How are griots and hip-hop artists similar? (Both use music to tell stories as well as entertain.)

Culture Close-up

Have students go online to myworldgeography.com to learn more about culture in the region.

ANSWERS

QUICK FACTS

Undernourishment According to the United Nations Food and Agriculture Organization, the Democratic Republic of the Congo has the highest percentage of undernourished people in the world—76 percent between 2003 and 2005. During that period, Gabon, also located in Central Africa, had one of the lowest rates of undernourishment in the world.

GUIDE ON THE SIDE

Hope for Change in the Future

- **Summarize** What are three major challenges facing West and Central Africa? (poverty, warfare, and disease)

- **Identify Details** What does it mean for a person to be undernourished? (They do not eat enough food to make a healthy diet.)

- **Draw Conclusions** Why might a large proportion of children be a problem for a developing economy? (Sample: It would be hard for a struggling economy to provide services for children who cannot work.)

Chart Skills Point out the graph and have students compare literacy rates.

- Why do you think the Democratic Republic of the Congo has a lower literacy rate than its neighbor Republic of the Congo? (because years of civil war have disrupted education)

 Data Discovery

Have students go to myworldgeography.com to learn more about literacy in West and Central Africa.

Hope for Change in the Future

Violence, poverty, and disease threaten daily existence for many in this region. Many countries are searching for <u>innovative</u> solutions to their problems. They seek to create better opportunities for the next generation of West and Central Africans.

innovative, *adj.,* fresh, new, or original

The Cost of Warfare Political instability and ethnic conflict threaten the safety of young people in this region. In some places, children are the victims of violence. For example, an estimated 10,000 child soldiers fought in Sierra Leone's ten-year civil war. In addition, thousands of people are forced to flee their homes to escape violence. In the Democratic Republic of the Congo alone, nearly 1.5 million people were internally displaced in 2007.

Poverty and Disease Poverty is another challenge faced by people in this region. Most people do not get to enjoy the benefits of the region's rich natural resources. Conflict, bad government, weak economies, and other factors lead to people being undernourished. A person who is undernourished does not have enough food to make a healthy diet. In West Africa, around 15 percent of the population is undernourished. In Central Africa, more than 50 percent of the population is undernourished.

Undernourishment makes people more vulnerable to diseases. Malaria and sleeping sickness affect millions of people every year. Another disease, acquired immunodeficiency syndrome (AIDS) is an epidemic in the continent of Africa south of the Sahara. Southern Africa has been hit the hardest. Still, many people in West and Central Africa suffer from this illness or know someone who does.

The African Union In 2002, an organization called the **African Union** was formed to promote unity among African states and to foster development and end poverty. The African Union continues the work of an earlier group called the Organization of African Unity, which was established in 1963. In recent years, the African Union has sent peacekeepers to several countries. It also works with international organizations to develop economic programs.

Literacy Rates in Central Africa

Republic of the Congo	83.8%
Cameroon	67.9%
Democratic Republic of the Congo	67.2%
Central African Republic	48.6%

SOURCE: CIA World Factbook Online, 2008

Chart Skills

1. Which country shown has the highest literacy rate?
2. What are the advantages of a high literacy rate?

Data Discovery

CHART SKILLS 1. Republic of the Congo **2.** Higher literacy rates create better-educated workers and more-involved citizens.

READING CHECK They are working to improve democracy, women's rights, infrastructure and social services.

SECTION 3 ASSESSMENT 1. Corruption hurts West and Central Africans by keeping them poor, but microcredit loans help some open their own businesses. Governments that are not corrupt invest in infrastructure such as roads.

CULTURE

Liberia's Iron Lady On January 16, 2006, Ellen Johnson-Sirleaf took office as the first elected female head of state in Africa. Her election is a sign of progress made by women in some parts of the region. Establishing gender equality is one way a country can help overcome poverty.

In an address to the United States Congress, Johnson-Sirleaf described the aspirations of women in Liberia: "Women, my strong constituency, tell me that they want the same chances that men have. They want to be literate. . . . We must not betray their trust."

An Eye Toward the Future The African Union, along with many foreign aid agencies, has identified these key factors in getting rid of poverty and promoting development in Africa:

- democracy
- women's rights
- development of infrastructure
- development of social services (such as education and healthcare)

The people of the region are working toward these goals by investing locally. Giving **microcredit,** or small loans usually less than $200, to individuals to fund their own businesses is a growing practice. Women use microcredit to start and run small businesses similar to Adede's bead business. The region is also investing in people by building new universities.

On a larger scale, others are developing new ways to meet people's needs. New technologies aim to improve lives without harming the environment. For example, many nations in the region have a huge potential for generating hydroelectricity.

Angola gets around 75 percent of its electricity from water power.

In all these ways, West and Central Africans are working to meet the challenges of their daily lives. The filmmaker Ousmane Sembene of Senegal sums up the hope for the future this way:

> 66 Forty years ago, we had nothing—no doctors, no engineers, no writers. We had no university. We thought a flag and a national anthem were enough for independence. . . . That is now a thing of the past. One has to count on the people. And despite all the problems, success for us is a certainty. Every day we're working hard, because we're dreaming of a better quality of life. 99
>
> —Ousmane Sembene

Reading Check How are West and Central Africans working to make their lives better?

my Story   📷 **Photo**

Evelyn looks forward to going to a university. ▶

Section 3 Assessment

Key Terms

1. Use the following terms to describe the obstacles standing in the way of progress in West and Central Africa, and how they might be overcome: infrastructure, microcredit, corruption.

Key Ideas

2. Describe how subsistence farming weakens economies.

3. How have neighboring countries made the Democratic Republic of the Congo's problems worse?

4. What health problems does undernourishment lead to?

Think Critically

5. **Analyze Cause and Effect** How do corruption and undemocratic governments contribute to poverty in West and Central Africa?

6. **Draw Inferences** How might other nations learn from the progress Ghana has made?

? Essential Question

Who should benefit from a country's resources?

7. How does unequal access to oil wealth affect the lives of Nigeria's people? Go to your Student Journal to record your answer.

- **Identify Details** What is the purpose of the African Union? (to promote unity among African states and to foster development and end poverty)

- **Predict** How will expanded higher learning benefit West and Central Africans? (Sample: It will allow them to become skilled workers and build their societies and economies.)

- **Analyze Text** What does Ousmane Sembene mean when he says "We thought a flag and a national anthem were enough for independence. . . . That is now a thing of the past."? (Sample: He means that Senegalese are now working hard for their own future instead of counting on independence to solve their problems)

ANSWERS

2. Subsistence farming limits improvements and education. 3. Countries such as Uganda and Rwanda have interfered, making the fighting more widespread and destructive. 4. Undernourishment leads to increased disease. 5. Corruption and undemocratic governments make it difficult for foreign companies to invest or for local people to start businesses. 6. Other countries can learn that stable, democratic governments support prosperity. 7. Some Nigerians live in dire poverty while others are very wealthy.

Things Fall Apart

OBJECTIVES

Students will

- understand the effects of British colonialism on Nigerian culture.
- **21st Century Learning** analyze literature as a source of information about Nigerian history.
- **ELL** understand multiple meanings of the words *value* (worth in money or core principle) and *custom* (tradition or something made to order).

SET EXPECTATIONS

In this lesson, students will

- read and analyze two excerpts from a Nigerian novel about the effects of European colonization.
- create a wall sampler that communicates Igbo values and customs.

1 Connect

Help students connect with ways in which cultures meet and blend together. Have students brainstorm times when they encountered another culture and had to change the way they do something. For example, perhaps they spent a holiday with a new family member who was used to celebrating in a different way, or perhaps they visited a friend's house and had to eat food they'd never had before. Discuss how they felt in these situations when they had no say about how to express their own culture.

ELL **Intermediate** Invite students to tell ways in which American culture has influenced their home life.

2 Learn

Preview Have students preview the two pages of images and documents. Read the Key Idea, glossary terms, and definitions before students begin reading. Clarify the meaning of terms by providing examples. Read the introduction to the documents.

Read Slowly read aloud the first excerpt without stopping. Read the excerpt again, this time stopping to read the questions at the left. Prompt students to analyze the meaning of the words. Have students answer the questions using the location of the letters to provide clues. Do the same for the second excerpt. Lead a discussion about the challenges of understanding and respecting another culture's values and customs, starting with students' responses to the questions. Ask, What happens in each excerpt? Do you think Okonkwo's punishment is fair? Why is the elder so upset about his people

changing their religion? What makes it hard for the Igbo and Europeans to understand each other or deal with their conflicts?

 **myWorld Activity: Cultural Sampler** Distribute *Activity Support: Values and Customs List,* which offers additional background on the Igbo and a place for students to record values and customs suggested by each excerpt. Have students list ideas and ways to illustrate those ideas. Finally, have students create an illustrated paper or fabric sampler to convey the values and customs to newcomers to an Igbo village. **(Visual/Verbal)**

25 min

L2 **Extra Support** Organize students in groups so that each student only has to identify and generate one custom or value for a group sampler.

3 Understand

Review Return to the Key Idea. Discuss how Okonkwo's experiences show the damage to Igbo traditions.

Assess Have students complete **Analyze the Documents.** Review their answers to determine if students have met the lesson objectives.

Remediate If students struggle to identify the excerpts as secondary sources, review criteria: A primary source is written by someone at the time discussed or described in the writing. A secondary source is one step removed. It usually describes, interprets, or builds on primary sources.

Name _____ Class _____ Date _____

myWorld Activity Support **Values and Customs List**

Cultural Sampler

Directions Read the information about the Igbo and make inferences about Igbo values and customs. List your ideas below. Describe ways you might illustrate the value or custom. Then create an illustrated sampler to post in the main square of an Igbo village. The sampler's goal is to show newcomers some of the local rules.

The Igbo

Igbo land was traditionally held by clans, or groups of families related somehow. People could use it for farming and building. In traditional times, clans clustered in villages. The villages were ruled by a council. Some council members were heads of clans and families. Others were wealthy. Villages in turn belonged to a group of villages that usually shared some common ancestors. Though many Igbo are now Christians, their traditional religion features many gods, including an earth goddess and a creator god.

Values related to	From Excerpt 1	From Excerpt 2	From This Page
Crime and Punishment			
Family			
Religion			
Land			

Ideas for Illustrations

Excerpt 1

- _____
- _____
- _____

Excerpt 2

- _____
- _____
- _____

T29

CULTURE

Chinua Achebe The author's life in some ways mirrors the meeting of cultures he describes in his novel. Achebe, himself of the Igbo people, grew up in Nigeria as the child of Christian missionary teachers. His youth was therefore influenced both by European culture through Christian religious teaching and by African culture through his family's Igbo ethnicity and language. He has described *Things Fall Apart* as a conversation between two languages in his life, English and Igbo. Trained as a scholar, Achebe is widely respected for describing history accurately and fairly in his novels.

GUIDE ON THE SIDE

Analyze Primary and Secondary Sources Use the lettered prompts to help students understand the text and analyze primary and secondary sources.

ANSWERS

A Clans are very important in Igbo society.

B A "male" type of crime is probably intentional.

C After seven years, Okonkwo will have been punished enough. Then he can return to the clan.

Primary Source

Things Fall Apart

Key Idea
- In his famous book *Things Fall Apart,* Chinua Achebe tells the story of Okonkwo, an Igbo leader whose traditions are hurt by European colonization.

The Nigerian author Chinua Achebe is considered by some to be the father of African literature. His most famous novel is *Things Fall Apart.* In the novel, Chinua Achebe tells the story of the meeting between Igbo and European colonizers in the late 1800s. He tells the story from the point of view of the Igbo. Achebe has said that he wrote *Things Fall Apart* to show his readers "that we in Africa did not hear of culture for the first time from Europeans." Below are two excerpts from the novel.

Read the text on the right. Stop at each circled letter. Then answer the question with the same letter on the left.

A Analyze How important are clans in Igbo society?

B Infer What do you think the "male" type of Okonkwo's crime might be?

C Draw Conclusions Why do you think Okonkwo will be able to return after seven years?

inadvertent, *adj.,* by accident

Okonkwo is exiled after accidentally killing a clansman.

66 The only course open to Okonkwo was to flee from the clan. It was a crime against the earth goddess to kill a clansman and a man who committed it **A** must flee from the land.
    The crime was of two kinds, **B** male and female. Okonkwo had committed the female, because it had been _inadvertent._ He could return to the clan after **C** seven years. 99
—Chinua Achebe, *Things Fall Apart*

▲ A traditional Igbo mask

21st Century Learning   ANALYZE PRIMARY AND SECONDARY SOURCES

To assist your students in analyzing primary and secondary sources, use the scaffolded questions at the left of each excerpt. In addition, you might use Core Concepts 9.2 Historical Sources to define each type of source and to discuss examples of each. Once students understand the source types, discuss how a work of fiction can function as a historical source and identify ways readers can determine if its history is reliable. For example, Achebe's statement of intention about his work suggests that he views his writing as historically reliable. Urge students to reread the excerpts dramatically and try to hear the message Achebe is communicating about the Igbo experience. For additional help, refer students to the **21st Century Online Tutor** *Analyze Primary and Secondary Sources*.

Read the text on the right. Stop at each circled letter. Then answer the question with the same letter on the left.

D Summarize   Why does the elder think Europeans cannot possibly understand Igbo customs?

E Develop Cultural Awareness   How have European attitudes affected Igbo who converted to Christianity?

F Analyze Cause and Effect   Why does the elder believe Europeans have caused things to fall apart?

tongue, *n.,* language

Okonkwo discusses the white man with an elder.

❝ 'Does the white man understand our custom about land?'

'How can he when he does not

D even speak our <u>tongue</u>? But he says that our customs are bad; and our own brothers who have taken up his religion also say that our customs are bad. How do you think we can fight when our own brothers have turned against us? The white man is very clever. He came quietly and peaceably with his religion. . . . Now

E he has won our brothers, and our clan can no longer act like one. He has put a knife on the things that

F held us together and we have fallen apart.' ❞

—Chinua Achebe, *Things Fall Apart*

▲ An Igbo town today

ANSWERS

D The elder believes that Europeans cannot understand Igbo culture because they don't speak the Igbo language.

E Igbo who have converted to Christianity have adopted European attitudes that look down on traditional customs.

F The elder believes that Europeans have divided the Igbo and turned them against one another, which has weakened the Igbo culture or made it fall apart.

Analyze the Documents

1. **Draw Conclusions** How does the first document show that the Igbo "did not hear of culture for the first time from Europeans?"

2. **Writing Task** These excerpts are taken from a work of fiction, based on real events. What do you think the author is trying to say about how the Igbo view their experience under colonial rule? Write a paragraph explaining your answer.

Chinua Achebe in his younger days ▶

ANALYZE THE DOCUMENTS 1. The first document shows that the Igbo society had a complex culture and legal structure in place before Europeans arrived. **2.** Answers will vary but should convey students' understanding that the author believes the Igbo viewed their experience under colonial rule as negative. He is saying that Igbo culture was complex and successful before colonial rule and that colonial rule did not respect this.

KEY TERMS AND IDEAS

1. different latitudes and different amounts of rainfall

2. The sahel is dryer than the savanna, and the savanna has more plant and animal life.

3. When trees are cut down, soil is loosened and can dry out and be blown away, leaving barren rock behind.

4. Imperialism destroyed traditional cultures and economies, and exploited Africans for European benefit

5. Subsistence farmers grow just enough food to feed their families.

6. Griots are like hip-hop artists in that both use music to tell stories and entertain.

7. Disease makes it difficult for countries to develop.

THINK CRITICALLY

8. The Democratic Republic of the Congo has been unstable largely because its different ethnic groups and neighbors have been fighting over its natural resources.

9. One of the lasting effects of European colonialism is that African borders split up some ethnic groups while putting rival groups together. This led to conflict. Also, Europeans left behind economies dependent on exporting a single-resource, leaving African countries vulnerable to unpredictable price shifts on the world market.

10. Islam and Christianity

11. The five themes are location, place, region, movement, and human-environment interaction. Geographers would talk about the location of West and Central Africa relative to the rest of the continent; the human and non-human features of West and Central Africa; why West and Central Africa could be considered a region; how people and goods move around West and Central Africa; and how West and Central Africans interact with their environment.

West and Central Africa

Chapter Assessment

Key Terms and Ideas

1. **Summarize** What produces the different climate zones of West and Central Africa?

2. **Compare and Contrast** How are the **Sahel** and **savanna** different from each other?

3. **Sequence** How does **deforestation** lead to **desertification**?

4. **Describe** In what ways did **imperialism** affect West and Central African countries?

5. **Explain** What do subsistence farmers do to make a living?

6. **Identify** What is a **griot**?

7. **Describe** What are some effects of disease on West and Central African people?

Think Critically

8. **Draw Inferences** Why has the Democratic Republic of the Congo been so unstable since independence?

9. **Draw Conclusions** What are some of the lasting effects of European colonialism?

10. **Categorize** Which religions were brought to West and Central Africa from other regions?

11. **Core Concepts: Five Themes of Geography** What are the five themes of geography? How would geographers use these themes to describe West and Central Africa?

Places to Know

For each place, write the letter from the map that shows its location.
Identify the following:

12. **Niger River**
13. **Congo River**
14. **Accra**
15. **Lagos**
16. **Kinshasa**
17. **Estimate** Using the scale, estimate the distance between Accra and Lagos.

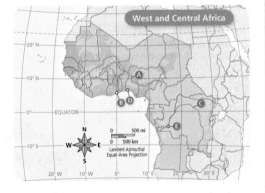

West and Central Africa

PLACES TO KNOW

12. A
13. C
14. B
15. D
16. E
17. about 400 km (250 miles)

 **myWorld Chapter Activity**

To Drill or Not To Drill Find Step-by-Step Instructions, Student Instructions and Rubric, and an Activity Support on pp. T5–T7. **(Verbal/Logical)**

 21st Century Learning

Make a Difference Students' presentations should show thorough research into the charity they have chosen. They should demonstrate that the charity helps people in West and Central Africa specifically. If students need help with this skill, direct them to the online tutorial *Make a Difference*.

→ **Online Assessment**

Tailor review and assessment to each student's needs with an array of online assessments.
• Self–Test
• On Assignment Article or Slideshow
• Success Tracker

? Essential Question
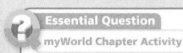 **myWorld Chapter Activity**

To Drill or Not To Drill? Follow your teacher's instructions to prepare advice for the president of a fictional African country that has just discovered oil deposits within its borders. Review evidence to see if you think developing the resource is a good idea or not. Prepare a report for the president recommending or advising against developing oil resources in your country.

21st Century Learning

Make a Difference

Research an aid organization in your community that helps people in West and Central Africa. Find out three things that you could do to help that organization. Present your findings to the class.

Document-Based Questions

Success ☆ Tracker™
Online at myworldgeography.com

Use your knowledge of West and Central Africa and Documents A and B to answer Questions 1–3.

Document A

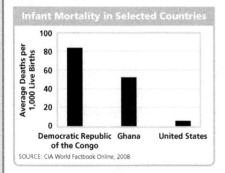

Infant Mortality in Selected Countries

SOURCE: CIA World Factbook Online, 2008

Document B

" We spent three days running from the rebels. We went 60 km [kilometers], walking in the day and sleeping in the bush at night. We ran with nothing. I saw so many people being killed that I just left without collecting my things. Even children are being killed."

—Woman in the Democratic Republic of the Congo

1. What did you learn in this chapter that explains the difference in infant mortality in the Democratic Republic of the Congo, Ghana, and the United States as shown in Document A?

   A Ghana has been very unstable in recent years.

   B The Democratic Republic of the Congo has an efficient healthcare system.

   C The United States is very diverse.

   D Conflict in the Democratic Republic of the Congo makes good healthcare impossible.

2. Who do you think the woman quoted in Document B is most afraid of?

   A the government of the Democratic Republic of the Congo

   B the rebel army

   C African Union peacekeepers

   D Belgian colonists

3. **Writing Task** How does civil violence affect a country and its people? Explain your answer.

WRITING TASK TIP

Use Data Demonstrate using data to prove a point before students complete Document-Based Question 3. Post an example such as, "The United States' low infant mortality rate of 6.3 per 1,000 live births, compared to the Democratic Republic of the Congo's higher rate at 83.11 per 1,000 live births shows that the United States has a more effective health care system." Draw students' attention to the way specific data is used to back up an argument.

DOCUMENT-BASED QUESTIONS

1. D

2. B

3. Students should connect the high infant mortality rate in the Democratic Republic of the Congo in Document A and the quote describing violence in Document B to comment on the results of civil war for average people. Students might write about aspects of life that are disturbed by civil violence. Students might also explain the effects of fear and insecurity on people such as the woman quoted in Document B.

Plan With Understanding by Design*

Chapter Objectives
Begin with the End in Mind

Students will demonstrate the following enduring understandings:
- Conflict shapes people's lives by demanding human and financial resources.

- Geographic factors create socio-economic benefits and challenges.
- Political and economic changes affect national stability and standards of living.

Connect
Make Learning Meaningful

Student Edition
- **Essential Question** Is conflict unavoidable?
- **myStory** Khulekani describes his life in rural South Africa and traces ways his country has changed since the fall of apartheid.

my worldgeography.com
myStory Online Get to know Khulekani through a video of his life and home.

Student Journal
Essential Question Preview

Experience
Teach Knowledge and Skills

Student Edition
- Read Sections 1, 2, and 3.
- Answer Reading Checks and Section Assessment questions.

my worldgeography.com
On Assignment Visual Glossary, Active Atlas, Data Discovery, Language Lesson, and Culture Close-up

Student Journal
- Sections 1, 2, and 3 Word Wise
- Sections 1, 2, and 3 Take Notes

Teacher's Edition
🏃 myWorld Activities
- Section 1: Cause-and-Effect Pairs, p. T38
- Section 2: Where I'm From, p. T44
- Section 3: Analyze Conflicts, p. T52

21st Century Learning Online Tutor
- Analyze Cause and Effect
- Read Special-Purpose Maps
- Sequence
- Categorize
- Compare and Contrast
- Identify Bias

Understand
Assess Understanding

Assessment Booklet
- Chapter Tests
- Benchmark Tests

Teacher's Edition
🏃 myWorld Chapter Activity Students role-play a historical meeting to explore how South African apartheid ended.

Success ✪ Tracker™
Online at myworldgeography.com
Administer chapter tests and remediate understanding.

my worldgeography.com
On Assignment Students write and submit an online article or multimedia slideshow about their virtual observations of conflicts in South Africa.

Student Edition
Chapter Assessment

Student Journal
Essential Question Writer's Workshop

---

* "Understanding by Design" is registered as a trademark with the Patent and Trademark Office by the Association for Supervision of Curriculum Development (ASCD). ASCD has not authorized, approved or sponsored this work and is in no way affiliated with Pearson or its products.

Connect to the Essential Question

Essential Question

Is conflict unavoidable?

Follow these steps to help students understand the Essential Question.

Connect to Their Lives

1. Ask students to think about reasons for conflict, or struggle, at their school or in their hometown. Ask, Why do people fight? Why can it be hard for everybody to get along? As students share their answers with the class, list them on the board.

2. Then post the diagram below and have students rate these reasons for conflict on a scale from 1 to 5, from unlikely source of conflict to likely, or have students turn to the Essential Question Preview page in their **Student Journal.**

REASON FOR CONFLICT	How likely is it to cause conflict?				
Misunderstanding	1	2	3	4	5
Power struggle	1	2	3	4	5
Difference	1	2	3	4	5
Other:_____	1	2	3	4	5

Connect to the Content

3. Now have students think about sources of conflict within a country or region. Ask, Are these reasons similar to the issues that divide people at school or in a town?

4. Post the following concept web. Have students list sources of conflict. Then have them color-code the conflicts as avoidable (first color) or unavoidable (second color).

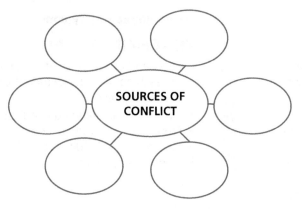

SOURCES OF CONFLICT

5. After previewing the chapter, have students make predictions on the Essential Question Preview page in the **Student Journal.** Also point out the Essential Question prompts on each section's Take Notes page in the **Student Journal.**

Explore worldgeography.com

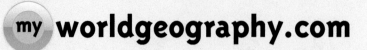

Welcome to myWorldGeography

http://www.myworldgeography.com

ON ASSIGNMENT: Southern and Eastern Africa

For this chapter's assignment, students will
- take a digital trip to the countries of Southern and Eastern Africa.
- take on the role of a journalist.
- gather notes, images, and data throughout their journey.
- write an article or create a multimedia slideshow on the Essential Question: *Is conflict unavoidable?*

ITINERARY

During their trip, students will make the following stops:

 myStory

Learn more from Khulekani about life in South Africa after apartheid.

 Active Atlas

Read physical, ecosystem, resource, and colonization maps of Southern and Eastern Africa.

 Data Discovery

Gather data about water use, religion, and literacy in Southern and Eastern Africa.

 Language Lesson

Learn to say "Hello" and "Thank you" in Xhosa.

 Culture Close-up

Experience a virtual safari.

 Self-Test

Assess their own knowledge of chapter content.

While on their trip, students will practice the following skills:

- **Analyze** maps and charts.
- **Synthesize** information from multiple sources.
- **Categorize** conflicts as avoidable or unavoidable.

TIGed
TakingITGlobal for Educators

Extend the reach of every lesson by helping students connect to a global community of young people with common interests and concerns. Visit myworldgeography.com to
- explore Country Pages relating to Southern and Eastern Africa.
- delve deeper into this chapter's Essential Question, *Is conflict unavoidable?*
- find online alternatives to and solutions for the Unit Closer 21st Century Learning Activity.

 worldgeography.com

TEACHER CENTER

Preview and assign student materials, enrich your teaching, and track student progress with the following resources:
- Online Lesson Planning and Resource Library
- Presentations for Projection
- Online Teacher's Edition and Ancillaries
- Google Earth Links

Assess Enduring Understandings

myWorld Chapter Activity   **Step-by-Step Instructions**   ⏱ 90 min

Agents of Change

Teach this activity at the end of the chapter to assess enduring understandings.

OBJECTIVES

Students will demonstrate the following enduring understandings:
- Conflict shapes people's lives by demanding human and financial resources.
- Political and economic changes affect national stability and standards of living.

Students will provide the following evidence of understanding:
- Meeting Role-Play
- Community Organization Name and Slogan

LEARNING STYLES
- Kinesthetic
- Interpersonal
- Intrapersonal

MATERIALS
- Activity Support: Student Instructions and Rubric, p. T34
- Activity Support: Note-Taking, p. T35
- Activity Cards: #79–84

  79. Nelson Mandela
  80. F. W. DeKlerk
  81. Desmond Tutu
  82. Miriam Makeba
  83. Sheena Duncan
  84. Information Card

Activity Steps

1. **Set Expectations** Tell students that they will use information from the chapter and Activity Cards to role-play real people involved in ending apartheid in South Africa. In character, they will attend the first meeting of a new community organization in South Africa. Their goal is to create a name and slogan that reflect the organization's beliefs about apartheid conflicts. Distribute and review *Activity Support: Student Instructions and Rubric.*

2. **South Africa: Agents of Change**
   - Review *Activity Support: Note-Taking.* Explain that students will complete it during the role-play.
   - Distribute each character card to a group of 4–5 students. Clarify that students will role-play that character for the entire meeting.

   L2 Extra Support Clarify that many students will play the same character. They should meet, greet, and ask questions of all characters in the role-play.

3. **Meet, Greet, and Question** With a volunteer, model an intermingling exchange. Begin 10–15 minutes of mingling and idea exchange.

   ELL Beginner Review English greeting customs.

4. **Call to Order** Call the meeting to order. Give students 5–10 minutes to silently record the names and beliefs of the characters they met. Then have students develop name and slogan ideas to share.

5. **Name and Slogan Brainstorm** Gather one of each character into new groups and have groups discuss name and slogan ideas for 5–10 minutes. Urge them to choose a name and slogan that honors members' shared beliefs about apartheid. Have them list their choices on Activity Support.

   L4 Challenge Ask students to write a press release announcing the new organization

6. **Wrap-up Questions and Discussion** Have students complete the final section of *Activity Support: Note-Taking.* Poll students—in their character roles—on the name and slogan ideas, and then discuss how they and their organization can help South Africa end apartheid without serious conflict.

KEY   ⏱ Time   👤 Individual   👥 Pairs   👨‍👨‍👦 Small Group   👨‍👨‍👧‍👦 Whole Class

Name _____ Class _____ Date _____

myWorld Chapter Activity Support   **Student Instructions and Rubric**

Agents of Change

Activity Instructions Read the following summary of your myWorld Chapter Activity. Follow your teacher's directions for more information.

1. You will attend a community organization meeting in the role of a person involved in the end of apartheid in South Africa.

2. Using information from the chapter and the Activity Cards, learn about the character you will role-play. Determine the beliefs and views you will have as this person.

3. Become the character you have been assigned, and meet, greet, and question the other characters in the role play.

4. Use *Activity Support: Note-Taking* to record names and beliefs of the characters you meet. Then, in a group, share ideas for a name and slogan for the organization. Choose a name and slogan that best describes your beliefs and goals. List your choices on the Activity Support.

5. Answer the wrap-up questions and participate in the organization's discussion of how it can work to end apartheid without serious conflict.

myWorld Chapter Activity	3 Exceeds Understanding	2 Reaches Understanding	1 Approaches Understanding
Meeting Participation	Always maintains character and shares accurate information	Mostly maintains character and shares mostly accurate information	Sometimes in character and shares some inaccurate information
Note-Taking	Records all information accurately	Records most information accurately	Records some information accurately
Slogan and Name Creation	Slogans and names suggested show creativity and clear understanding of the group's role in ending apartheid.	Slogans and names suggested show clear understanding of the group's role in ending apartheid.	Slogans and names suggested show some understanding of the group's role in ending apartheid.

Name _____ Class _____ Date _____

Agents of Change

Directions While you role-play meeting different leaders of the movement to end apartheid in South Africa, complete the sections below. Remember to stay in character.

Meet, Greet, Question You are _____. Find someone . . .

. . . from the same country as you. _____

. . . against apartheid. _____

. . . that was prime minister or president. _____

. . . that spent time in prison. _____

. . . that was part of the National Party. _____

. . . that was part of the African National Congress. _____

. . . that was famous worldwide. _____

Call to Order Complete the table with information from the meet, greet, and question. Later, record name and slogan choices.

Names	Beliefs

Community Group Name	Community Group Slogan

Wrap-up Prepare to respond to the following questions in character.

Which name and slogan matches the organization's shared beliefs? _____

What events show the need for the organization's work? _____

How can the organization help end apartheid without serious conflict? _____

Southern and Eastern Africa

- Introduce the Essential Question so that students will be able to understand the big ideas of this chapter (see earlier page, Connect to the Essential Question).

- Help students prepare to learn about Southern and Eastern Africa by looking at the chapter's maps, charts, and photos.

- Have students make and record chapter predictions with the *Essential Question Preview* in the **Student Journal.**

- Ask them to analyze maps on this page.

GUIDE ON THE SIDE

Explore the Essential Question . . .

Have students complete the Essential Question Writer's Workshop in their **Student Journal** to demonstrate in-depth understanding of the question in the context of this chapter.

Analyze Maps Point out the political map.

- Which country is an island? (Madagascar)

- Which countries have no coastline? (Uganda, Rwanda, Swaziland, Zambia, Zimbabwe, Botswana, Malawi, Ethiopia, Burundi, Lesotho)

- Why might countries such as Somalia and Namibia struggle with water shortages? (They appear to have no permanent lakes or rivers.)

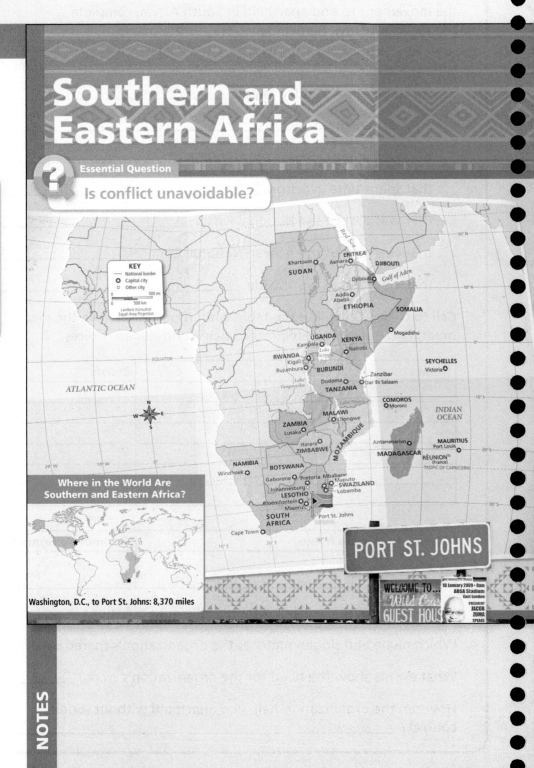

Southern and Eastern Africa

Essential Question

Is conflict unavoidable?

Where in the World Are Southern and Eastern Africa?

Washington, D.C., to Port St. Johns: 8,370 miles

PORT ST. JOHNS

INTRODUCE my Story

Get students excited to learn about Southern and Eastern Africa by first experiencing the region through the eyes of Khulekani, a young South African student.

- Read myStory and watch the myStory Video about his life.

- Have students complete *A Hopeful Song* in the **Student Journal** to prepare to learn about challenges and hopes of young people in the region.

my Story

A Hopeful Song

In this section, you'll read about Khulekani, a young South African man who lives in Port Saint Johns. What does Khulekani's story tell you about life in Southern and Eastern Africa today?

Explore the Essential Question
- at my **worldgeography.com**
- using the myWorld Chapter Activity
- with the **Student Journal**

Story by Greg Fell for myWorld Geography Online

At 19, Khulekani is a young man with strong principles and big dreams. Khulekani is a member of the Xhosa (KOH sah) people, the second-largest ethnic group in South Africa. His parents passed away ten years ago. Now he lives with his aunt and his sister.

Khulekani lives in a settlement called Nonyevu, on a hill that overlooks the town of Port Saint Johns, in the Transkei region of South Africa. Behind the town is the mighty Umzimvubu River. From Khulekani's home, the view of the lush, tropical landscape is spectacular. Still, life can be difficult for Khulekani and his family.

"We have no water or electricity in Nonyevu. This is a problem for me because I often get homework that requires me to watch television. Without electricity I cannot watch television. When my school shirt gets dirty and there is no rainwater I have to use water from the tap in town, and this water is not clean enough for washing."

Along with water and electricity, healthcare is also lacking in parts of Transkei. The HIV/AIDS epidemic has taken a heavy toll in this area.

my Story

A Hopeful Song

- **Summarize** Why is daily life difficult for Khulekani and his family? (There is no water or electricity in the settlement. Good healthcare is also hard to find.)

- **Cause and Effect** How do the daily challenges in his life make it harder for Khulekani at school? (Lack of electricity means that he may not be able to do homework that requires watching something on television. Lack of water means that he may not be able to wash his school shirt.)

On Assignment

Have students go to myworldgeography.com and complete various tasks as investigative journalists in Khulekani's hometown and the surrounding region.

NOTES

QUICK FACTS

Running Water and Electricity In 2008, a survey by South Africa's government showed that more South Africans had gained access to running water. There was an even greater increase in the number of South African households with electricity for lighting, heating, and cooking.

Households with running water:

2001 72.1 percent   **2007** 74.4 percent

Households using electricity for lighting:

2001 69.7 percent   **2007** 80 percent

GUIDE ON THE SIDE

Khulekani doing the laundry

Filling a water jug to bring home

Cooking breakfast

- **Compare and Contrast** How has South Africa changed since the end of apartheid? How has it stayed the same? (The main change since the end of apartheid is that Africans of all races share power while under apartheid, white South Africans controlled the country. Still, most blacks continue to have lower standards of living than whites.)

- **Draw Conclusions** Do you think Khulekani's attitude about equality and fairness are typical among black South Africans? (Sample: Perhaps, but there are probably some people that are more angry about the continued gap between living standards for black and white South Africans.)

Until 1994, the apartheid system oppressed black South Africans. Under apartheid, white South Africans controlled the country, even though black South Africans are a majority. Since the fall of apartheid, South Africans of all races have shared power. The racial divide is slowly healing. Like most young South Africans today, Khulekani has moved past the racial divisions of the past.

"You see, now everything is right," he says, "because we are equal. White people can help black people if they are suffering. Black men have also oppressed other black men, so all in all, it just depends on how good or nice you are, rather than your skin color. Either way you are equal."

Still, like all South Africans, Khulekani is aware of the huge gap between developed and undeveloped areas in his country. He and his family struggle to get by, but many South Africans, mostly white, live more comfortable lives.

On a a typical morning, Khulekani wakes up at 6 A.M. and boils water on his gas stove for a bath. He makes his breakfast, usually bread and tea. Then it's time to go to school. Khulekani walks to school, where he is in 11th grade. When he finishes school next year, he hopes to study at a nearby university. His goal is to graduate and become an accountant.

NOTES

CULTURE

Schools Education in post-apartheid South Africa remains a huge challenge for the government. Inequality between blacks and whites will take more time to correct. In 2006, only 27 percent of black South Africans who were over 19 years old had finished high school and some six to eight million adults were not fully literate. The government spends the largest part of its budget on education, and

has two particular programs in place to improve the situation for the poorest South Africans. It is paying all school fees in areas such as Khulekani's Eastern Cape province so that poor families need not contribute. It is also providing school gardens and other food to feed poor students who may come to school hungry.

An assembly at school

Khulekani meets his friends in town.

Having breakfast and rushing off to school are things teenagers do all over the world. But because Khulekani's family is so poor, everyday routines can be challenging. For example, just to have enough water for drinking, cooking, and washing, Khulekani must carry six-gallon jugs of water more than a half a mile. He is responsible for carrying all the water his family needs.

"You must not waste things like water and just throw them away. I don't have the means to get new things so I must look after what I have. The things we have must only be used in the right way in order to survive."

Despite the challenges he faces, Khulekani remains positive, "Yes, things like carrying water from town and doing homework without electricity can affect my schoolwork but I can work past those things."

Today, being involved at school helps Khulekani enjoy his life. He runs a local youth leadership group, for example. "I like to be involved with the youth group. I like to do positive things."

Khulekani is also a part of the school choir. He is optimistic about the choir. He tells us it is the highlight of his day, "The reason why I want to sing in the choir is because I want to take advantage of my opportunities. I want to learn how to do everything in life."

They sing mostly Xhosa hymns, and Khulekani finds joy when he is singing with the choir.

"I like to be happy, and singing with other kids makes me happy. It's very nice. It takes away the worries."

Khulekani believes in his future and the future of South Africa. He believes that once he has made his own way in the world, he can come back and help fix the problems in his town.

Meet the Journalist
Name Greg Fell
Favorite Moment Choir practice: everything that Khulekani had said to us about the joy singing brought him was true.

myStory Online
Join Khulekani as he shows you more about his life in South Africa.

Choir practice

- **Identify Details** What are some activities Khulekani is involved with at school? (He runs a youth leadership group and he sings in the school choir.)
- **Infer** What qualities do you think Khulekani has? (He is an optimistic person. He has a lot of energy. He is a hard worker. He likes people.)
- **Predict** What kind of role do you think young people like Khulekani will play in South Africa's future? Explain. (Young people will be very important in South Africa's future. Like Khulekani, they will get educated and will use their knowledge to help solve problems.)

myStory Video
Have students watch the video at myworldgeography.com about Khulekani's life at home and at school.

NOTES

Chapter Atlas

OBJECTIVES

Students will know

- the region's major landforms, bodies of water, and ecosystems.
- benefits and challenges from uneven distribution of resources.

Students will be able to

- label an outline map of Southern and Eastern Africa.
- analyze effects of physical geography on people in the region.

SET EXPECTATIONS

In this section, students will

- read Chapter Atlas.
- diagram cause-and-effect relationships between physical and human geography in the region.
- go On Assignment in Southern and Eastern Africa and experience a virtual safari.

CORE CONCEPTS

You may wish to teach or reteach the following lessons from the Core Concepts Handbook:

- Types of Climate, pp. 40–41
- Ecosystems, pp. 42–43
- Environment and Resources, pp. 48–49

KEY

Differentiated Instruction	English Language Instruction
L1 Special Needs **L2** Extra Support	**ELL** Beginner **ELL** Early Intermediate **ELL** Intermediate
L3 On-Level **L4** Challenge	**ELL** Early Advanced **ELL** Advanced

1 Connect
Make learning meaningful

Make Connections Discuss the typical climate, resources, and geographic challenges or shortages in your community. Then list parallel features for a very different U.S. community. Contrast how each community's climate and resources might affect its geographic or economic challenges. Ask students how similar contrasts might affect people's lives in Southern and Eastern Africa, a region where resources are spread very unevenly.

L2 **Extra Support** Provide an example: Our community is hot and dry. A key resource is tourism. A key challenge is shortage of water.

Activate Prior Knowledge Recall that the previous chapter discussed seasonal rains and forest clearing in West and Central Africa. Ask students how these geographic factors might affect nearby Southern and Eastern Africa.

ELL **Early Intermediate** Use visuals of West and Central Africa to recall the image of forest clear-cutting and its impact.

Prepare Follow the steps in the section **Preview.** Preteach the Key Terms. Then have students complete *Word Wise* in their journals using in-text clues and the glossary for help.

2 Experience
Teach knowledge and skills

Read Use **Background** notes and **Guide on the Side** questions to model active reading. Have students use *Take Notes* in their **Student Journal** to record important places to know in Southern and Eastern Africa on an outline map. Students should use the maps in the Chapter Atlas and the Active Atlas at myworldgeography.com for assistance.

L1 **Special Needs** Have students who prefer computer reading use the **Online Student Edition.**

ELL **Intermediate** To help students link physical and human geography, review English cause-and-effect signal words: *because, cause,* and *as a result of.*

L3 **On-Level** Have students read *Enrichment: Victoria Falls* to learn more about an ambitious bridge that responds to dramatic geography.

Practice: myWorld Activity Students will identify and depict cause-and-effect relationships between physical and human geography in Southern and Eastern Africa. They will also discuss ways to maximize positive effects and minimize negative effects. **Step-by-Step Instructions** and **More Activities** follow on pp. T38–T39. Have students complete **21st Century Online Tutor** *Analyze Cause and Effect* and apply this skill to the activity.

SECTION 1 RESOURCE GUIDE

FOR THE STUDENT

my worldgeography.com Student Center

- Active Atlas
- Data Discovery
- Culture Close-up

Student Edition (print and online)
- Chapter Atlas

Student Journal (print and online)
- Section 1 Word Wise
- Section 1 Take Notes

21st Century Learning Online Tutor

- Analyze Cause and Effect
- Read Special-Purpose Maps

FOR THE TEACHER

my worldgeography.com Teacher Center

- Online Lesson Planner
- Presentations for Projection
- SuccessTracker

ProGuide: Africa
- Lesson Plan, pp. T36–T37
- 🏃 myWorld Activity Step-by-Step Instructions, p. T38
- Activity Support: Picture Cards, p. T39
- myWorld Geography Enrichment, p. T40
- Section Quiz, p. T41

Accelerating the Progress of ELLs
- Peer Learning Strategies, p. 46

3 Understand
Assess understanding

Review Review *Word Wise* and *Take Notes* in the Student Journal.

Assess Knowledge and Skills Use the Section Assessment and Section Quiz to check students' progress.

Assess Understanding Review students' responses to the Section Assessment Essential Question prompt.

Remediate Use these strategies to review and remediate.

If students struggle to . . .	Try these strategies.
Describe the region's physical geography	Post a word bank for describing the region's physical geography.
Label an outline map	Suggest labeling countries first and then major landforms.
Read an ecosystems map	Help students label reminder images of each ecosystem.

ELL Support

ELL Objective Students will be able to use prefixes to define new words.

Cultural Connections To reinforce the link between physical and human geography in Southern and Eastern Africa, invite students to use home languages to describe a way that physical geography has affected their lives recently.

ELL Early Advanced/Advanced Content Tip Post the key term *ecotourism*. Circle the prefix *eco*. Explain that it stands for the word *ecology*, which means "environment." Ask students what *ecotourism* might mean.

🏃 **ELL Activity** Provide three cause-and-effect frames related to the region's physical environment. For each frame, provide either a cause statement and/or picture *or* an effect statement and/or picture. Pair students to discuss the frames and suggest statements or pictures that could complete it. Have students work individually to complete their frames. **(Visual/Verbal)**

myWorld Activity   **Step-by-Step Instructions**   20 min

Cause-and-Effect Pairs

OBJECTIVES

Students will

• identify cause-and-effect relationships between physical and human geography in Southern and Eastern Africa.

• draw inferences about additional benefits and challenges of physical geography in the region.

LEARNING STYLE

• Visual
• Logical

21st Century Learning

• Analyze Cause and Effect

MATERIALS

• Activity Support: Picture Cards, p. T39
• Scissors
• Tape or glue

Activity Steps

1. Tell students they will be asked to identify three ways that the region's physical geography affects its people. They will draw pictures representing the three cause-and-effect relationships. Class members will then randomly select cards and discuss ways the region's people can maximize benefits and resolve challenges of their geography.

2. Review cause-and-effect relationships using Africa's weather: *If it rains, then* . . . Have students share positive (crops grow) and negative effects (floods).

3. Using the *Chapter Atlas* and *Activity Support: Picture Cards*, students should draw pictures representing three cause-and-effect relationships in the text.

L1 Special Needs Provide simple picture ideas, such as a diamond ring for South African mining or a miner's hat for dangers of mining.

4. Have students cut out and create two-sided cards. Collect the cards and mix well. Invite volunteers to draw cards at random and read one side aloud. Listeners must guess the missing cause or effect.

L4 Challenge Have students make cards that show causes with multiple effects or chains of linked causes and effects.

5. Discuss these questions: If the effect is a benefit, how can people in the region maximize it? If the effect is a problem, how might people minimize it?

ELL Early Intermediate Use ELL Activity to review cause-and-effect relationships for use in the discussion.

More Activities From myWorld Teachers

 Local Connections Have students make handbooks on the rules in your community that protect the environment or the animals in it. For example, there might be rules about when people can fish or where to throw away chemicals. **(Logical)**

Ecotourism Ad To reinforce the important interaction between human and physical geography, have students create ads for ecotourism safaris on the Serengeti. **(Visual)**

 Team Teaching Assign partners to develop ways to teach the region's key landforms and natural resources to a pre-school audience. Teaching teams should use visual props and gestures to explain the features. **(Kinesthetic/Verbal)**

my worldgeography.com   **Teacher Center** ⊙   Find additional resources in the online Teacher Center.

Name _____ Class _____ Date _____

myWorld Activity Support   **Picture Cards**

Cause-and-Effect Pairs

Directions Draw pictures to represent cause-and-effect relationships in *Chapter Atlas*. Then cut out cards on the single dotted lines. Fold on the double lines and secure with tape.

Cause	**Effect**
Cause	**Effect**
Cause	**Effect**

T39

Name _____ Class _____ Date _____

Enrichment: Victoria Falls

Directions Read the selection below and study the diagram. Then
answer the questions that follow and complete the activity.

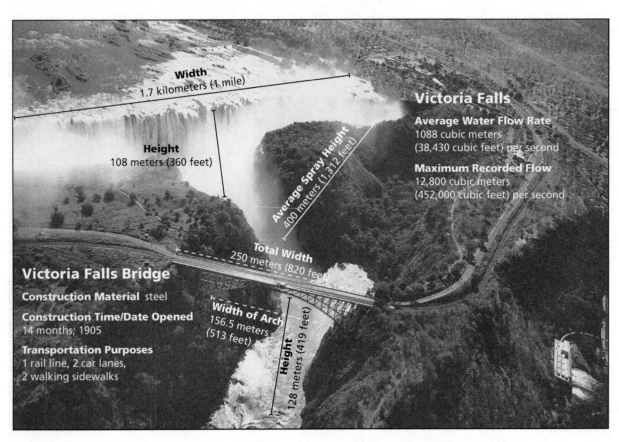

Width
1.7 kilometers (1 mile)

Height
108 meters (360 feet)

Average Spray Height
400 meters (1,312 feet)

Victoria Falls

Average Water Flow Rate
1088 cubic meters
(38,430 cubic feet) per second

Maximum Recorded Flow
12,800 cubic meters
(452,000 cubic feet) per second

Total Width
250 meters (820 feet)

Victoria Falls Bridge

Construction Material steel

Construction Time/Date Opened
14 months; 1905

Transportation Purposes
1 rail line, 2 car lanes,
2 walking sidewalks

Width of Arch
156.5 meters
(513 feet)

Height
128 meters (419 feet)

1. What might cause the flow rate over the falls to change so much at
   certain times? What does this suggest about the climate upriver?

   _____

   _____

2. Cecil John Rhodes, who commissioned the bridge, said "Build the
   bridge across the Zambezi where the trains as they pass will catch
   the spray from the falls." How does this location affect the bridge's
   transportation and recreational purposes? How do you think it
   influenced the height and width of the bridge?

   _____

   _____

3. **Activity** Speculate on how the bridge's builders built across the
   gorge. Then briefly research to prove or adjust your ideas.

Name _____ Class _____ Date _____

Section Quiz

Directions Answer the following questions using what you learned in Section 1.

1. _____ What feature of Southern and Eastern African is a long, unusually flat land area between areas of higher ground?
   a. the Great Rift Valley
   b. the Kalahari
   c. the Namib
   d. the Eastern African Plateau

2. _____ How does ecotourism affect Southern and Eastern Africa?
   a. fighting different diseases
   b. creating zoos for animals
   c. helping conserve the environment
   d. cutting down forested areas

3. _____ What is the definition of *poaching*?
   a. the conservation of wildlife
   b. the act of protecting natural resources
   c. the illegal hunting of wildlife
   d. the destruction of forests

4. _____ What does the Serengeti Plain look like?
   a. grass-covered with few trees
   b. mountains covered with forest
   c. large areas of treeless sand dunes
   d. dense forest that blocks out the sun

5. _____ Which country in the region does coffee come from?
   a. Zambia
   b. Ethiopia
   c. Tanzania
   d. South Africa

6. Complete the table below with one cause and effect statement about each topic in relation to Southern and Eastern Africa.

Landforms and Bodies of Water	Ecosystems
Natural Resources	**Challenges for People**

SECTION PREVIEW

Chapter Atlas

- Model preparing to read by previewing the Key Ideas, Key Terms, headings, visuals, and captions. Have students make predictions about what they will learn. For ELL support, post the prompt, "I predict I will read about . . ."

- Preview and practice reading special-purpose maps by looking at the Ecosystems Map. Help students make predictions about information the map might contain. Ask, How do ecosystems unite nations in Southern and Eastern Africa?

- Preteach this section's high-use Academic Vocabulary and Key Terms using the table on the next page and in-text definitions. Have students practice Key Terms by completing the *Word Wise* page in their journals.

GUIDE ON THE SIDE

Remarkable Land and Water

- **Identify Main Ideas** What is the Great Rift Valley? How did it form? (It is a long, very flat area of land between two areas of higher ground. It formed when two of Earth's plates spread apart, letting the land between them sink.)

- **Compare and Contrast** How might the land of the valley be different from the land next to it? (The land next to the valley will be much higher than that in the valley.)

- **Predict** What else do you predict will be different about the geography of the Great Rift valley and the lands near it? (Sample: The climate and ecosystems of the valley will be different from those in the lands next to it.)

Reading Skill

Label an Outline Map While they read, have students identify the Places to Know! on the outline map of the region in the **Student Journal**.

Section 1

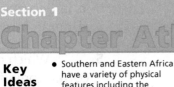
Chapter Atlas

| Key Ideas | • Southern and Eastern Africa have a variety of physical features including the Great Rift Valley, highland plateaus, and Africa's great lakes. | • The region's ecosystems vary greatly, and include tropical areas, savannas, highlands and arid zones. | • Some parts of the region are rich in natural resources, but feeding the population has proved difficult. |

Key Terms • Great Rift Valley   • Serengeti Plain   • poaching   • ecotourism   Visual Glossary

 Reading Skill: Label an Outline Map Take notes using the outline map in your journal.

◄ Mount Kilimanjaro, Africa's highest mountain

◄ A woman from Tanzania

Remarkable Land and Water

Southern and Eastern Africa, where Khulekani lives, are home to diverse and impressive physical features. From the huge desert of the Sahara to Africa's great lakes, this region has some of Earth's most breathtaking landscapes and wildlife.

One of Southern and Eastern Africa's unique features is the **Great Rift Valley.** This is a long, unusually flat area of land between areas of higher ground in Eastern Africa. It was formed when two of Earth's plates moved away from each other. This movement caused the land in between them to sink and form a valley.

ANSWERS

ACADEMIC VOCABULARY

High-Use Word	Definition and Sample Sentence
transportation	*n.* system used to move people or things *Transportation in our community includes cars, trains, and buses.*
irrigate	*v.* to bring water to an area *Farmers must irrigate or their crops will dry up in a place where so little rain falls.*

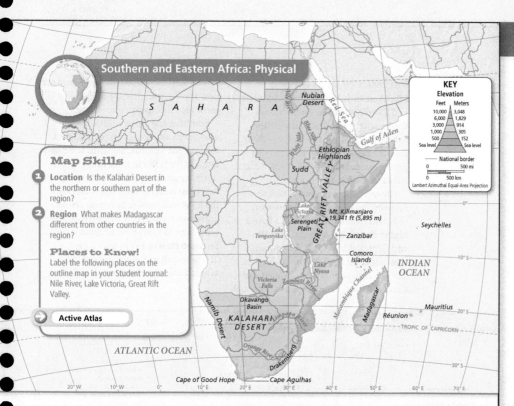

Southern and Eastern Africa: Physical

SAHARA

Nubian Desert

Red Sea

Gulf of Aden

Blue Nile

White Nile

Ethiopian Highlands

Sudd

GREAT RIFT VALLEY

Lake Victoria

Mt. Kilimanjaro
19,341 ft (5,895 m)

Serengeti Plain

Lake Tanganyika

Zanzibar

Seychelles

Comoro Islands

Lake Nyasa

Mozambique Channel

INDIAN OCEAN

Victoria Falls

Zambezi River

Madagascar

Mauritius

Réunion

TROPIC OF CAPRICORN

Okavango Basin

Namib Desert

Limpopo River

KALAHARI DESERT

Orange River

Drakensberg

ATLANTIC OCEAN

Cape of Good Hope   Cape Agulhas

20°W 10°W 0° 10°E 20°E 30°E 40°E 50°E 60°E 70°E

0°

10°S

20°S

30°S

KEY
Elevation

Feet	Meters
10,000	3,048
6,000	1,829
3,000	914
1,000	305
500	152
Sea level	Sea level

— National border

0   500 mi
0   500 km
Lambert Azimuthal Equal-Area Projection

Map Skills

1. **Location** Is the Kalahari Desert in the northern or southern part of the region?
2. **Region** What makes Madagascar different from other countries in the region?

Places to Know!
Label the following places on the outline map in your Student Journal: Nile River, Lake Victoria, Great Rift Valley.

⊙ **Active Atlas**

The valley's sides rise steeply into mountains and high plateaus. Africa's highest point, Mount Kilimanjaro, sits along the Great Rift Valley. There are also large plains between mountain ranges.

Near the Great Rift Valley lie a group of large and beautiful lakes. One of these, Lake Victoria, is the largest lake in Africa. Africa's great lakes support plant, animal, and human life in areas around them. So do the large rivers that originate, or start, in this region. The Nile, the Zambezi, the Orange, and the Limpopo are the largest. A spectacular waterfall called Victoria Falls is on the Zambezi River.

Rivers serve as a <u>transportation</u> network. But the Sudd swamps block movement between East Africa and Egypt, in North Africa. In the Sudd, floating mats of vegetation and tall papyrus reeds make it difficult for ships to pass.

Parts of Southern and Eastern Africa are very dry. Deserts ring the region: the Sahara, Nubian, Kalahari, and Namib. The Namib Desert, along the coast of Namibia, has some of the world's tallest sand dunes.

Reading Check How do lakes and rivers affect plant, animal, and human life in Southern and Eastern Africa?

transportation, *n.,* system used to move people or things

MAP SKILLS 1. southern 2. It is an island. 3. Students should correctly locate and label each place on the outline map in their **Student Journal.**

READING CHECK Rivers and lakes support life in areas around them. Rivers provide a transportation system.

GUIDE ON THE SIDE

- **Identify Details** What are the main bodies of water in Southern and Eastern Africa? (a group of large lakes including Lake Victoria, the Nile, Zambezi, Orange, and Limpopo rivers, the Sudd swamps)

- **Categorize** On which river are the Victoria Falls? (Zambezi River)

- **Predict** Why might some people in Southern and Eastern Africa struggle to find enough water? (Some parts of the region are desert and get very little rainfall.)

Map Skills Have students locate physical features on the map.

- If physical features contribute to conflicts, how might the conflicts in different parts of Southern and Eastern Africa compare? (They are probably similar because the physical geography is fairly similar.)

⊙ **Active Atlas**

Point out the map of Southern and Eastern Africa's physical geography.

- Have students go to myworldgeography.com to learn more about the physical geography of Southern and Eastern Africa.

GEOGRAPHY

Monsoon Winds The seasonal wind patterns that influence East Africa's weather are also known as monsoon winds. Monsoon winds occur because land warms and cools more quickly than water. In warmer months, the land heats up but the water stays cooler. The hot air rises, which allows the cooler air to flow onto land. That cooler air brings moisture from the ocean with it. In cooler months, this process is reversed. The land cools more quickly than the water, drawing cool and dry air from the land toward the water. These seasonal shifts cause wet seasons—when the winds flow from water to land—and dry seasons—when the winds flow from land to water. In Africa, however, even the wet seasons are relatively dry.

Patterns of Ecosystems

- **Compare and Contrast** How is the climate in Southern and Eastern Africa different than in West and Central Africa? (Southern and Eastern Africa has areas of higher elevation that have lower temperatures and less precipitation, even at the Equator.)

- **Infer** How do you think elevation affects temperature? (Temperature decreases with increased elevation.)

- **Identify Main Ideas** What is the best-known ecosystem in Southern and Eastern Africa? Give an example. (the savanna; the Serengeti Plain)

Map Skills Have students identify ecosystems on the map.

- How might the vegetation in Zimbabwe compare to that in Sudan? Explain. (It is probably similar, because both nations have tropical or subtropical grassland ecosystems.)

21st Century Learning

Read Special-Purpose Maps Have students develop this skill by using this interactive online tutorial and activities. Students will learn how to read special-purpose maps and apply this skill to new situations.

Patterns of Ecosystems

Like West and Central Africa, Southern and Eastern Africa lie on both sides of the Equator. This region also has the Sahara in the north and wetter regions near the Equator. Wind patterns that cause seasonal rains in West and Central Africa also affect this region.

However, there is a major difference between the two regions. Many parts of Southern and Eastern Africa have a higher elevation, or height, than West and Central Africa. This height means that areas near the Equator are less hot and wet than similar areas in West and Central Africa. For example, even though Mount Kilimanjaro and Mount Kenya are near the Equator, they are so high that snow caps their peaks year-round.

Southern and Eastern Africa have woodlands and forests on both sides of the Equator. Gorillas, leopards, and many kinds of birds live in these areas.

The savanna is one of the most important ecosystems in this region. It is also the most well known. Savannas are flat, grass-covered plains with few trees. The most famous part of the savanna is the **Serengeti Plain** in Kenya and Tanzania. The Serengeti and other parts of the savanna are home to many animals.

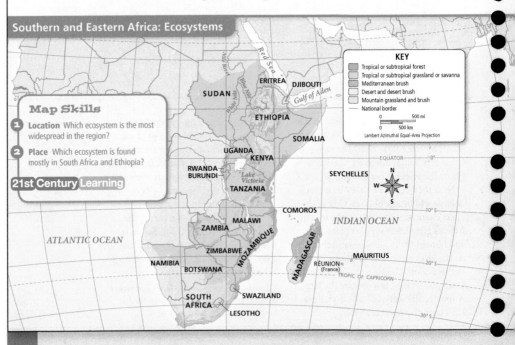

Southern and Eastern Africa: Ecosystems

Map Skills

1. **Location** Which ecosystem is the most widespread in the region?
2. **Place** Which ecosystem is found mostly in South Africa and Ethiopia?

21st Century Learning

KEY
- Tropical or subtropical forest
- Tropical or subtropical grassland or savanna
- Mediterranean brush
- Desert and desert brush
- Mountain grassland and brush
- — National border

Lambert Azimuthal Equal-Area Projection

MAP SKILLS 1. tropical or subtropical grassland or savanna **2.** mountain grassland and brush

QUICK FACTS

Adaptable Wildebeests Over a million wildebeests live on the Serengeti, where they have adapted to the unique landscape. They face two main challenges. First, food and water vary dramatically by location, season, and even by year. Second, wildebeests must avoid meat-eating predators. To overcome the first challenge, wildebeests have adapted in key ways. For example, their mouths are built to eat the Serengeti's very nutritious short grasses quickly and in large amounts. They are built to migrate, and do so when food supplies fall. To overcome the second challenge, wildebeests have changed behaviors. For example, they deliver all their young in a short time and the young can run more quickly than other similar animals. This allows wildebeests to keep moving to find food and to avoid predators.

Large herds of elephants, lions, wildebeests, zebras, giraffes, gazelles, and other animals live on the plains. This wildlife shapes the way people see the region. Still, many Africans live in towns and cities and may never see one of these animals in the wild.

Many African animals have become endangered. This can happen because they are hunted too much or because people move into places they live. Governments have tried to protect the animals. However, **poaching,** or illegal hunting, is still a problem. Kenya, South Africa, and other countries have set up national parks to protect animals. At the same time, these countries promote **ecotourism**. This is a kind of tourism in which people learn about conservation and try to do little or no harm to the environment.

As in West and Central Africa, the trees in many forested areas in Southern and Eastern Africa have been cut down. Cleared land is used for farmland or mining. South Africa, Madagascar, Kenya, and other countries in the region are trying to grow new forests in some areas.

Reading Check What type of ecosystem supports zebras and lions?

my World IN NUMBERS
150,000 gazelles and **3,000** lions live in Tanzania's Serengeti National Park.

Mountain gorillas live in high tropical woodlands in Rwanda, Uganda, and neighboring countries.

Gazelles, lions, elephants, zebras, and many other animals thrive on the wide-open plains of the savanna.

Culture Close-up

READING CHECK savanna

- **Cause and Effect** Why are many African animals endangered? (They have been hunted too much or pushed from their habitat.)
- **Compare Viewpoints** Think of some arguments in favor of and against hunting animals. (In favor: Animals are harming crops; Against: Animals will become extinct.)
- **Problem Solve** What problems might wildlife parks cause for people in the area? How can governments solve these problems? (The parks might reduce hunting and so create food shortages. Governments can suggest other ways to get food or adapt the park's borders.)

myWorld in Numbers

Analyze Data What might happen if there were more lions? Explain. (There would be fewer gazelles. Lions eat gazelles.)

 Culture Close-up

Have students go to myworldgeography.com to experience a virtual safari.

ANSWERS

ECONOMICS

Mining Industries South African mining dominates the production of some mineral resources. For example, it supplies 80 percent of the world's platinum. The industry employs nearly 500,000 people directly and another 400,000 through industry suppliers. Mining is the country's biggest employer. In 2009, record high gold prices put even more pressure on South Africa's miners. Companies began to drill even deeper into the ground, and some miners have illegally broken into closed shafts in search of gold. Unfortunately, both actions have led to increased accidents and deaths. Tanzanian mining is also important to that nation's economy. Recent changes in government policies have led to a mining boom, especially in gold mining. Mining exports rose from $45 million in 1995 to $384 million in 2002.

GUIDE ON THE SIDE

Riches from the Land

- **Identify Details** List the main mineral resources of Southern and Eastern Africa. (diamonds, gold, platinum, copper, tin, iron, uranium)
- **Categorize** Where are most of the mineral resources located? (South Africa, Botswana, Tanzania)
- **Cause and Effect** What problems has mining caused for the region and its people? (Mining has poor and dangerous working conditions.)

Map Skills Have students locate each resource on the map.

- Looking at where resources can be found, would you predict that Somalia will be a rich or a poor country? Why? (Somalia will be a poor country because, according to the map, it has no important natural resources.)

Active Atlas

Point out the map of Southern and Eastern Africa's Resources.
- Have students go to myworldgeography.com to see more data about the resources of Southern and Eastern Africa.

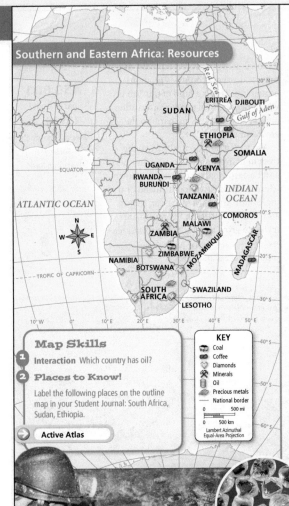

Map Skills

1. **Interaction** Which country has oil?
2. **Places to Know!**
Label the following places on the outline map in your Student Journal: South Africa, Sudan, Ethiopia.

Active Atlas

Riches From the Land

Southern Africa has more mineral and ore resources than many other parts of the world. It also has some areas where farming is very productive.

Mining Some of the region's resources are precious stones or metals like diamonds, gold, and platinum. Others, such as copper, tin, iron, and uranium, are important for business and industry.

Not all countries have an abundance, or large amount, of minerals. Some have many resources, while others have few. South Africa has by far the richest deposits of mineral resources. It is among the world's leading producers of gold, platinum, and chromium. Diamonds are another big moneymaker.

Mining helps countries like South Africa and Botswana build strong economies. It brings jobs to local people. It yields products to sell to people abroad. However, miners often work for long hours in poor conditions. Some underground mines are very dangerous. Many miners have lost their lives when mines collapsed or other accidents occurred.

Mining is difficult work, but it can also bring wealth to a region. At the left are diamonds as they look when they are mined. Below is a cut diamond.

ANSWERS

MAP SKILLS **1.** Sudan **2.** Students should correctly locate and label each place on the outline map in their **Student Journal.**

368 Eastern Hemisphere
534 World Geography

CORE CONCEPTS: PEOPLE'S IMPACT ON THE ENVIRONMENT

Review Core Concepts 4.3 before discussing the impact of mining on the environment in South Africa. Recall ways that people can affect the environment negatively, such as deforestation, pollution, and destruction of wildlife. Then have students identify positive and negative ways that South Africans have affected their environment.

Mining can also hurt the environment. Some types of mining leave large scars on the land. Mining can cause pollution. Air and water can be polluted when minerals are processed and when fuel is burned to run drills.

Farming People also use the land in this region to farm and raise animals. Farmlands can be found in most of the countries in the region. But there are many areas that are very dry. These places cannot rely on regular rainfall for crops. Sudan, Ethiopia, Somalia, and Namibia struggle to find enough water to grow their crops.

Because so much of the region is dry, many farmers <u>irrigate</u> their land. Cotton, tobacco, and tea are grown in irrigated areas. People also raise cattle and other livestock in drier parts of the region. In some of these areas, wild animals are a threat to the herds. Herders must defend their animals at night.

Some of the region has very fertile land. In South Africa and other countries, people grow many crops. They run large commercial farms or plantations. These farms grow crops such as sugar cane, cotton, avocados, and tropical fruits. They often export their crops.

Coffee is Ethiopia's most important export. In fact, the plant was probably first grown in Ethiopia's highlands. The word *coffee* may even come from the Kaffa region of Ethiopia, where the crop is grown.

Reading Check What are the advantages and disadvantages of diamond mining?

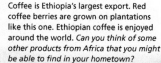
irrigate, *v.,* to bring water to an area

Coffee is Ethiopia's largest export. Red coffee berries are grown on plantations like this one. Ethiopian coffee is enjoyed around the world. *Can you think of some other products from Africa that you might be able to find in your hometown?*

GUIDE ON THE SIDE

- **Summarize** What big problem must farmers in Southern and Eastern Africa solve in order to succeed? (They must get enough water in areas where rain doesn't always supply that water.)

- **Cause and Effect** How do the region's farmers solve their main problem? (They irrigate.)

- **Identify Details** What are some of the main crops in Southern and Eastern Africa? (cotton, tobacco, tea, coffee, sugar cane, avocados, tropical fruits)

- **Categorize** Which crops grow in dry areas? (cotton, tobacco, tea)

READING CHECK advantages: jobs, income for the economy. disadvantages: poor working conditions, pollution

CAPTION Sample: sugar, cotton

ANSWERS

PRIMARY SOURCE

Homemade Electricity in Uganda Share these remarks about small hydroelectric dams that people are building in Uganda. One such dam cost about $15,000 to build and creates electricity for a single hospital. Others bring power to small villages. They also divert less water from downstream than large dams. Ask if the efforts should be supported by African governments and by the international aid community.

"The government has promised and promised to bring electricity to the village and never has. So we did it ourselves."

—Sabuni Seezi, Kagando Christian Hospital, western Uganda

"We're embracing a forgotten technology that . . . lets us control our own destiny."

—Jim Melrose, managing director Lujeri Tea Estates, Malawi

GUIDE ON THE SIDE

Challenges of the Environment

- **Identify Details** What are some challenges for countries that lack water resources? (They struggle to feed their populations or build economies.)

- **Identify Main Ideas** What are some causes of famine in the region? (lack of water and good farmland)

- **Infer** Why are Sudan and Ethiopia the main recipients of food aid? (Both have dry climates and lack the rain needed to grow sufficient food.)

Map Skills Have students trace the flow of water on the map.

- Which country takes the most water? (Egypt)

 myWorld Activity

Cause-and-Effect Pairs Find Step-by-Step Instructions and an Activity Support on pp. T38–T39. **(Visual/Logical)**

> **Active Atlas**

Point out the water flow map.
- Have students go to myworldgeography.com to learn more about water use in the region.

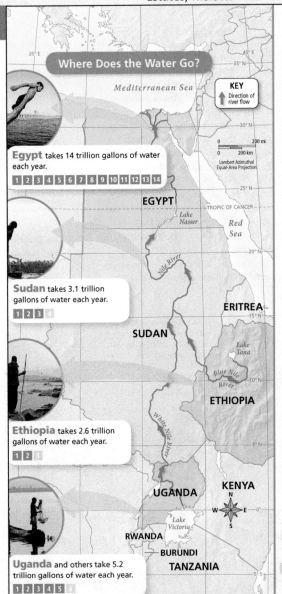

Where Does the Water Go?

KEY
↑ Direction of river flow

Mediterranean Sea

Egypt takes 14 trillion gallons of water each year.
`1 2 3 4 5 6 7 8 9 10 11 12 13 14`

EGYPT

Lake Nasser

Red Sea

TROPIC OF CANCER

Nile River

Sudan takes 3.1 trillion gallons of water each year.
`1 2 3 4`

ERITREA

SUDAN

Lake Tana

Blue Nile River

ETHIOPIA

White Nile River

Ethiopia takes 2.6 trillion gallons of water each year.
`1 2 3`

UGANDA

KENYA

Lake Victoria

RWANDA

BURUNDI

TANZANIA

Uganda and others take 5.2 trillion gallons of water each year.
`1 2 3 4 5 6`

0   200 mi
0   200 km
Lambert Azimuthal Equal-Area Projection

Challenges of the Environment

Water—who has it and who doesn't—is a huge challenge for countries in this region. Countries that have enough water resources have a better chance of feeding their populations. Countries that do not have enough water struggle to support their populations. Lack of water and good farmland leads to famine, or a shortage of food. Sudan and Ethiopia receive more food aid than many other countries in the world for this reason.

The region's many rivers provide a valuable benefit to some countries. Dams have been built along major rivers to generate hydroelectricity. They also provide water for nearby farms.

But these dams can cause conflict. For example, the Nile flows through Sudan and other countries before reaching Egypt. Dams built in Uganda take water away from Sudan. Who gets to decide how much water each country can take?

Reading Check What are the advantages and disadvantages of building dams?

> **Map Skills**
>
> This map shows the amounts of water taken from the Nile River by different countries each year.
>
> **Interaction** What might happen if Uganda took more water? How would this affect Sudan?
>
> > **Active Atlas**
>
> **myWorld Activity** Cause-and-Effect Pairs

MAP SKILLS There will be less for the nations downriver, such as Sudan.

READING CHECK Dams create electricity and supply water but reduce water for people downstream.

SECTION 1 ASSESSMENT 1. Two of Earth's plates moved apart, causing land between them to sink into a valley. **2.** Ecotourism raises awareness; Poaching threatens wildlife. **3.** Kenya and Tanzania **4.** elephants, lions, wildebeests, zebras, giraffes, gazelles **5.** Mineral resources help make South Africa prosperous.

GEOGRAPHY

Diseases Sleeping sickness is actually called African trypanosomiasis. It is found only in sub-Saharan Africa because it is spread only by the bite of the tsetse fly. The most recent epidemic was in the 1970s, when the disease surprised doctors by appearing again after a long period of little sickness. Sleeping sickness gets its name because people very ill with it experience trouble with their sleep.

In river blindness (oncheocerciasis), people can become blind. The disease is transmitted by the bite of the black fly that lives in Africa's fast-moving streams and rivers. Cholera is not at all unique to Africa. This disease is transmitted by polluted water and food, and can be controlled by providing access to clean water and food.

Disease

As in West and Central Africa, disease causes many problems in Southern and Eastern Africa. Some diseases stem from the environment. Just as mosquitoes carry malaria, tsetse flies carry sleeping sickness. The flies live in many areas between the Sahara and the Kalahari Desert. These areas are known as the tsetse belt.

Sleeping sickness can be deadly to both people and the cattle they raise. The disease makes it impossible to raise cattle in the tsetse belt.

Many people in Southern and Eastern Africa do not have access to clean water, and so they contract diseases carried by water. For example, cholera and river blindness have crippled and killed many Southern and Eastern Africans.

AIDS, which does not stem from the environment, has reached epidemic proportions in this region. You will read more about AIDS later.

Reading Check What harm does the tsetse fly cause?

A doctor and patient in Kenya

Southern and Eastern Africa Adult HIV/AIDS Incidence Rate

| United States 0.6% | Somalia 1% | South Africa 18.1% | Swaziland 38.8% |

People with HIV/AIDS   People without HIV/AIDS   SOURCE: *CIA World Factbook*, 2009

Chart Skills

The United States population is 307,000,000. Swaziland has 1,123,000 people. Which country has more people living with HIV/AIDS?

> **Data Discovery**

Section 1 Assessment

Key Terms

1. How was the Great Rift Valley formed?

2. How do ecotourism and poaching affect the environment?

3. In which nations is the Serengeti Plain located?

Key Ideas

4. What are some animals that live on the savanna?

5. What resources help make countries like South Africa more prosperous than others?

6. Why might a dam in Uganda cause trouble in Sudan?

Think Critically

7. **Compare Viewpoints** Why do some people believe mining helps people in the region while others say it is harmful? Give evidence.

8. **Compare and Contrast** Somalia and Botswana have different resources. How might this difference affect the lives of their people?

Essential Question

Is conflict unavoidable?

9. How do you think the lack of resources in some countries might cause conflict? How might the abundance of resources in other countries cause conflict? Go to your Student Journal to record your answers.

READING CHECK The tsetse fly carries sleeping sickness.

CHART SKILLS The United States has more people living with HIV/AIDS.

6. A dam in Uganda might reduce water for Sudan. 7. Mining brings jobs, but they are hard and dangerous. Mining can also pollute the environment. 8. With limited water Somalis struggle to get enough food. Mineral resources probably give people in Botswana jobs, so they can afford to fulfill their needs. 9. People fight both over access to limited resources and to control valuable resources.

GUIDE ON THE SIDE

Disease

- **Identify Details** What diseases cause problems in this region? (sleeping sickness, cholera, river blindness, HIV/AIDS)

- **Predict** How does disease make a community struggle economically? (Workers cannot work. Medical care costs the community money.)

- **Problem Solve** What are some ways that people could avoid getting these diseases? (Stay away from rivers, wear insect repellent to avoid fly bites, and try to use clean water.)

Chart Skills Have students use the chart to compare HIV/AIDS rates in the different countries.

- How could disease rates increase conflict? (Conflicts might occur over who will care for the sick or who gets medical care.)

> **Data Discovery**

Have students go to myworldgeography.com to learn more about disease in the region.

History of Southern and Eastern Africa

OBJECTIVES

Students will know

- early cultures in Southern and Eastern Africa.
- effects of Arab and European trade, rule, and influence on the region.

Students will be able to

- sequence key events in regional history.
- categorize people and ideas in regional history.

SET EXPECTATIONS

In this section, students will

- read History of Southern and Eastern Africa.
- complete a category card about regional history and sequence the card on a timeline.
- go On Assignment in Southern and Eastern Africa and learn more about the history of the region.

CORE CONCEPTS

You may wish to teach or reteach the following lessons from the Core Concepts Handbook:

- Trade, pp. 66–67
- Migration, pp. 78–79
- Cultural Diffusion and Change, pp. 96–97

KEY

Differentiated Instruction

L1 Special Needs   **L2** Extra Support
L3 On-Level   **L4** Challenge

English Language Instruction

ELL Beginner   **ELL** Early Intermediate   **ELL** Intermediate
ELL Early Advanced   **ELL** Advanced

1 Connect
Make learning meaningful

Make Connections Ask students to name familiar languages, foods, or consumer items that came to your community from other cultures. As a class, discuss ways that these features have influenced your community. Ask students to predict how movement of people and ideas affects communities in a region.

L2 **Extra Support** Offer examples, such as the influx of foods from other cultures leading to diverse food on the school lunch menu or at local markets and restaurants

Activate Prior Knowledge Remind students that in the previous chapter they learned about European colonization in West and Central Africa. Help students to review the effects of colonialism. Ask them to predict how colonization might affect Southern and Eastern Africa.

L4 **Challenge** Have students create and present two-column tables recalling pros and cons of colonization in West and Central Africa.

Prepare Follow the steps in the section **Preview.** Preteach the Key Terms. Then have students complete *Word Wise* in their journals using in-text clues and the glossary for help.

2 Experience
Teach knowledge and skills

Read Use **Background** notes and **Guide on the Side** questions to model active reading. Have students use *Take Notes* in their **Student Journal** to sequence events in the history of Southern and Eastern Africa. Have them complete **21st Century Online Tutor** *Sequence* and apply this skill to reading the section.

L1 **Special Needs** Have students place sticky notes with questions on areas of text that they find confusing. Review the questions in small groups.

ELL **Intermediate/Early Advanced** Preteach pronunciation for the Key Terms *Boers* and *apartheid,* noting that these words reflect the pronunciation patterns of the South African language Afrikaans.

L4 **Challenge** Have students read *Enrichment: Homo Erectus* to learn more about the discovery of early humans in Africa.

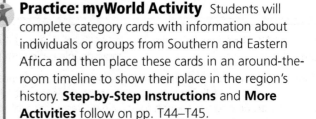

Practice: myWorld Activity Students will complete category cards with information about individuals or groups from Southern and Eastern Africa and then place these cards in an around-the-room timeline to show their place in the region's history. **Step-by-Step Instructions** and **More Activities** follow on pp. T44–T45.

SECTION 2 RESOURCE GUIDE

FOR THE STUDENT

my worldgeography.com Student Center
- Active Atlas

Student Edition (print and online)
- History of Southern and Eastern Africa

Student Journal (print and online)
- Section 2 Word Wise
- Section 2 Take Notes

21st Century Learning Online Tutor
- Sequence
- Categorize

FOR THE TEACHER

my worldgeography.com Teacher Center
- Online Lesson Planner
- Presentations for Projection
- SuccessTracker

ProGuide: Africa
- Lesson Plan, pp. T42–T43
- 🏃 myWorld Activity Step-by-Step Instructions, p. T44
- Activity Support: Identity Cards, p. T45
- myWorld Geography Enrichment, p. T46
- Section Quiz, p. T47

Accelerating the Progress of ELLs
- Organizing Information Strategies, p. 48

---

3 Understand
Assess understanding

Review Review *Word Wise* and *Take Notes* in the **Student Journal.**

Assess Knowledge and Skills Use the Section Assessment and Section Quiz to check students' progress.

Assess Understanding Review students' responses to the Section Assessment Essential Question prompt.

Remediate Use these strategies to review and remediate.

If students struggle to . . .	Try these strategies.
Sequence regional historical events	Have them list dates from the text on sticky notes, then put these in order.
Categorize individuals or groups in the region	Discuss characteristics that define each group in the text.
Understand the fall of apartheid	Replay the **myStory Video** and review life in post-apartheid South Africa.

ELL Support

ELL Objective Students will be able to use English proper nouns and adjectives to name nations and express nationality.

Cultural Connections To connect students to the movement of ideas in regional history, let them use home languages to describe cultural features brought from home countries to America.

ELL Early Intermediate Content Tip Point out the word *apartheid and* circle *apart* within it. To define the term, hold your hands together and then apart. Explain that *apartheid* means "apartness," the key principle of the *apartheid* policy.

ELL Activity Post and review a word bank of nations and nationalities for the section, such as *Kenya/Kenyan.* Have students write the appropriate nouns and adjectives on index cards—nouns on one side and adjectives on the other. They can use these cards to bookmark section text about these nations and nationalities, and to complete *Activity Support: Identity Cards.* **(Verbal)**

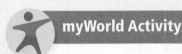

myWorld Activity   **Step-by-Step Instructions**

 25 min

Where I'm From

OBJECTIVES

Students will
- categorize important individuals and groups from regional history.
- sequence individuals and events from regional history.

LEARNING STYLE
- Logical
- Kinesthetic

21st Century Learning
- Categorize

MATERIALS
- Paper roll or long ribbon
- Markers
- Activity Support: Identity Cards, p. T45

Activity Steps

1. Tell students that they will be asked to identify an individual or group from the history of Southern and Eastern Africa. Students will use section text to describe and categorize the individual or group on a card and then work with other students to place the card in proper sequence on a timeline.

2. Distribute copies of *Activity Support: Identity Cards* and assign the listed people and groups evenly among students, repeating as needed.

   L2 Extra Support Assign cards that correspond to boldfaced subheadings, such as *Nubians* or *Aksum People* or Key Terms.

3. Allow students 5 minutes to locate the pertinent chapter text about their person or group.

4. Give students 10 minutes to complete their Identity Cards. Clarify how to describe sequence without a specific date.

ELL Early Advanced Read through the names on *Activity Support: Identity Cards,* confirming that students can identify and pronounce them.

5. Use a paper roll to create a large timeline on a wall or floor. Start the timeline with the label *2 million years ago* and end it with the label *1994.* Invite students to read their cards aloud, place them in the appropriate place on the timeline, and add a date label.

6. As a class, discuss each card's placement. Focus on how the person or group influenced Southern and Eastern African history. Have students record dates or sequence descriptions for each new card in the table on *Activity Support: Identity Cards.*

   L4 Challenge Invite students to briefly research their person or group, sharing additional information orally.

More Activities From myWorld Teachers

Local Connections Have students create "Where I'm From" cards about people in your community that have made an impact and order the cards on a timeline. **(Verbal/Logical)**

Art Exhibit Using online sources, have students locate photographs of art and artifacts from the cultures of Southern and Eastern Africa. Work as a class to create a printed or online art exhibit. Discuss how a culture's art relates to its resources, i.e. diamonds, or its culture, i.e. iron making. **(Logical/Visual)**

Charades Post important events or terms from the section. Have student teams convey events or terms with gesture and pantomime, as other students guess. For example, they might pass notes to one another to show the spread of ideas, or angrily point away to show independence movements. **(Kinesthetic)**

 worldgeography.com **Teacher Center** ➔ Find additional resources in the online Teacher Center.

Name _____ Class _____ Date _____

myWorld Activity Support   Identity Cards

Where I'm From

Directions On the table, underline or circle the person or group you are assigned. Then complete and cut out the identity card from the bottom of the page. As you learn about other groups or people, list important dates next to the name on the table. If you don't have a specific date, use words like *before Europeans* to place people or groups in sequence.

Bantu migrants Date _____	Nubians Date _____	Arab Muslims Date _____	Boers Date _____	Mau Mau Date _____
Great Zimbabwe people Date _____	Portuguese traders Date _____	British colonists Date _____	Nelson Mandela Date _____	F.W. de Klerk Date _____
Aksum people Date _____	Jomo Kenyatta Date _____	African National Congress Date _____	*Homo erectus* Date _____	

✂ -

Where I'm From

Name _____

I am from _____

I was important when _____

I am important in the history of Southern and Eastern Africa because

_____

_____

_____

_____

Name _____ Class _____ Date _____

Enrichment: Homo Erectus

Directions Read the selection below. Then answer the questions that follow and complete the activity.

The first *Homo erectus* discovered by archaeologists wasn't found in Africa. It was found on the island of Java in Indonesia. Since that discovery in 1891, scientists have found several other important fossils of *Homo erectus*. Two of these were found at Lake Turkana, Kenya. The first was found in 1975 and represents the oldest African fossil of *Homo erectus*. It is 1,800,000 years old. The second was found in 1984 and is the most complete fossil of *Homo erectus*—a young boy.

Many different scientists study these fossils and the places where they were found. Some study the bones and teeth. Others study pottery or tools found nearby to figure out how *Homo erectus* lived. Some study the remains of any plants or animals of the same age. Others study the rocks that contain the fossils. All of this information helps us figure out what *Homo erectus* looked like and how he lived.

Scientists believe that *Homo erectus* walked upright (*erectus* means "upright"). They also believe that *Homo erectus* figured out how to use fire, made stone tools, and perhaps wore clothing. *Homo erectus* ate fruit, plants, and meat, which they cut with tools. Their brains were nearly the size of modern humans but were contained in very differently shaped skulls. Some were as tall as today's humans.

There are many questions still to answer about how *Homo erectus* is linked to modern humans *(Homo sapiens)*. However, many scientists believe in the theory that *Homo erectus* came from Africa, near the Lake Turkana discovery, and then moved to other continents. They believe that *Homo erectus* eventually became *Homo sapiens*.

1. What clues do scientists use to figure out what *Homo erectus* looked like and how he lived?

_____

_____

2. According to most scientists, where did *Homo erectus* come from?

_____

3. Activity The largest collection of *Homo erectus* fossils was found near Beijing, China between 1921 and 1966. Use this information and the selection above to map where and when scientists have found *Homo erectus*. Label each find with location, date, and a description such as "largest collection."

Name _____ Class _____ Date _____

Section Quiz

Directions Answer the following questions using what you learned
in Section 2.

1. _____ What scientific discovery helps teach
   us about the earliest humans?
   a. slave trade
   b. fossils
   c. iron tools
   d. ivory

2. _____ In which modern country did the
   Boers settle?
   a. South Africa
   b. Sudan
   c. Mozambique
   d. Kenya

3. _____ How did the policy of apartheid
   separate people in South Africa?
   a. by colony
   b. by language
   c. by race
   d. by religion

4. _____ Which colonists were overthrown by
   the Mau Mau rebellion?
   a. Egyptian
   b. Dutch
   c. Portuguese
   d. British

5. _____ What was the main goal of the
   African National Congress?
   a. to expand Nubian civilization
   b. to expand the slave trade
   c. to gain national independence
   d. to end the apartheid system

6. Complete the table below with one example for each category
   dealing with the geography of Southern and Eastern Africa.

Event	Effects
Bantu migration	
European colonialism	
Fall of apartheid	

History of Southern and Eastern Africa

- Model preparing to read by previewing the Key Ideas, Key Terms, headings, visuals, and captions. Have students make predictions about what they will learn. For ELL support, post the prompt, "I predict I will read about . . ."

- Preview and practice sequencing by helping students to order important events in the course of the school year or your community's history.

- Preteach this section's high-use Academic Vocabulary and Key Terms using the table on the next page and in-text definitions. Have students practice Key Terms by completing the *Word Wise* page in their journals.

GUIDE ON THE SIDE

Early Humans and Great Civilizations

- **Identify Main Ideas** Where do scientists believe the earliest humans may have lived? (in Africa)

- **Infer** What evidence helps scientists learn about early humans? (Fossils tell about early humans.)

Analyze Visuals Ask students to relate the two images on this page.

- How could the scientists' activities lead to the discovery of the skull? (Scientists carefully dig to reveal buried items such as the skull.)

┼┼┼┼┼┼ **Reading Skill**

Sequence While they read, have students practice this skill by completing the *Take Notes* graphic organizer in the **Student Journal.**

Section 2

History of Southern and Eastern Africa

Key Ideas
- Earth's first people lived in Africa.
- Humans settled throughout Africa, creating societies, states, and trade networks.
- Contact with Arabs and Europeans influenced the culture, religions, and ethnic makeup of the region.
- In the 1800s, Europeans colonized and settled in the region, but African nations gained independence in the 1900s.

Key Terms • fossil • Boers • ethnocentrism • Mau Mau • apartheid
• African National Congress

 Visual Glossary

┼┼┼┼┼┼ **Reading Skill: Sequence** Take notes using the graphic organizer in your journal.

▲ Scientists searching for fossils
◄ The skull of an early ancestor of human beings who lived in South Africa 2.5 million years ago

Southern and Eastern Africa may have been home to the earliest humans. From ancient times to the present, many different cultures and civilizations have left their mark on the region.

Early Humans and Great Civilizations
The first humans may have lived in Africa two million years ago. In particular, the remains of early humans have been found in countries such as Ethiopia and Tanzania.

Earth's First People Scientists have found fossils of early human beings in Eastern Africa. **Fossils** are the remains of ancient humans or animals. Most early humans lived in warm places. They moved around in search of food. One kind of early human called *Homo erectus* lived in Africa between 1 and 2 million years ago. Early humans spread out from Africa to other continents.

ACADEMIC VOCABULARY

High-Use Word	Definition and Sample Sentence
constant	*adj.* continuing; not stopping *Constant rain has kept the ground from drying out this week.*
trend	*n.* general change in a given direction *Reality shows are the most recent trend in popular TV shows.*

Nubia and Aksum The first civilization in this part of Africa was in Nubia. Nubia is a region in modern-day Sudan. It was home to the states of Kush and Meroë. Civilization in Nubia grew from around 2000 B.C. Nubia became a center of trade. It traded with its neighbor, Egypt. Skills and technologies from Egypt were introduced into Nubia. Nubians passed these on to other parts of Africa. The most important technology was iron-making.

The kingdom of Aksum was located in what is today Ethiopia. Aksum had a port on the Red Sea. This location helped make Aksum a center for trade in and beyond Africa. Aksum's traders sold gold, ivory, and other goods. They traded with Rome and India. Roman traders may have brought Christianity to Aksum. It became a Christian kingdom. Ethiopia still is mostly Christian today.

The Bantu Migrations Around A.D. 500 the population of the Bantu people in western Africa grew until their land could not accommodate them. They left their homeland and migrated across Southern Africa. This migration spread the Bantu language. The Bantu brought with them their farming methods, including the raising of cattle. They also spread their knowledge of iron tools. Many groups the Bantu met adopted their language. They began raise to cattle and make iron.

Great Zimbabwe In Southern Africa, Great Zimbabwe thrived in the 1400s. It was a large trading city founded by Bantu speakers. Great Zimbabwe's traders took gold and ivory to Africa's east coast ports. There they traded for goods from China, India, and Southeast Asia.

Arab Influence Traders who spoke Arabic came to Eastern Africa by sea and across the Sahara. They practiced Islam. Some settled in the region, mostly along the eastern coast and on the island of Zanzibar. Zanzibar and coastal areas were tied into a large trading network. It included the Mediterranean, India, and Southeast Asia. Arab traders widened East Africa's slave trade. They brought their language, religion, and cultural influence to the region. Arab merchants also founded cities, including Mogadishu in modern-day Somalia.

Reading Check How did early civilizations spread ideas in Africa?

This doorway from Zanzibar shows the artistic influence of Arab merchants who lived and traded in the region.

▼ This large enclosure is one of the most impressive remains of the city of Great Zimbabwe. *What can you infer about the culture that built it?*

GUIDE ON THE SIDE

• **Sequence** Explain the sequence of movement of Bantu languages and culture and Arab-Muslim culture in Southern and Eastern Africa. (Bantu languages and farming methods moved from the Bantu culture into many cultures in Southern Africa. Arab-Muslim culture moved from the Arab Muslim empire into Africa, across the Sahara, and to Eastern Africa.)

• **Summarize** Describe the results of cultural movement in the region. (Cultures blended with other cultures, exchanging languages and ways of life.)

Analyze Visuals Have students study the photo of the ruins.

• Why do you think the people of Great Zimbabwe built a circular enclosure? (Perhaps they wanted protection from other people.)

READING CHECK by trade and migration

CAPTION The culture was advanced enough to build a city.

ANSWERS

COMMON MISCONCEPTIONS

African Slave Trade Clarify that only about 5 percent of slaves sent to the Americas came from Southern and Eastern Africa. However, long before the trans-Atlantic slave trade developed, Southern and Eastern Africans were enslaved and sent to other parts of the world. For example, Bantu people from what is now Tanzania, Malawi, and Mozambique were brought to Somalia and sold as slaves. In Eastern Africa, many slaves were owned by Arabs or sold through Swahili Coast ports to southwest Asia. After the Arabs took Zanzibar back from Portugal, they enslaved 60–90 percent of the population to work on clove plantations. Many people were also enslaved in southern Sudan and shipped up the Nile to Egypt and then to Southwest Asia.

GUIDE ON THE SIDE

Europeans in Southern and Eastern Africa

- **Cause and Effect** How did Portugal's arrival change the slave trade? (It expanded the trade.)

- **Infer** Why would warfare and loss of population make societies more vulnerable? (People would be exhausted. Plus there would be fewer warriors and resources for fighting invaders.)

- **Identify Main Ideas** How did trade lead to colonies? (Trading companies needed supply posts for their traders. They sent settlers to create those posts and many stayed and spread into nearby areas.)

Map Skills Have students identify the colonies ruled by each European nation.

- What effect would a war between European powers have in this region? Why? (If European powers fought in Europe, their colonies might fight one another in Africa.)

→ **Active Atlas**

Point out the map of European rule in Southern and Eastern Africa.
- Have students go to myworldgeography.com to learn more about colonial rule in Southern and Eastern Africa.

Europeans in Southern and Eastern Africa

In the 1400s, Europeans began to come to Southern and Eastern Africa. They came first to trade and later to set up colonies.

First Meetings and the Slave Trade
Portugal began to trade with Eastern Africa in the 1400s. Around 1500, the Portuguese took control of parts of Eastern Africa. They wanted to control trade along the Eastern African coast. They expanded the slave trade.

Southern and Eastern Africans, like the West and Central Africans, suffered from the effects of the trans-Atlantic slave trade. Constant warfare and loss of population weakened their societies. They became vulnerable to European empires.

constant, *adj.*, continuing; not stopping

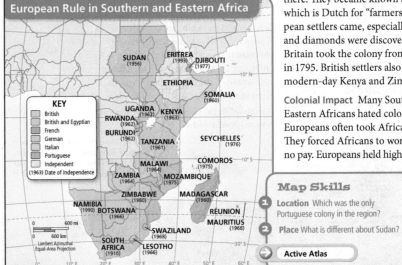

European Rule in Southern and Eastern Africa

KEY
- British
- British and Egyptian
- French
- German
- Italian
- Portuguese
- Independent
- (1963) Date of Independence

SUDAN (1956) · ERITREA (1993) · DJIBOUTI (1977) · ETHIOPIA · SOMALIA (1960) · UGANDA (1962) · KENYA (1963) · RWANDA (1962) · BURUNDI (1962) · TANZANIA (1961) · SEYCHELLES (1976) · MALAWI (1964) · COMOROS (1975) · ZAMBIA (1964) · MOZAMBIQUE (1975) · ZIMBABWE (1980) · MADAGASCAR (1960) · NAMIBIA (1990) · BOTSWANA (1966) · RÉUNION · MAURITIUS (1968) · SWAZILAND (1968) · SOUTH AFRICA (1910) · LESOTHO (1966)

0 600 mi
0 600 km
Lambert Azimuthal Equal-Area Projection

Map Skills
1. **Location** Which was the only Portuguese colony in the region?
2. **Place** What is different about Sudan?

→ **Active Atlas**

European Rule Many European nations spread their empires into Africa in the late 1800s. As in West and Central Africa, Europeans traded and conquered territory in Southern and Eastern Africa. They also founded colonies of settlers there. By around 1900, European nations ruled most of Africa.

Some European colonies were founded by trading companies. These companies needed to send supplies to traders traveling to Asia. They sent settlers to build supply posts. For example, the Dutch East India Company started a settlement in South Africa. It was called Cape Town. Over many years, Dutch settlers spread out to create the Cape Colony. Many farmers from the Netherlands, France, and other European countries settled there. They became known as **Boers,** which is Dutch for "farmers." More European settlers came, especially when gold and diamonds were discovered. Great Britain took the colony from the Dutch in 1795. British settlers also moved to modern-day Kenya and Zimbabwe.

Colonial Impact Many Southern and Eastern Africans hated colonial rule. Europeans often took Africans' lands. They forced Africans to work for little or no pay. Europeans held high positions.

MAP SKILLS 1. Mozambique **2.** It was ruled by two countries, one European and one African.

HISTORY

Education and Healthcare Germany colonized parts of East Africa in the 1880s, including the modern nations of Burundi, Rwanda, and part of Tanzania. More than other European colonizers, the Germans left their mark on local education systems, raising teacher standards and using excellent textbooks and materials. One area of education that most Westerners in Africa supported was tropical medicine. This is in part because African diseases were so devastating to European traders, explorers, and settlers. By around 1900, most of the colonial powers had created medical schools to focus on tropical diseases. At first, the medical advances just helped colonists rule, but eventually the advances were also extended to some members of the local population.

Colonialism: Positive and Negative

▼ Europeans built up Southern and Eastern Africa's infrastructure, including railways. This helped Africans, although Europeans built them for their own purposes.

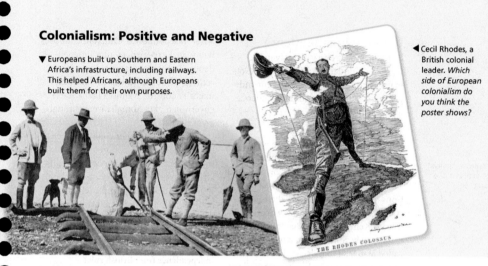

◄ Cecil Rhodes, a British colonial leader. *Which side of European colonialism do you think the poster shows?*

THE RHODES COLOSSUS

But Africans had little political power. Many Europeans also looked down on African cultures. They believed their own cultures were superior, an attitude called **ethnocentrism.** For example, colonial leader Cecil Rhodes believed that British people were better than others.

66 I contend that we are the first race in the world, and that the more of the world we inhabit the better it is for the human race. 99
—Cecil Rhodes

However, not everything European colonialists did was negative. Though the British had held African slaves for centuries, they outlawed slavery in 1833. They then helped fight the slave trade across Africa. Europeans brought modern healthcare to Southern and Eastern Africa. They built up infrastructure to access resources.

This infrastructure also helped Africans. Europeans built schools. More Africans had access to education. With that education, Africans felt ready to take charge of the governments of their own countries.

Reading Check **How was the first colony in South Africa founded?**

◄ Haile Selassie, the Emperor of Ethiopia from 1930 to 1974, resisted European aggression. He fought the Italian army, which invaded his country in the 1930s. Ethiopia was never colonized by Europeans.

READING CHECK The first colony in South Africa was founded by the Dutch East India company to supply its traders.

CAPTION negative

GUIDE ON THE SIDE

- **Summarize** Why did many Southern and Eastern Africans hate colonial rule? (Colonial rulers took Africans' land, forced them to work without pay, and left them with little political power.)

- **Analyze Text** What does the text mean by "Europeans looked down on African cultures"? (It means Europeans believed that African cultures were not as advanced or worthwhile as European cultures.)

- **Identify Evidence** What evidence can you find for European ethnocentrism? (Cecil Rhodes believed British people were better.)

Analyze Visuals Have students relate the images of colonialism to the text.

- What are some positive effects of colonialism? (Europeans built up infrastructure, helped end slavery in Africa, and improved healthcare and education in the region.)

- How might these effects make Africans "ready to take charge of the government" in their countries? (Infrastructure helped Africans build up their economies. Education helped them run governments. Modern healthcare reduced disease and made societies stronger.)

QUICK FACTS

President Obama's Kenyan Roots America's 44th president, Barack Obama has roots in Southern and Eastern Africa. His father, Barack Obama senior, was born in Kenya. He was a member of the Luo tribe, which forms the third-largest ethnic group in Kenya.

The Obama family comes from a western Kenyan village called Kogelo. Barack Obama is the first American of African heritage to become president. News of his election was greeted with widespread celebration in Kenya and in other African countries.

Winning Independence

- **Analyze Text** What does the text "the road was very bumpy" mean? (African nations faced many problems to gain independence.)

- **Categorize** What were some positive and negative effects of urbanization and industrialization after independence? (Countries got richer but traditional rural life suffered.)

The Rise and Fall of Apartheid

- **Summarize** What was the main goal of apartheid? (to separate blacks and whites; to keep economic and political power in white control)

- **Identify Details** What were some ways that apartheid affected black South Africans? (Jobs, neighborhoods, schools, and hospitals were segregated. Travel was restricted and blacks could not vote. Interracial marriage was illegal.)

Winning Independence

In 1900, almost every country in the region was under colonial rule. By 1960, many African nations had become independent. But the road to independence was very bumpy.

Trouble in Kenya The Kikuyu (kee KOO yoo) people of Kenya were one group that opposed colonial rule. The British had taken much of their land, and British ethnocentrism made good relations difficult. In the 1940s, the Kikuyu started a political party that worked toward Kenya's independence. Change came slowly. Some began a movement called **Mau Mau** that decided to use force to end British rule in Kenya more quickly. The British and the Mau Mau fought for four years. Finally, Kenya gained independence in 1963. Kikuyu leader Jomo Kenyatta led the new nation.

trend, *n.,* general change in a given direction

British soldiers guard Kenyan villagers while looking for Mau Mau fighters.

After Independence Different countries had varied experiences after independence. Zimbabwe was ruled by white settlers, while Kenya was under black majority control. Namibia had a stable government, but Somalia went through great conflict.

In Kenya, as in other countries such as South Africa, urbanization and industrialization were important <u>trends</u> after independence. Factories were built in major cities. Rural people left farms behind to find work in factories. These trends made Kenya and South Africa richer but hurt traditional rural life.

Reading Check Why did the Kikuyu want independence from British rule?

The Rise and Fall of Apartheid

South Africa gained independence from Britain in 1910. However, the white minority kept political and economic power for themselves.

South Africa Under Apartheid In 1948, the white minority in South Africa adopted **apartheid,** an official government policy of keeping white and black South Africans apart. It was similar to American segregation in many ways. Apartheid laws secured power for white South Africans. Black people could only live and work in certain places, and harsh laws made travel difficult. Schools and hospitals were segregated. Black people could not vote. The Prohibition of Mixed Marriages Act made marriage between people of different races illegal.

READING CHECK The Kikuyu were angry that the British had taken their land. They also disliked British ethnocentrism.

READING CHECK Nelson Mandela, F.W. de Klerk

SECTION 2 ASSESSMENT **1.** Ethnocentrism is the view that one's culture is superior. **2.** The Boers were European settlers in South Africa. *Boer* means "farmer" in Dutch. **3.** The ANC opposed apartheid. **4.** Africa **5.** Bantu Migrations

ECONOMICS

Divestment and Sanctions In the late 1980s, the anti-apartheid movement grew in the United States. Protests called for individuals and institutions to stop investing in companies doing business with South Africa. City and state governments followed suit and eventually the U.S. Congress passed the 1986 Comprehensive Anti-Apartheid Act, which banned U.S. investment in South Africa. Not all anti-apartheid activists agreed with this approach. Helen Suzman was a white South African member of Parliament who believed that economic pressure would hurt blacks more than whites. Still, she spoke out passionately against apartheid, and frequently visited Nelson Mandela during his years in prison. Helen Suzman died in 2009.

Mandela and the End of Apartheid Many people inside and beyond South Africa believed apartheid was wrong. Black South Africans organized and protested. White police all too often responded with violence. The government banned groups like the **African National Congress** (ANC), a political party that worked for black civil rights. Many ANC leaders were jailed. Other nations criticized South Africa sharply. Some refused to trade with South Africa. That hurt its economy.

One man who played a key role in ending apartheid was Nelson Mandela. He was an ANC leader who was jailed in 1962. He continued to protest from his prison on Robben Island. Another man who played a role was F. W. de Klerk, South Africa's president from 1989 to 1994. Although he was white, de Klerk realized that apartheid was destroying South Africa. In 1990, he released Nelson Mandela from prison. Together, Mandela

myWorld Activity
Where I'm From

◄ Nelson Rolihlahla Mandela led the struggle against apartheid and became South Africa's president. He shared a Nobel Peace Prize with F. W. de Klerk in 1993.

and de Klerk worked to end apartheid. In 1994, South Africans of all races voted together. Mandela became president. South Africa was truly independent.

Reading Check Who were two people who helped end apartheid?

Section 2 Assessment

Key Terms
1. What is ethnocentrism?
2. Who were the Boers? What does the word *boer* mean and what language does it come from?
3. What system did the African National Congress fight?

Key Ideas
4. Where do scientists believe the first human beings came from?
5. What were some effects of the Bantu migrations?
6. How did contact with Arabs influence Southern and Eastern Africa?
7. How did apartheid hurt black South Africans?

Think Critically
8. **Analyze Cause and Effect** What caused Kenyans to fight British rule?
9. **Compare and Contrast** How was Kenya's path to independence different from South Africa's?

Essential Question
Is conflict unavoidable?
10. Apartheid in South Africa ended without civil war or large-scale ethnic conflict. What do you think made this possible? Go to your Student Journal to record your answer.

spread Bantu languages, cattle-raising methods, and iron tools. **6.** Arabs brought their language, culture, and Islamic religion. **7.** Apartheid separated black South Africans and restricted their education, jobs, homes, voting, and travel. **8.** Kenyans wanted independence. **9.** Kenya's independence was achieved by force and led to black majority rule. South African independence occurred by political means and led to white minority rule. **10.** Cooperation between white and black South Africans helped end apartheid without civil war or major conflict.

ANSWERS

Literature of Southern and Eastern Africa

OBJECTIVES

Students will

- use primary sources to appreciate different literary traditions in Southern and Eastern Africa.
- **21st Century Learning** compare and contrast kingdoms described in the literature of the region.
- **ELL** use English words to identify different forms of communication.

SET EXPECTATIONS

In this lesson, students will

- read and analyze two stories from the literature of Ethiopia and South Africa.
- illustrate and retell one of the stories to emphasize how it reflects its culture of origin.

1 Connect

To help students connect with different storytelling traditions, ask them to list ways in which people communicate ideas and values today. List these in general categories, such as print, digital, and oral. Discuss the features of each. For example, electronic communication offers speed and easy access, while oral communication is often more personal. Then ask, What does each way of communicating say about a culture? How does it reflect the values of that culture?

ELL Intermediate Use examples to review meaning and terms for print, digital, and oral communication.

2 Learn

Preview Have students preview the two pages of images and documents. Read the Key Idea, glossary terms, and definitions before students begin reading. Clarify the meaning of terms by providing examples. Read the introduction to the documents.

Read Slowly read aloud the excerpt of Galawdewos's story without stopping. Read the document again, this time stopping to read the questions at the left, and prompt students to analyze the meaning of the words. Have students answer the questions using the location of the letters to provide clues. Do the same for the tale of the Shining Princess. Lead a discussion about the different approaches to storytelling, starting with students' responses to the questions. Ask, What is each story about? How do the topics and methods for communicating these stories help us understand what was important to the cultures that created them?

L2 Extra Support Write a sentence on the board, and have students read it. Then read it aloud. Connect the difference between reading and listening to the stories.

myWorld Activity: Storytelling Festival Have your own festival of storytelling in your classroom. Assign half the class to retell one story and half to retell the other. Distribute *Activity Support: Cultural Illustrations*, on which students will record important ideas and images suggested by each story text, and then draw an illustration to reflect these ideas. Invite each large group to retell its story and present its illustrations. Give students the option of a dramatic retelling. **(Visual/Verbal)**

25 min

3 Understand

Review Return to the Key Idea. Discuss ways in which each story reflects its culture and traditions, for example, by emphasizing what is important to the storyteller.

Assess Have students complete **Analyze the Documents.** Review their answers to determine if students have met the lesson objectives.

Remediate If students struggle to add to the stories, have them summarize the events in the existing text. Ask guiding questions to help students predict possible future events such as, How might Mar Galawdewos rule from his palace? What might he see from the tower? Who might be dazzled by the Shining Princess? What might he or she do to show admiration?

Name _____ Class _____ Date _____

myWorld Activity Support   **Cultural Illustrations**

Storytelling Festival

Directions To be part of your class's storytelling festival, retell
one of the two stories. Pick a story, and then figure out the
most important ideas and images from the story. Next, draw an
illustration that you think captures the ideas and reflects the
images or words in the story. Use your illustration to help you
retell the story to the class. You may choose to act out your story
as you tell it.

Your Story (Circle One)   Galawdewos   The Story of the Shining Princess

Cultural Ideas Shown in the Story

_____

_____

_____

Vivid Images in the Story

_____

_____

_____

Illustration for Retelling the Story

What cue (signal word or phrase) from the text will tell storytellers
when to show your illustration?

_____

PRIMARY SOURCE

Storytelling and Culture Share and discuss these comments about the relationship between storytelling and culture around the world:

"The storyteller tells us who we are, who the other is, and what kind of relationship we can establish. . . . The storyteller can give us clues to our social and individual identity."

Discuss with students how the stories in this lesson give them clues to the social and individual identities of their storytellers. Then ask them if they agree with this statement: "[I]t is the story, not time, that travels."

—Alberto Manguel, 2007 CBC Massey Lecturer, quoted in "Building a City of Words Transforms Storytellers into Society's Masons" by Jay Smith, vueweekly.com

GUIDE ON THE SIDE

Compare and Contrast Use the lettered prompts to help students analyze the documents and compare and contrast the kingdoms described.

ANSWERS

Ⓐ King Solomon from the Bible

Ⓑ The kingdom's wealth includes a beautiful tower with marble, gold, and silver, a palace decorated with gold and precious stones, and a building for the church.

Ⓒ You can tell that the king and his people were religious because the chronicles credit God for choosing the king, compare the king to Solomon, and describe constructing a building for the church.

Primary Source

Literature of Southern and Eastern Africa

Key Idea • Stories from Southern and Eastern Africa show the varied cultures and traditions of this large region.

▲ A page from an Ethiopian religious book

The cultures of Southern and Eastern Africa have a long tradition of storytelling. Some parts of the region, such as Ethiopia, have used writing to record their history for centuries. In other parts of the region, such as South Africa, stories were passed down orally from one generation to another. In Ethiopia, Christian themes influenced the literature. Ethiopian monks wrote about the lives of their kings, often comparing them to kings from the Bible. One of these stories tells about King Galawdewos, who ruled in the 1500s. In Southern Africa, people like the 'Msuto were cattle herders. They passed down stories about the lives of their chiefs and important people. A beautiful princess is the main character in one of these stories.

Stop at each circled letter on the right to think about the text. Then answer the question with the same letter on the left.

Ⓐ Identify Details Who is Galawdewos compared to?

Ⓑ Identify Evidence What are some signs of this kingdom's wealth?

Ⓒ Make Inferences How can you tell that the king and his people were religious?

Mar, *n.,* a local term meaning "Lord"
reign, *v.,* to rule
surmounted, *v.,* topped; covered

Galawdewos

❝ God made <u>Mar</u> Galawdewos <u>reign</u> over the beautiful country of Ethiopia and placed him on the throne of his father, giving him wisdom . . . like that of Solomon the son **Ⓐ** of David. . . .

He built in [his capital] a beautiful tower the corners of which were <u>surmounted</u> with . . . precious marble and the interior engraved with figures of gold and silver. He also constructed a palace which was decorated and adorned **Ⓑ** inside and outside with gold and precious stones. . . .

Ⓒ In the town a building belonging to the church was also constructed. ❞

—*The Ethiopian Royal Chronicles*

ANALYZE THE DOCUMENTS 1. Both stories describe kingdoms in beautiful countries that contain admired figures with great power. Both describe kingdoms that include beautiful buildings that show great wealth. Both stories describe kingdoms that have a main leader. "Galawdewos" describes a city kingdom with a King who rules from elaborate palaces, while "The Story of the Shining Princess" describes a rural kingdom with a chief who rules from a hut. In the first story, the person of power is a man—the

21st Century Learning COMPARE AND CONTRAST

To assist your students in comparing and contrasting the stories, begin with the scaffolded questions at the left of each excerpt. Encourage students to view each story as a window into the culture that created it. Suggest that they reread each excerpt for specific nouns, verbs, and adjectives that create a picture of the story's originating culture. For example, in "Galawdewos," the details that describe the king's tower and palace offer information about the kingdom. Urge students to work with partners to listen to the stories read out loud, closing their eyes or sketching a drawing in order to identify details about each kingdom. Have students group similar details under headings such as "Buildings" or "Leaders" and then use these headings to organize the paragraphs of their essays. For additional help, refer to **21st Century Learning Online Tutor** *Compare and Contrast*.

Stop at each circled letter on the right to think about the text. Then answer the question with the same letter on the left.

D **Identify Details** What is the countryside like?

E **Analyze Primary Sources** What details make this household seem prosperous?

F **Identify Main Ideas** Why was Maholia called the Shining Princess?

kraal, *n.*, a traditional dwelling encircled by a fence; a livestock pen

calabash, *n.*, gourd used for holding liquid

beheld, *v.*, saw

The Story of the Shining Princess

❝ Far up in the mountains, nestling in a cool green valley,

D stood a most beautiful <u>kraal</u>. The hut was a bright green, for it was finely thatched with grass, and the floor within was of the firmest and most brilliantly polished red earth.

E Around the inner walls stood the cooking pots made of red clay, and along with these were shining green <u>calabashes</u> overflowing with the richest milk and cream. . . . This was the home of a great Chief's wife. The Chief, who had been dead for many years, had left his Queen alone in the world with only one little daughter named Maholia. . . .

As [Maholia] grew up, she became more and more celebrated for her beauty and charm; in fact she was so lovely that she dazzled the eyes of all who <u>beheld</u> her, and she became known among her people as the Shining

F Princess. ❞

—Traditional 'Msuto tale
from *Black Fairy Tales*, by Terry Berger

Analyze the Documents

1. **Compare and Contrast** How do these sources describe kingdoms that are both alike and different?
2. **Writing Task** Write another paragraph to add to one of these documents. Try to make your writing match the style and content of the existing story.

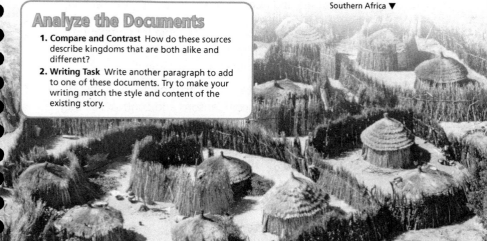

A traditional kraal in Southern Africa ▼

D The countryside is very green and cool.

E The household seems prosperous because it is finely thatched and has a good floor. It also has many cooking pots and a store of rich milk and cream.

F Maholia was called the Shining Princess because she was so beautiful that she dazzled the eyes of people who saw her, as if she were shining.

King. In the second story, it is a young woman—the princess. **2.** Students' stories should include events appropriate to the story they are continuing, and should reflect an attempt to continue the original story's voice.

Southern and Eastern Africa Today

OBJECTIVES

Students will know

- the effects of ethnic, language, and religious diversity on the region.
- ethnic, political, and economic challenges for the region.

Students will be able to

- compare and contrast groups, nations, and governments in the region.
- generate opinions about conflicts in the region, and then identify bias.

SET EXPECTATIONS

In this section, students will

- read Southern and Eastern Africa Today.
- complete a fact-and-opinion tree about regional conflicts.
- go On Assignment in Southern and Eastern Africa, and learn more about religion and literacy in the region.

CORE CONCEPTS

You may wish to teach or reteach the following lessons from the Core Concepts Handbook:

- Economic Development, pp. 64–65
- Cultural Diffusion and Change, pp. 96–97
- Conflict and Cooperation, pp. 110–111

KEY

Differentiated Instruction	English Language Instruction
L1 Special Needs **L2** Extra Support	**ELL** Beginner **ELL** Early Intermediate **ELL** Intermediate
L3 On-Level **L4** Challenge	**ELL** Early Advanced **ELL** Advanced

1 Connect
Make learning meaningful

Make Connections Ask students to think about what happens when members of a group disagree. Ask them to list possible results on a positive to negative continuum. Have students predict challenges nations might face if different groups in the nation disagree about the nation's goals and future.

L2 Extra Support Provide examples of disagreements, such as among friends over an activity, in a family over distribution of chores, or in the community over how to use resources.

Activate Prior Knowledge Remind students that in the previous section they learned about ways that language, culture, and ideas spread throughout the region. Ask them to predict how the resulting mix of cultures, languages, and ideas might affect people living in modern Southern and Eastern Africa.

Prepare Follow the steps in the section **Preview.** Preteach the Key Terms. Then have students complete *Word Wise* in their journals using in-text clues and the glossary for help.

2 Experience
Teach knowledge and skills

Read Use **Background** notes and **Guide on the Side** questions to model active reading. Have students use *Take Notes* in their **Student Journal** to compare and contrast groups, governments, and nations in modern Southern and Eastern Africa. Have students complete **21st Century Online Tutor** *Compare and Contrast* and apply this skill to reading the section.

L2 Extra Support Identify criteria for comparing and contrasting in the chapter, such as language and type of government.

ELL Intermediate Preteach signal terms to help students identify comparisons and contrasts as they read: *most, also, sometimes, different, others, but,* and *in other instances.*

L4 Challenge Have students generate an additional graphic organizer to map section content according to cause and effect.

Practice: myWorld Activity Students will list facts about regional conflicts on a graphic organizer, generate opinions about the facts, and then work in groups to identify bias in their opinions. **Step-by-Step Instructions** and **More Activities** follow on pp. T52–T53.

SECTION 3 RESOURCE GUIDE

FOR THE STUDENT

my worldgeography.com Student Center
- Data Discovery

Student Edition (print and online)
- Southern and Eastern Africa Today

Student Journal (print and online)
- Section 3 Word Wise
- Section 3 Take Notes

21st Century Learning Online Tutor
- Compare and Contrast
- Identify Bias

FOR THE TEACHER

my worldgeography.com Teacher Center
- Online Lesson Planner
- Presentations for Projection
- SuccessTracker

ProGuide: Africa
- Lesson Plan, pp. T50–T51
- myWorld Activity Step-by-Step Instructions, p. T52
- Activity Support: Fact-and-Opinion Tree, p. T53
- myWorld Geography Enrichment, p. T54
- Section Quiz, p. T55

Accelerating the Progress of ELLs
- Reading Support Strategies, p. 42

3 Understand
Assess understanding

Review Review *Word Wise* and *Take Notes* in the **Student Journal.**

Assess Knowledge and Skills Use the Section Assessment and Section Quiz to check students' progress.

Assess Understanding Review students' responses to the Section Assessment Essential Question prompt.

Remediate Use these strategies to review and remediate.

If students struggle to . . .	Try these strategies.
Describe specific ethnic and political conflicts	Have students describe goals of different groups and obstacles each faced.
Identify bias	Assign additional practice with the **21st Century Online Tutor.**
Understand the distribution of language in the region	Have students listen to Language and Religion in the **Online Student Edition**, and label a map with places mentioned.

ELL Support

ELL Objective Students will be able to differentiate fact and opinion.

Cultural Connections To stress the link between economic and political stability, allow students to use home languages to describe how decisions by governments in home countries might affect those countries' economies (jobs, trade, etc.).

ELL Early Advanced Content Tip Explain that each red subheading relates to a Key Idea. Blue subheadings then name topics within the large topics of the red subheadings. Help students create a simple outline with the Key Ideas and subheadings, and then briefly paraphrase text under each subheading.

ELL Activity Review fact and opinion: Facts are information that can be proven as true, such as today's temperature. Opinions state a person's beliefs, such as *Cold days are fun*. Have pairs take turns stating facts or opinions and categorizing each statement. Rule out opinions about students. **(Logical/Verbal)**

myWorld Activity   **Step-by-Step Instructions**

 20 min

Analyze Conflicts

OBJECTIVES

Students will

- list facts and generate opinions about conflicts in Southern and Eastern Africa.
- identify bias in their opinions and explore how bias contributes to conflicts.

LEARNING STYLE

- Logical
- Visual

21st Century Learning

- Identify Bias

MATERIALS

- Activity Support: Fact-and-Opinion Tree, p. T53

Activity Steps

1. Tell students that they will be asked to identify facts about conflicts in Southern and Eastern Africa. They will then generate opinions based on the facts. Finally, students will meet in groups to identify bias, or unfair preference, in their opinions and discuss how the text has changed their views.

   L2 Extra Support Review and compare the definitions of fact and opinion.

2. Explain that bias is an unfair preference for or against something. For example, a government leader from one ethnic group might have a bias in favor of his group. A newspaper reporter might be biased toward one sports team over another and blame a loss on injuries instead of poor play.

3. Distribute *Activity Support: Fact-and-Opinion Tree.* Allow students twenty minutes to review Section 3 for facts about a conflict in Southern and Eastern Africa, and to generate opinions based on those facts.

ELL Early Intermediate Direct students to text that discusses conflicts. Read aloud as students follow. Have students choose a conflict and then identify facts about it.

   L2 Extra Support Demonstrate how to add boxes and arrows to *Activity Support: Fact-and-Opinion Tree.*

4. Have groups share fact-and-opinion trees and discuss bias in each other's views. After students record evidence of bias in their own views, have them complete and discuss Reflection.

   L4 Challenge Ask students to list additional facts they'd like to have in order to better understand conflicts in the region.

More Activities From myWorld Teachers

Local Connections Have students identify conflicts in their school or community and then stand on a continuum to show their view about the conflict issue. Brainstorm possible solutions. **(Kinesthetic/Logical)**

Presentation To expand class knowledge, have student groups research one of the conflicts in the section. Invite groups to share their findings in a brief computer presentation. **(Verbal/Visual)**

Interview Have pairs script and role-play an interview between a government budget officer and an NGO or other aid worker in which they debate ways to fight poverty and disease in Africa. **(Verbal/Interpersonal)**

 my worldgeography.com **Teacher Center** ⊙ Find additional resources in the online Teacher Center.

Name _____ Class _____ Date _____

myWorld Activity Support   Fact-and-Opinion Tree

Analyze Conflicts

Directions On a blank piece of paper, create a fact-and-opinion tree like the one below. Add as many boxes and lines as you need. Record information about a conflict from *Southern and Eastern Africa Today*. Identify bias with classmates and record it on your tree. Complete **Reflection** to explore how your opinions have changed.

Roots Record facts about a conflict in Southern and Eastern Africa on the roots of your tree.

Branches Use the facts to form opinions about the conflict. Write your opinions on the branches of your tree.

Fruit Are your opinions biased? If so, draw a fruit next to your opinion statements. Add + in the fruit for positive bias or − for negative bias.

Reflection List one opinion each from before and after your reading. What has changed?

Before _____

After _____

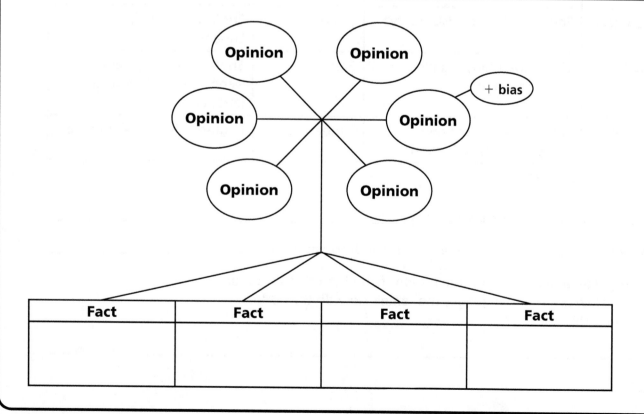

Name _____ Class _____ Date _____

Enrichment: Culture Spread

Directions Read the table below. Then answer the questions that follow and complete the activity.

Country	Main Languages	Country	Main Languages
Botswana	English*; Setswana	Mozambique	Emakhwa; Zichangana; Portuguese*
Burundi	Kirundi*; French; Swahili	Namibia	English*; Afrikaans; German
Comoros	Arabic*; French*; Comorian (Arabic-Swahili mix)	Rwanda	Kinyarwanda (Bantu)*; French*; English*; Swahili
Djibouti	French*; Arabic*; Somali	Seychelles	Creole (related to French); English*
Egypt	Arabic*; English; French	Somalia	Somali*; Arabic; English
Eritrea	Arabic; Araf; Tigrinya	South Africa	Zulu*; Xhosa*; English*; Afrikaans*; Sotho*
Ethiopia	Amharic; Oromo; Somali; Tigrinya; English	Sudan	Arabic*; Nubian; English
Kenya	English*; Swahili	Swaziland	English*; SiSwati*
Lesotho	Sesotho; English*; Zulu; Xhosa	Tanzania	Swahili*; English; Arabic
Madagascar	English*; French*; Malagasy*	Uganda	English*; Swahili; Arabic; Luganda
Malawi	Chichewa; Chinyanga; other local languages	Zambia	English*; Lunda, Bemba, Kaonda and other local languages
Mauritius	Creole (related to French); Bhojpuri; French; English*	Zimbabwe	English*; Shona; Sindebele

* Official Language(s)

1. In what nations is Arabic spoken today? _____

2. With what other nations can people in Burundi communicate? _____

3. **Activity** Use a map to find three nations from the chart that share borders. How are their languages the same? How do they differ? What does this tell you?

_____

_____

Name _____ Class _____ Date _____

Section Quiz

Directions Answer the following questions using what you learned
in Section 3.

1. _____ What are two major ethnic groups in
   Rwanda?
   a. Hutu and Tutsi
   b. Zulu and Xhosa
   c. Muslims and Hindus
   d. Janjaweed and Kikuyu

2. _____ Which language helped form
   Swahili?
   a. English
   b. Dutch
   c. Arabic
   d. Portuguese

3. _____ What is the definition of genocide?
   a. an election of government officials
   b. an attempt to destroy a whole people
   c. the removal of an elected government
   d. the changing of a nation's borders

4. _____ What is the name for privately
   funded groups that try to solve
   environmental, social, and health problems
   during regional conflicts?
   a. military relief organizations (MROs)
   b. student political organizations (SPOs)
   c. pro-environmental organizations (PEOs)
   d. nongovernmental organizations (NGOs)

5. _____ What effect does HIV/AIDS have on
   Southern and Eastern Africa?
   a. It provides peacekeeping troops to the
      region.
   b. It kills people and blocks economic
      development.
   c. It contributes to poor transportation
      networks.
   d. It reduces racial inequality in South
      Africa.

6. Complete the table below with one conflict for each country.
   Then draw a conclusion about the effect of these conflicts on
   development in the Southern and Eastern region of Africa.

Country	Sudan	Zimbabwe	South Africa	Rwanda
Conflict				
Conclusion				

Southern and Eastern Africa Today

- Model preparing to read by previewing the Key Ideas, Key Terms, headings, visuals, and captions. Have students make predictions about what they will learn. For ELL support, post the prompt, "I predict I will read about . . ."

- Preview and practice comparing and contrasting, using examples of popular sports among your students.

- Preteach this section's high-use Academic Vocabulary and Key Terms using the table on the next page and in-text definitions. Have students practice Key Terms by completing the *Word Wise* page in their journals.

GUIDE ON THE SIDE

A Variety of Ethnic Groups and Religions

- **Summarize** Describe the relationship between ethnic groups and country borders in Southern and Eastern Africa. (Some ethnic groups live in a single country. Others live in many countries. Few countries have only one ethnic group.)

- **Predict** What do you think might happen when people from different ethnic groups all live in the same country? (Sample: There may be conflict between those groups about how the government should act or how people should live.)

Categorize

- Which is largest ethnic group in Kenya? (the Kikuyu)

- In which countries do Maasai live? (Kenya and Tanzania)

- Which groups live in South Africa? (Zulu and Xhosa)

Reading Skill

Compare and Contrast While they read, have students practice this skill by completing the *Take Notes* graphic organizer in the **Student Journal.**

Section 3

Southern and Eastern Africa Today

Key Ideas
- This region's many different historic influences and ethnic groups have produced vibrant and varied cultures.
- Many nations in the region struggle with ethnic conflict and corrupt or underperforming governments.
- Despite the many challenges facing the region, there are reasons to hope that it will overcome its obstacles.

Key Terms • indigenous • Swahili • genocide • AIDS • nongovernmental organization (NGO)

 Visual Glossary

Reading Skill: Compare and Contrast Take notes using the graphic organizer in your journal.

◄ Kenyan runners have won many Olympic gold medals.

Southern and Eastern Africa have a wealth of natural resources. But the region also faces unique and serious challenges. Some of its nations have had more success than others in building peace and prosperity.

A Variety of Ethnic Groups and Religions

Most people in Southern and Eastern Africa are **indigenous,** or native, to the region. There are many different groups of people in the region. They belong to hundreds of different ethnic groups, speak different languages, and practice different religions.

Ethnic Groups Some ethnic groups live in a single country. Others stretch across borders. Few countries are made up of a single ethnic group. Some of the largest groups are the Zulu and Xhosa, who live in South Africa; the Kikuyu in Kenya; and the Hutu and Tutsi in Rwanda. In the past, different ethnic groups lived different lifestyles. For example, the Maasai, in Kenya and Tanzania, herded cattle. The Baganda in Uganda farmed and lived in large villages. However, today many people in the region live in cities. They no longer make a living in the ways that their ancestors did.

ACADEMIC VOCABULARY

High-Use Word	Definition and Sample Sentence
ethnic	*adj.* group of people with the same nationality, language, or religion *At our class ethnic festival, we ate Korean food and learned Native American dances.*
integrate	*v.* bring together, particularly people from different groups *As the first African American to play Major League baseball, Jackie Robinson helped to integrate sports.*

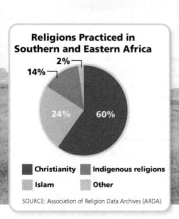

Religions Practiced in Southern and Eastern Africa

- 60% Christianity
- 24% Indigenous religions
- 14% Islam
- 2% Other

SOURCE: Association of Religion Data Archives (ARDA)

A procession of Ethiopian Christians

Chart Skills

1. Which two religions are most widely practiced in this area?
2. What percentage of people practice Islam?

➔ **Data Discovery**

Languages The diverse people of Southern and Eastern Africa speak many different languages. Most belong to the Bantu language family. This fact is a legacy of the Bantu migrations. Languages from outside the region have also made inroads. English is spoken as a second language in countries that were once part of the British Empire. In South Africa, Afrikaans (af rih KAHNZ) is widely spoken. It comes from the Dutch spoken by early colonists.

Arab influence is widespread throughout the region. Arabic is spoken in Sudan. It also helped create the Swahili language. **Swahili** is a Bantu language. It is unique because it has many Arabic elements and words from other languages. For example, when you count from one to ten in Swahili, three of the numbers come from Arabic, while seven are Bantu. Swahili developed because of trade between Eastern Africa and Arab countries. It is now used as a common language throughout much of Eastern Africa.

Religions Many people in Southern and Eastern Africa practice indigenous African religions. Others practice Islam or Christianity. Some mix their indigenous religions with one or the other. Christianity is strongest in the southern part of the region. Islam is mostly practiced in northern parts of the region. Although Islamic countries surround Ethiopia, it has been a center of Christianity for many centuries.

Reading Check What are three indigenous groups in Southern and Eastern Africa?

Ndebele (un duh BEE lee) people from South Africa paint their homes in bright colors. ▶

Build Cultural Awareness

- What cultural effects did the British and Dutch leave behind? (English and Afrikaans languages)

- What is one Arab influence on the region? (Arabic is widely spoken.)

- How did Swahili develop? (Arabic and Bantu speakers interacted through trade or other contacts. A blended language developed.)

- **Synthesize** What is the benefit of a "common language" in a region? (Sample: It allows people from different countries and ethnic groups to communicate. It creates a regional community.)

Chart Skills Have students use the circle graph to identify percentages for each religion in the region.

- Are Christians a minority or a majority in the region? (a majority)

➔ **Data Discovery**

Have students go to myworldgeography.com to learn more about religion in the region.

CHART SKILLS 1. Islam, Christianity **2.** 24 percent

READING CHECK Any three of: Zulu, Xhosa, Kikuyu, Hutu, Tutsi, Maasai, Baganda

CULTURE

Hotel Rwanda The 2004 film *Hotel Rwanda* told the true story of Paul Rusesabagina, the Hutu manager of a luxury hotel in Rwanda's capital of Kigali. Rusesabagina is married to a Tutsi woman, and when the Hutu extremists led violence against Tutsi, Rusesabagina sheltered more than 1200 Tutsi countrymen by calling them guests. Critics and activists praised the film's ability to inspire and educate people, including foreign policy expert Samantha Power, "Hotel Rwanda is particularly powerful because it's not a black-and-white genocide from ancient history. It's genocide shot in color in the present day . . . Maybe the next film will be about Darfur. It can't come soon enough." Source: "Filming the Unfilmable" by Katrina Onstad, http://www.cbc.ca/arts/film/genocide.html

GUIDE ON THE SIDE

Conflict in Southern and Eastern Africa Today

- **Compare and Contrast** How are the people in northern and southern Sudan different? (North: Most people are Arabs and Muslims. South: Most people belong to other ethnic groups and are not Muslims.)

- **Cause and Effect** How did these differences lead to civil war? (Muslims dominated the country so southern Sudanese rebelled.)

myWorld Activity

Analyze Conflicts Find Step-by-Step Instructions and an Activity Support on pp. T52–T53. **(Logical/Visual)**

Darfur Refugee Crisis

- **Cause and Effect** How did fighting in Sudan lead to the Darfur refugee crisis? (Attacks on civilians have forced people to flee their homes in search of safety.)

- **Infer** Why do you think some refugees end up in eastern Chad? (The camps inside Darfur could be full or not as safe.)

Conflict in Southern and Eastern Africa Today

As Europeans carved up Africa and then left their colonies, they created many new countries. They often drew borders without regard to where different <u>ethnic</u> groups lived. Sometimes one ethnic group was divided between two different countries. In other places, opposing ethnic groups were included in the same country. These ethnic groups fought for power after Europeans left. Some of these conflicts are still going on. Two of the most deadly conflicts in recent years have taken place in Sudan and Rwanda.

ethnic, *adj.,* group of people with the same nationality, language, or religion

myWorld Activity
Analyze Conflicts

Conflicts in Sudan Sudan is divided among many different ethnic groups. In the north, most people are Arabs and practice Islam. In the south, most people belong to other ethnic groups and are not Muslims. After independence, northerners dominated the country. Southerners rebelled twice. This led to two civil wars between north and south. The wars continued until 2005 and killed several million people.

Since 2003, Darfur has been the scene of another bloody conflict. Darfur is a region in the west of Sudan. Black farmers have fought Arab herders over scarce water resources. The herders support the Sudanese government, while the farmers oppose it. Militias of herders with government backing have attacked civilian farmers. Hundreds of thousands of people, mostly black farmers, have been killed. Many more have been forced to flee their homes. Many people call the Darfur conflict a **genocide,** or an attempt to destroy a whole people.

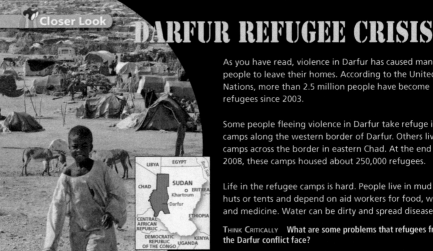

Closer Look
DARFUR REFUGEE CRISIS

As you have read, violence in Darfur has caused many people to leave their homes. According to the United Nations, more than 2.5 million people have become refugees since 2003.

Some people fleeing violence in Darfur take refuge in camps along the western border of Darfur. Others live in camps across the border in eastern Chad. At the end of 2008, these camps housed about 250,000 refugees.

Life in the refugee camps is hard. People live in mud huts or tents and depend on aid workers for food, water, and medicine. Water can be dirty and spread disease.

THINK CRITICALLY What are some problems that refugees from the Darfur conflict face?

THINK CRITICALLY Refugees lack clean water, food, and medicine, and have lost their homes.

ANSWERS

CORE CONCEPTS: POLITICAL SYSTEMS

Review Core Concepts 8.2 before discussing the success and failure of governments in Southern and Eastern Africa. Help students identify features of democratic governments and of dictatorships.

Have students list qualities they think a government needs to function for its people, such as clear chain of command and the ability to supply basic needs to citizens.

Genocide in Rwanda Rwanda has had a troubled history since the colonial period. The country is divided between two ethnic groups, the majority Hutu and the minority Tutsi. Before Belgium colonized the region, the Tutsi formed an elite class that ruled the Hutu. The Belgians favored the Tutsis and used them to keep control of the Hutus. After independence, violence flared up against the Tutsi and the Hutu took control. Further fighting and struggles for power between the groups continued.

Eventually the situation exploded into a horrible genocide. During a few months in 1994, Hutu military and militia groups killed an estimated 800,000 to 1 million Tutsis. The United Nations sent French, Canadian, and other troops to Rwanda to stop the killings. However, they were not effective. The murders stopped when the Tutsi once again came to power. Millions of Hutus fled the country to neighboring Zaire, today called the Democratic Republic of the Congo. Fighting between the two groups continues in that country.

Many people abroad regret that foreign countries could not or did not do more to stop the killing. Kofi Annan, former Secretary General of the UN and a high UN official during the genocide, believes more should have been done to stop it.

> 66 The international community failed Rwanda and that must leave us always with a sense of bitter regret. 99
> —Kofi Annan

Reading Check How did colonialism lead to conflicts in Southern and Eastern Africa?

Governing the Region

Southern and Eastern African countries have many different forms of government. Some are democratic, while others are ruled by dictators.

Democracy Today, one of the most democratic governments in the region is South Africa. Since the end of apartheid, fair and free elections have produced a stable government. Citizens participate in their government and can freely join voluntary organizations. But the new multiracial democracy has experienced growing pains as it tries to <u>integrate</u> and improve South African society. The lingering legacy of apartheid is that black South Africans are still, on average, much poorer than white South Africans. Inequalities remain in areas such as healthcare, unemployment, education, and landownership.

Dictatorship Unlike South Africa, Sudan is a dictatorship. Though the country calls itself a republic, President Omar al-Bashir rules by force. People cannot participate in the government or choose their leaders.

Zimbabwe has also been a dictatorship. A single political party has held on to power for more than 28 years. Even though there is a constitution, President Robert Mugabe has ruled like a dictator. Corruption and oppression have become common. Failed policies have led to economic collapse. Millions of people from Zimbabwe have fled to South Africa.

Reading Check What is a major social problem in South Africa after apartheid?

integrate, *v.,* bring together, particularly people from different groups

- **Summarize** Which ethnic group was responsible for the Rwandan genocide? How did the genocide end? (The Hutu were responsible for the Rwandan genocide. It ended when the Tutsis took power again.)

- **Express an Opinion** What do you think outside nations should do about genocide? (Sample: Try to stop it, using force if necessary.)

Governing the Region

- **Categorize** What is the role of citizens in South Africa? (They participate in government and freely join organizations.)

- **Summarize** Describe the status of blacks and whites in South Africa today. (Black South Africans are still poorer than white South Africans, with less access to health care and education, higher rates of unemployment, and lower rates of land ownership.)

- **Categorize** What type of government rules Sudan? (dictatorship)

- **Analyze Text** What do you think it means to say Mugabe rules "like a dictator" (Sample: Mugabe does not share power or respect human rights.)

READING CHECK Colonialism created national borders that divided ethnic groups or pushed opposing ethnic groups into the same country.

READING CHECK inequality between whites and blacks

ANSWERS

PRIMARY SOURCE

Despair in Zimbabwe Share this 2009 diary entry about attempts to get corrupt president Robert Mugabe to share power with opposition led by Morgan Tsvangirai:

"When I started doing this diary I was so on fire—I wanted to talk about what was happening in my country. I hoped it would somehow bring the story to a lot more ordinary people—and there'd be action and something would change for the better. But it's been a long 10 months and my passion and my hope in politicians is gone."

—Esther (not her real name), in Zimbabwe's capital city of Harare, quoted in "Harare Dairy: 'Hope has died'" at http://news.bbc.co.uk/2/hi/africa/7842562.stm

---

GUIDE ON THE SIDE

Problems and Potential

- **Infer** Describe the rate of economic development in Southern and Eastern Africa. (slow)

- **Cause and Effect** Choose one problem facing the region and explain how it gets in the way of development. (Sample: Political instability means that people and businesses can't count on their government for basic services. For example, businesses cannot thrive in dangerous situations or when they cannot get supplies or bring their goods to market. Children may not have access to schools, so they will not be trained as workers.)

- **Infer** Explain why unevenly distributed resources and corruption make development difficult. (Unevenly distributed resources give some countries money to invest in roads, schools, etc. while other countries struggle just to feed their people. Corruption causes problems for businesses and may lead to stolen foreign aid.)

Problems and Potential

Serious obstacles stand in the way of economic development in the region. Political violence hurts economic growth. Poor transportation systems and low literacy rates also hold back development. On the other hand, the region possesses rich natural resources. It could one day use them to build up economies. Countries like Kenya and South Africa have proved that progress is possible in Southern and Eastern Africa.

Barriers to Development One major obstacle to development is the lack of stable governments in some countries. Somalia, for example is ruled by competing militias and warlords. Without a government, theft and violence are common. Piracy has become a serious problem. Gunmen off the Somali coast have attacked ships, seizing cargoes and holding crews for ransom.

Another obstacle to development is the lack of resources in some countries. For example, frequent droughts have helped keep Ethiopia among the world's poorest

African Union Peacekeepers
Former South African President Thabo Mbeki reviews African Union peacekeeping troops.

countries. Corruption also hurts development, because corrupt countries are unreliable places to do business. Corrupt leaders also steal foreign aid. Lack of education is another serious obstacle. Many families in the region cannot afford to send their children to school. Boys often have more access to education than girls. This makes it difficult for women to get better jobs and improve their situation.

Another problem is disease. Of all the regions in the world, Southern and Eastern Africa have been hit hardest by HIV and AIDS. **AIDS** is an often-deadly disease caused by the HIV virus. It attacks the immune system. It kills about 1.5 million people in this region each year, and that number is rising. Many countries are too poor to properly treat the sick. Also, when so many people get sick or die, work that is necessary to the economy does not get done. This holds back development and hurts everybody.

Hope for the Future While Southern and Eastern Africa have difficult obstacles to overcome, there are positive signs for the future. Governments are

Piracy in Somalia
Pirates in small, fast boats attack larger, slower cargo ships.

ANSWERS

READING CHECK political instability, violence, poor transportation, lack of education, uneven resource distribution, corruption, disease

CHART SKILLS 1. South Africa **2.** Yes, in South Africa; in Kenya and Sudan, boys probably have greater access than girls.

SECTION 3 ASSESSMENT 1. Darfur or Rwanda **2.** HIV attacks the immune system. **3.** NGOs focus on environmental problems, poverty, disease, and conflict. **4.** HIV takes workers out of the economy. **5.** Mostly-Arab herders are

QUICK FACTS

PEPFAR In 2003, the United States launched PEPFAR (President's Emergency Plan for AIDS Relief.) The program has worked to provide AIDS treatment and prevention for more than 10 million people in 15 focus countries, 10 of which are in Southern and Eastern Africa (Ethiopia, Botswana, Kenya, Mozambique, Namibia, Rwanda, South Africa, Tanzania, Uganda, and Zambia). In 2008, PEPFAR was extended for another five years.

making serious efforts to fight AIDS. For example, the Ugandan government sends text messages on mobile phones to educate people about the epidemic. Globalization makes international trade faster and easier. It lets countries like Kenya and South Africa ship more export goods and improve their economies.

Foreign governments and **nongovernmental organizations (NGOs),** groups that operate with private funding, are helping to deal with environmental problems, poverty, disease, and conflict. They also help provide more opportunities for education, especially for women. Nations in the region have formed different organizations to cooperate in solving common problems. The African Union (AU) is the most important. Recently, it has sent peacekeeping troops to Sudan and Somalia.

Reading Check What are some barriers to development in this region?

Literacy Rates and Gender

SOURCE: *CIA World Factbook* ■ Male ■ Female

Chart Skills

1 In which country are literacy rates most similar for men and women?

2 Do you think boys and girls have equal access to education in all of these countries? Explain.

➡ **Data Discovery**

Section 3 Assessment

Key Terms
1. Name one example of a genocide from this region.
2. What part of the body does the HIV virus attack?
3. How do NGOs (nongovernmental organizations) help improve life in Southern and Eastern Africa?

Key Ideas
4. How does HIV/AIDS hold back development?
5. Which groups are fighting in Darfur, and what are they fighting about?
6. Describe some of the successes and failures of South Africa since the fall of apartheid.

Think Critically
7. **Compare and Contrast** How are the recent histories of Rwanda and South Africa similar? How are they different?
8. **Solve Problems** What do you think are the most effective ways Southern and Eastern Africans are improving their region? Why do you think these are the most effective?

Essential Question
Is conflict unavoidable?
9. In the countries of Sudan, Rwanda, Kenya, and South Africa, what has caused ethnic violence? Go to your Student Journal to record your answer.

fighting mostly-Arab farmers over scarce water resources. **6.** Successes: democratic government with free elections; Failures: social and economic inequality between blacks and whites. **7.** Similar: ethnic conflict; Different: violence and genocide in Rwanda, the peaceful end of apartheid in South Africa **8.** Sample: Cooperation is the most effective way to improve the region because it lets people share good ideas. **9.** The biggest causes of ethnic violence are unequal access to power and anger between groups that follow different religions.

ANSWERS

- **Summarize** Who is trying to solve development problems in the region? (Governments inside and outside the region are working with NGOs and regional organizations on the region's problems.)
- **Draw Conclusions** What role does cooperation play in efforts to solve the region's problems? Give an example to explain. (Everyone involved has to cooperate for efforts to work. For example, relief agencies and local governments must work together to get medicine to sick people.)

Chart Skills Have students use the chart data to compare literacy by gender and country.
- What events could explain the levels of literacy in Sudan? (Ethnic conflict and war may be keeping some Sudanese from studying.)

➡ **Data Discovery**

Point out the graph of literacy and gender in South Africa, Kenya, and Sudan.
- Have students go to myworldgeography.com to see more data about literacy in Southern and Eastern Africa.

The Effects of Colonialism

OBJECTIVES
Students will

- compare and contrast the impact of colonialism on Sudan, Tanzania, and South Africa.
- **21st Century Learning** sequence colonial rule and independence in Sudan, Tanzania, and South Africa.
- **ELL** use proper adjectives to identify nations and their citizens.

SET EXPECTATIONS
In this case study, students will

- read The Effects of Colonialism.
- create a decorative timeline showing European colonial control and independence for three nations.

1 Connect

Have students think about how people sometimes react to direction from authority figures. Ask students: What does it feel like when you want more independence than you have? What happens when you try to act more independently than your parents wish? Tell them that the people of Sudan, Tanzania, and South Africa wanted freedom and independence from European authority. Many people in these countries were tired of the discrimination that Europeans directed toward them and felt that European leaders treated them without respect.

L1 Special Needs Have students role-play confrontations between students and adults as a way to focus their attention on obstacles to increased independence.

2 Learn

Preview Have students preview Key Ideas, Key Terms, visuals, and headings. Ask which countries and colonial powers they see represented. Have them predict the kinds of changes you will be reading about for each African country.

Read While students read The Effects of Colonialism, ask questions found in the **Guide on the Side** to build understanding of Key Ideas and lesson objectives.

ELL Intermediate List all the nations discussed in the case study. Next to each, write the proper adjective for that nation or its citizens, i.e., *Britain* and *British*. Have students practice with flashcards.

myWorld Activity: Colonialism on the Clock Distribute *Activity Support: Country Events*. Assign each student a nation, and then have them use the Case Study to identify and record important events in their nation's colonial history. Students should then make or find illustrations to show these events. Have triads combine their work in a three-nation giant timeline. Groups should use a single color for each colonial power on the timeline, such as red for all periods of British control. Ask groups to conclude which colonial power had the widest and longest-lasting influence on these three countries. Discuss as a class. **(Verbal/Visual)**

25 min

L4 Challenge Have students add a fourth line to their timeline, showing major events in America's colonial history.

3 Understand

Review Have students list the nations that controlled each African country. Then summarize the effects of each nation's control.

Assess Check students' answers to the Assessment questions for completeness and accuracy. Evaluate students' timelines for accurate and descriptive reflection of historical events and their conclusion about colonial effects.

Remediate If students are struggling with the Key Ideas, have them make three-column tables with headings for each African nation. In each column, students should list ways in which colonial rule affected the nation.

Name _____ Class _____ Date _____

myWorld Activity Support **Country Events**

Colonialism on the Clock

Directions Create a timeline for one of the three countries in the Case Study. First, record dates of important events, such as changes of power. Then, create four pictures to describe how your country changed over time, such as a star to show the nation's independence. Add your information and pictures to a timeline showing all three nations. Color-code each government that ruled the different countries, using the same color for each ruling power throughout the timeline.

Your Country _____

Important Event _____ **Date** _____

Important Event _____ **Date** _____

Important Event _____ **Date** _____

Important Event _____ **Date** _____

ECONOMICS

Exports Then and Now European colonial powers were greatly interested in the money they could make from products found in African nations, such as gold and diamonds. In many cases, these African nations continue to make money from these same products, exported to the world. For example, Tanzania still exports gold and cotton, and South Africa still exports gold and diamonds.

GUIDE ON THE SIDE

Tanzania

- **Cause and Effect** Why did the Portuguese go to Tanzania? (They wanted to trade with Tanzanians and Arab merchants.)

- **Identify Evidence** How did their settlement patterns reflect their goals for being in Tanzania? (They set up forts on the coasts rather than permanent settlements. This shows that their interest was primarily in trade.)

Analyze Maps Have students link the dates and countries on the map.

- In what order did European countries rule Tanzania? (Portugal, Germany, Great Britain)

- On the basis of their 2009 standards of living, which African country do you think suffered the most from colonial rule? (Tanzania)

Case Study

The Effects of Colonialism

Key Idea	• Southern and Eastern African peoples had varying experiences under European rule.	• Each modern society shows the effects of its colonial past.

Key Terms • Scramble for Africa • abolish • Great Trek

Colonialism had a major effect on Southern and Eastern Africa. Countries such as Tanzania, Sudan, and South Africa were deeply changed by colonial rule. During the late 1800s, European powers raced to seize giant pieces of territory before their rivals arrived in the region. This race was called the **scramble for Africa**. At the Berlin Conference in 1884, European countries met and divided up Africa. The effects of the division and colonization of Africa can still be seen.

Tanzania

In what is now Tanzania, the first Europeans to arrive were the Portuguese. They came to trade with local Africans and Arab merchants. They set up forts along the coast in the early 1500s.

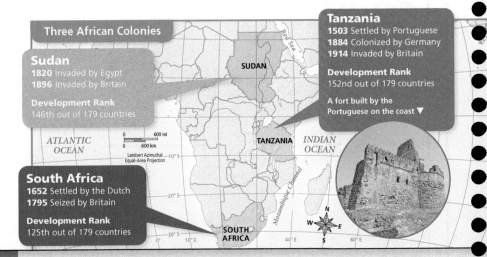

Three African Colonies

Sudan
1820 Invaded by Egypt
1896 Invaded by Britain

Development Rank
146th out of 179 countries

ATLANTIC OCEAN

0   600 mi
0   600 km
Lambert Azimuthal Equal-Area Projection

South Africa
1652 Settled by the Dutch
1795 Seized by Britain

Development Rank
125th out of 179 countries

Tanzania
1503 Settled by Portuguese
1884 Colonized by Germany
1914 Invaded by Britain

Development Rank
152nd out of 179 countries

A fort built by the Portuguese on the coast ▼

Red Sea

SUDAN

TANZANIA   INDIAN OCEAN

Mozambique Channel

SOUTH AFRICA

GEOGRAPHY

Suez Canal The Suez Canal creates a way for ships to get from the Mediterranean Sea to the Red Sea. This made the trip from Britain to its colonies in India much shorter than it had been. Prior to the Suez Canal, ships had to travel around the southern tip of Africa. Though Egyptian leaders since ancient times had built canals to reach the Red Sea, it wasn't until 1869 that a modern and fully functional canal was built. To protect its interests, Britain bought shares in the company that built the canal and later occupied the canal zone in Egypt.

The Portuguese traded gold, ivory, and slaves. Their presence caused resentment. In 1698, Arabs and local Africans forced them out.

In 1884, Germany colonized the area. Germans set up plantations to grow crops such as cotton and rubber for export. They also built railroads and schools. But German rule was harsh. In 1905 Tanzanians rebelled. The Germans brutally put down the rebellion.

Britain seized the German colony in modern-day Tanzania after World War I. The British ruled with a lighter hand. They governed through local leaders. In the process, however, they created tribal organizations, groupings, and divisions that had not existed before. In this way, they changed local society.

Tanzania became a united and independent nation in 1961. But the British left it with a weak economy that relied on export crops. The country remained poor.

Reading Check **Which three European powers colonized modern-day Tanzania?**

Sudan

Sudan was ruled by both Egypt and Britain. Egypt invaded Sudan in 1820. It wanted to control the upper Nile River and to have access to resources in Sudan. Egypt ruled Sudan harshly.

In the late 1800s, the British invaded Egypt and then Sudan. They wanted to protect the Suez Canal, the route by sea from Britain to its colony of India.

For the next six decades, Britain and Egypt ruled Sudan together, although the British held the real power. The British tried to modernize Sudan. They put an end to, or **abolished,** the slave trade. They built rail and telegraph lines. They built schools and educated new leaders.

Despite these benefits, colonial rule also harmed Sudan. You have read that Sudan is divided between a largely Arab Muslim north and a black non-Muslim south. This division developed before the colonial period. However, Britain worked to keep the two regions separate. It wanted to limit Muslim influence in the south. This policy helped divide Sudan and keep the south less developed.

Sudan gained independence in 1956, but the country has remained divided. Power rests mainly with Arab Muslims in the north. Southern rebels fought two civil wars for independence but failed. As you read, conflict today is especially severe in the western region of Darfur.

Reading Check **What is the most important division in Sudanese society?**

Sudan
Troops from the British colony of India helped conquer Sudan for Britain.

GUIDE ON THE SIDE

- **Categorize** What did Portugal and Germany export from Tanzania? (Portugal: gold, ivory, slaves; Germany: cotton, rubber)
- **Cause and Effect** How did Tanzanians react to both Portuguese and German rule? (They resented it and rebelled.)

Sudan

- **Sequence** Which country first colonized Sudan? (Egypt) Which country took over next? (Great Britain)
- **Categorize** What were Egypt and Great Britain's main interests in Sudan? (Egypt: natural resources, control of the Nile; Great Britain: control of Suez Canal trade)

Cause and Effect

- Why did Britain try to separate Sudan into regions? (It wanted to limit Muslim influence.)
- How did the separation affect Sudan over time? (Separation kept Sudan's southern region from developing and created divisions that continue today.)

ANSWERS

COMMON MISCONCEPTIONS

Africans and Afrikaners Explain that in the discussion of South Africa, *Africans* refers to black Africans who had lived in the region before Europeans arrived. *Afrikaners* refers to white Europeans who settled in what is now South Africa in the mid-1600s. Afrikaners were originally of Dutch (from Holland, today called The Netherlands) ancestry, but intermarriage with German employees of the Dutch East-India company added German ancestry, as well. Historians say that the Afrikaners themselves coined the term to tell people back in Holland that they felt Africa was their home, not Europe.

GUIDE ON THE SIDE

South Africa

- **Identify Details** How did Afrikaners treat Africans? (Afrikaners killed and enslaved Africans, and pushed them off of their land.)

- **Compare and Contrast** How was British policy toward Africans the same as Dutch policy? How was it different? (At first, Britain also enslaved Africans and seized land. It later ended slavery.)

- **Summarize** What happened to the Zulu Kingdom? (The British conquered it.)

Map Skills Discuss the map of colonial rule in South Africa.

- What happened to the Boers between the Great Trek and 1910? (The British conquered them.)

- Which areas on the map were part of South Africa after 1910? (Transvaal, Orange Free State, Cape Colony)

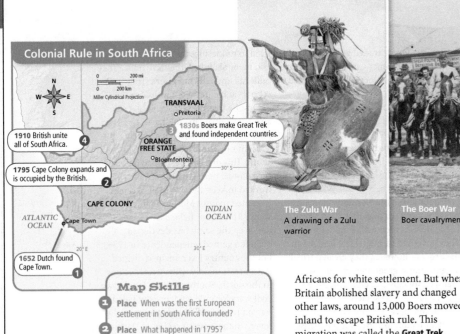

The Zulu War A drawing of a Zulu warrior

The Boer War Boer cavalrymen

Map Skills

1. **Place** When was the first European settlement in South Africa founded?
2. **Place** What happened in 1795?

South Africa

The Dutch were the first Europeans to settle in South Africa. They founded Cape Town near the southern tip of Africa. The settlement grew into the Cape Colony.

Dutch and British Rule Dutch and other non-British Europeans who settled in Cape Colony are called Boers or Afrikaners. As the Boers moved inland, they set up large farms. They pushed Africans off the land. They killed or enslaved Africans who resisted.

In 1795, Britain took over the Cape Colony. At first the British continued Boer policies. They seized lands from Africans for white settlement. But when Britain abolished slavery and changed other laws, around 13,000 Boers moved inland to escape British rule. This migration was called the **Great Trek.** Boer migrants formed several small, independent countries known as Boer republics. They maintained white rule.

After the discovery of diamonds and gold inland from the Cape Colony, the British moved to expand their rule. In 1879, they attacked the Zulu Kingdom, a powerful African state. Although the Zulus fought back fiercely, the British were able to defeat them.

In 1899, the British went to war against the Boer republics. The fight dragged on for four brutal years. The British imprisoned tens of thousands of Boer and African civilians before winning the war.

In 1910, a united South Africa gained independence. Afrikaners and English-speaking whites shared power. The black

READING CHECK Both were defeated by the British.

MAP SKILLS 1. The Dutch founded Cape Town in 1652. **2.** The British took over the Cape Colony.

QUICK FACTS

Diversity in Black South Africa The Zulu remain one of the main groups of black South Africans, but there are many others. The Xhosa, Ndebele, and Swazi are Nguni people like the Zulu. Other groups include the Sotho-Tswana, the Tsonga, and the Venda. Even within these groups, there are differences, for example, of language.

The Zulu language is the most commonly spoken home language, but, as of 2001, Xhosa was spoken by 17.6 percent of South Africans. This means that while the Xhosa and the Zulu are similiar in many ways, they often do not speak the same language.

Apartheid
◀ A sign marking a segregated beach in South Africa

▲ Soldiers in the all-white military of the apartheid era

Today
A multiracial crowd in modern South Africa

GUIDE ON THE SIDE

Cause and Effect

• How did expanded British control of South Africa affect black South Africans? (It didn't change their lives much. The black majority was still powerless.)

• What effects remain even though white majority rule has ended? Explain. (Racial inequality remains. Black South Africans are more likely than whites to be poor, sick, or without access to basic services and safe places to live.)

majority remained powerless. As you read, the apartheid system of white rule lasted until 1994.

New Migrants While the British ruled South Africa, many non-Europeans migrated there. Some came from other British colonies like India and Malaysia. Most worked as contract laborers on large farms. They were treated poorly by the white-ruled government.

Apartheid's Aftermath Racial inequality is still a major problem in South Africa. It is a legacy of the colonial rule and apartheid. Black South Africans are more likely than white South Africans to live in poverty, to have HIV or AIDS, and to go without basic services such as clean water. Khulekani, for example, lacks running water. Many black South Africans also live in dangerous urban slums.

However, the widespread violence and oppression that plagued South Africa during the apartheid period are a thing of the past. South Africans from different races and ethnic groups are working to overcome the divisions left by the difficult history of their country.

Reading Check **What did the Boers and the Zulu have in common?**

Assessment

1. How did Germany govern Tanzania?

2. How did colonial British rule affect the society of Sudan?

3. Which European power united South Africa?

4. What was similar about the colonial experiences of these three countries?

5. How does the legacy of apartheid affect South Africa today?

ASSESSMENT **1.** Germany ruled Tanzania harshly, putting down rebellions with brutal force. **2.** British rule divided the society of Sudan and kept parts of it from developing. **3.** Great Britain **4.** In all three countries, Europeans ruled for their own benefit, often with negative effects on Africans. **5.** Racial inequality continues.

ANSWERS

KEY TERMS AND IDEAS

1. People clear forests to reach the region's abundant mineral resources.

2. Water is scarce in the region, and its location determines where people have enough water for crops and other living needs.

3. The Bantu came from West Africa and went to Southern and Eastern Africa.

4. Sample: Nubia, iron-making; Bantu, language spread; Great Zimbabwe: large city.

5. European control brought settlers and created colonies. It expanded the slave trade, which disrupted African society and enslaved many. Regional economies and education improved in some places.

6. Inequality between blacks and whites still exists in economic status, healthcare, unemployment, education, and land ownership.

7. NGOs are important because they work on many different problems. They are also neutral, which is useful in a region with many conflicts and underperforming governments.

THINK CRITICALLY

8. Uneven distribution of resources and water, remaining effects of European rule, ethnic and religious conflicts, disease, and inequality of many kinds contribute to the problem. Government and private efforts to educate people, reduce disease, create political solutions, and stop genocide allow progress.

9. Unlike citizens in the United States, citizens in Sudan cannot participate in government or choose their leaders.

10. The white minority mostly supported apartheid, which separated whites and blacks and gave power to whites. The black majority opposed apartheid and pushed for greater political power and equality.

11. Beginning with the movement of human beings out of Eastern Africa, movement has spread human culture. Early African cultures, such as the Nubians and the Bantu, spread iron-making and language, as they moved throughout the region. Arab traders spread the religion of Islam, as well as the Arabic language and other learning from beyond Africa. European colonists brought additional languages and cultural ideas into the region.

Southern and Eastern Africa

Chapter Assessment

Key Terms and Ideas

1. **Discuss** Why do Southern and Eastern Africans clear forests for mining?

2. **Summarize** Why is the location of water resources so important in Southern and Eastern Africa?

3. **Recall** Where did the Bantu come from and where did they migrate to?

4. **Categorize** Give three examples of early civilizations in the region and name a feature of each.

5. **Analyze Cause and Effect** How did European control change Southern and Eastern Africa?

6. **Summarize** What have been some of the main consequences of **apartheid** in South Africa?

7. **Synthesize** Given the challenges that the region's people and governments face, why are **nongovernmental organizations (NGOs)** important in Southern and Eastern Africa?

Think Critically

8. **Solve Problems** Economic progress has been slow for the nations of this region. What geographic and human factors contribute to the problem? What factors allow or contribute to progress?

9. **Compare and Contrast** How is the role of citizens in Sudan today different from their role in the United States?

10. **Compare Viewpoints** During the apartheid era in South Africa, what main views were held and by whom?

11. **Core Concepts: Cultural Diffusion and Change** How has the movement of people influenced religion, culture, and language in Southern and Eastern Africa?

Places to Know

For each place, write the letter from the map that shows its location.

12. South Africa
13. Madagascar
14. Kenya
15. Lake Victoria
16. Khartoum
17. Kalahari Desert
18. **Draw Inferences** What might be some geographic reasons for South Africa being the region's economic superpower?

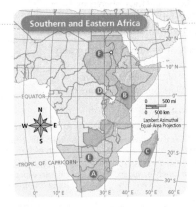

Southern and Eastern Africa

PLACES TO KNOW

12. A
13. C
14. B
15. D

16. F
17. E
18. Sample: It has access to good ports, so it could be a trade center.

myWorld Chapter Activity

Agents of Change Find Step-by-Step Instructions, Student Instructions and Rubric, and an Activity Support on pp. T33–T35. **(Kinesthetic/ Interpersonal/Intrapersonal)**

21st Century Learning

Analyze Media Content Students' report cards should show a successful search and thoughtful and accurate selection of data. If students need help with this skill, direct them to the online tutorial *Analyze Media Content*.

 Online Assessment

Tailor review and assessment to each student's needs with an array of online assessments.
- Self-Test
- On Assignment Article or Slideshow
- Success Tracker

Essential Question
myWorld Chapter Activity

Agents of Change Follow your teacher's instructions to participate in a community group meeting attended by important individuals involved in the fall of apartheid in South Africa. Learn how different individuals helped take down apartheid. Think about ways that different groups of people can live together peacefully, and about what causes conflicts to occur.

21st Century Learning
Analyze Media Content

Using reliable sources in the library or online, research an ethnic conflict in the region. Find three examples and create a report card for each.
- type of media (print, online, TV, or radio)
- accuracy in describing conflict and participant views
- reliability (Is the source objective?)

Document-Based Questions

Success Tracker™
Online at myworldgeography.com

Use your knowledge of Southern and Eastern Africa, as well as Documents A and B, to answer Questions 1–3.

Document A

Document B

Bantu Genes		
Country or Region	Number of People Tested for Gene Type	Number of People With Bantu Gene Type
Kenya	227	223
Tanzania	41	41
Mozambique	4	2
Southern Africa	23	20

SOURCE: *Genetics and Molecular Biology*, volume 24 (1998), no. 4

1. Where was the Bantu people's original homeland?
   A Europe
   B North Africa
   C West Africa
   D Southern Africa

2. Which of the following can you conclude from Document B?
   A Very few Tanzanians are of Bantu heritage.
   B Most Kenyans are of Bantu heritage.
   C Most Mozambicans are of European heritage.
   D Most people in the world are of Bantu heritage.

3. **Writing Task** Based on what you have learned from the chapter and the documents above, explain the information presented in Document B.

WRITING TASK TIP

SUPPORT CONCLUSIONS Before students complete the Writing Task, tell them that explaining information in a document usually requires drawing a conclusion. Review that conclusions are based on clues in the text and on the reader's prior knowledge. Model how to identify clues in the documents, such as the time indicators on the map that show when Bantu speakers arrived in Kenya and the table information that shows how many Kenyans are Bantu-speakers.

DOCUMENT-BASED QUESTIONS

1. C

2. B

3. Answers will vary but should point out that Bantu speakers arrived in Kenya earliest and so had the greatest time to establish and spread throughout the local community. As a result, it makes sense that most Kenyans today are of Bantu heritage.

Plan With Understanding by Design*

Chapter Objectives
Begin With the End in Mind

Students will demonstrate the following enduring understandings:
- Conquest and conflict have shaped people's lives in history and in the present.
- A region's physical features and climate affect the people who live there in many ways, including socio-economic benefits and challenges.
- Political and economic situations affect the stability and standards of living in a given place.

Connect
Make Learning Meaningful

Student Edition
- **Essential Question** How much does geography shape a country?
- **Shaimaa's Neighborhood** Shaimaa describes her life in Cairo, Africa's largest city.

my worldgeography.com
myStory Video Get to know Shaimaa through a video of her life and home.

Student Journal
Essential Question Preview

Experience
Teach Knowledge and Skills

Student Edition
- Read Sections 1, 2, and 3.
- Answer Reading Checks and Section Assessment questions.

my worldgeography.com
On Assignment Visual Glossary, Active Atlas, Data Discovery, Language Lesson, Culture Close-up, and Self-Test

Student Journal
- Sections 1, 2, and 3 Word Wise
- Sections 1, 2, and 3 Take Notes

Teacher's Edition
✖ **myWorld Activities**
- Section 1: On the Move, p. T66
- Section 2: The Farmer's Pitch, p. T72
- Section 3: Human Bar Graph, p. T80

21st Century Learning Online Tutor
- Draw Conclusions
- Use Parts of a Map
- Give Effective Presentations
- Use Charts and Graphs
- Analyze Cause and Effect
- Identify Main Ideas and Details

Understand
Assess Understanding

Assessment Booklet
- Chapter Tests   • Benchmark Tests

Teacher's Edition
✖ **myWorld Chapter Activity**
Students make entries for a new national crest contest in a North African nation, including crest drawings and persuasive paragraphs to contest judges.

Student Edition
Chapter Assessment

my worldgeography.com
On Assignment Students will write and submit an online article or multimedia slide show about the effect of geography on North African countries.

Success ☆ Tracker™
Online at myworldgeography.com
Administer chapter tests and remediate understanding.

Student Journal
Essential Question Writer's Workshop

Connect to the Essential Question

 Essential Question

How much does geography shape a country?

Follow these steps to help students understand the Essential Question.

Connect to Their Lives

1. Have students discuss how they think geography has shaped their lives. (If students have already studied this Essential Question, encourage them to note changes to their opinion.) As students respond, emphasize the diversity of ways that geography can shape their lives. Students might focus on parks, nearby lakes, local weather, crops grown in their region, the size of their school, and recreational activities. Ask, Have you ever lived in a place that had different geographic influences? Explain.

2. Have students identify how geographic elements mentioned in the table below have affected their lives. Post the following table for them to complete or have students turn to the *Essential Question Preview* page in their **Student Journal.**

Personal Influence of Geographic Elements				
Parks, Lakes, Rivers	Local Weather	Local Crops	Size of school	Recreational Activities

3. Discuss students' responses. Ask, In what ways can these elements affect each other? For example, in what way can cold weather affect the type of recreational activities in a region?

Connect to the Content

4. Now have students brainstorm ways that geographic elements can influence a country. For instance, amount of rainfall can affect what crops are grown.

5. In the table below, have students list possible influences of geographic elements on a country.

Influences of Geographic Elements on a Country				
Physical Features	Climate	Natural Resources	Population	Culture

6. After previewing the chapter, have students make chapter-related predictions on the *Essential Question Preview* page in the **Student Journal.**

7. Remind students that they will answer a prompt related to the Essential Question on each section's Take Notes page in the **Student Journal.**

Explore worldgeography.com

Welcome to myWorldGeography

http://www.myworldgeography.com

ON ASSIGNMENT: North Africa

For this chapter's assignment, students will
- take a digital trip to North Africa.
- take on the role of a journalist.
- gather notes, images, and data throughout their journey.
- write an article or make a multimedia slideshow connecting the information and images gathered during their trip and this chapter's Essential Question: How much does geography shape a country?

ITINERARY

During their trip, students will make the following stops:

myStory Video

Learn more from Shaimaa about life in Cairo.

Active Atlas

Read physical, ecosystems, and colonial maps of North Africa.

Data Discovery

Read a graph of GDP and GDP Per Capita.

Language Lesson

Learn to say a few words in Egyptian Arabic.

Culture Close-up

Explore the ruins of the temple at Abu Simbel in Egypt.

Self-Test

Assess their own knowledge of chapter content.

While on their trip, students will practice the following skills:

- **interpret** graphic representations of data.
- **synthesize** information in an article or slideshow.
- **evaluate** effects of geography on North Africa.

TakingITGlobal for Educators

Extend the reach of every lesson by helping students connect to a global community of young people with common interests and concerns. Visit myworldgeography.com to
- explore Country Pages relating to North Africa.
- delve deeper into this chapter's Essential Question, *How much does geography shape a country?*
- find online alternatives to and solutions for the Unit Closer 21st Century Learning Activity.

 worldgeography.com

TEACHER CENTER

Preview and assign student materials, enrich your teaching, and track student progress with the following resources:
- Online Lesson Planning and Resource Library
- Presentations for Projection
- Online Teacher's Edition and Ancillaries
- Google Earth Links

Assess Enduring Understandings

 myWorld Chapter Activity **Step-by-Step Instructions**   **90 min**

National Crest Contest

Teach this activity at the end of the chapter to assess enduring understandings.

OBJECTIVES

Students will demonstrate the following enduring understandings:
- Conquest and conflict have shaped the lives of people through history and in the present.
- A region's physical features and climate affect the people who live there.
- Political and economic situations affect the stability and standards of living in a given place.

Students will provide the following evidence of understanding:
- National Crest Drawing
- Crest Statement

LEARNING STYLES
- Visual
- Verbal

MATERIALS
- Activity Support: Student Instructions and Rubric, p. T62
- Activity Support: Country Crests, p. T63
- Poster board
- Colored pencils or markers
- Activity Cards: #85–90
  - 85. Morocco
  - 86. Algeria
  - 87. Tunisia
  - 88. Libya
  - 89. Egypt
  - 90. Compare to the United States

Activity Steps

1. **Set Expectations** Tell students that they will use information from the chapter and Activity Cards to make contest entries suggesting a new national crest for a North African country. Entries will include a drawing of the national crest showing history, government, geography, and economy, as well as a paragraph arguing for the entry. Assign countries.

2. **Provide Background**
   - Using the Activity Support, model the process by discussing what might be included in a United States crest. Show a sample state or family crest.
   - Review directions for *Activity Support: Country Crests* and *Student Instructions and Rubric*.

   ELL Early Intermediate Clarify the category names on the crests. Provide visual examples.

3. **Gather Information** Allow students 30 minutes to read the Activity Cards, review chapter text, and take turns using computers to conduct online image research. Urge them to take notes.

   L1 Special Needs Provide an illustrated list of common flag and crest symbols and the ideas or qualities they typically represent.

4. **Draw Crests** Have students plan representative pictures or symbols for each category, using blank paper, then sketching lightly in pencil onto the crest, and then adding permanent ink and color. Have students add a national motto, using original mottos or locating appropriate quotations.

   ELL Beginning Provide sample motto frames and suitable motto concepts, for example liberty, honor, and agriculture.

5. **Write Statements** Tell students to write a statement of a few paragraphs to persuade judges to choose their entry. Students should explain why each image effectively represents an aspect of the country.

   L4 Challenge Have students use Card 90 to write additional sentences comparing each aspect of their country to the United States.

6. **Publish and Display** Have students mount crests and statements on poster board or heavy paper. Group completed entries by nation in a class display.

KEY **Time** **Individual** **Pairs** **Small Group** **Whole Class**

Name _____ Class _____ Date _____

myWorld Chapter Activity Support   **Student Instructions and Rubric**

National Crest Contest

Activity Instructions Read the following summary of your myWorld Chapter Activity. Follow your teacher's directions for more information.

1. You will make an entry for a contest choosing a new national crest for a North African country. Your entry will include a proposed new crest and a persuasive paragraph to convince judges to choose your entry.

2. Using information from the chapter and Activity Cards, learn about your assigned nation and identify its most important features.

3. Draw pictures or symbols that clearly show your country's history, government, geography, and economy. If you wish, find ideas online or in books. Show your ideas on *Activity Support:* Country *Crests*.

4. Write a few paragraphs urging judges to choose your crest. Describe each image and argue how it will help viewers get to know your country and its personality. Support your ideas with information from the Activity Cards and the chapter.

5. Display your statement and your national crest in class for viewing by contest judges.

myWorld Chapter Activity Rubric	3 Exceeds Understanding	2 Reaches Understanding	1 Approaches Understanding
Crest Artwork	Draws colorful and detailed pictures	Draws pictures with some color and limited detail	Draws pictures with no color and few details
Content	Draws pictures that accurately represent information from each category	Draws pictures that accurately represent information from at least two categories	Draws pictures that do not accurately represent information about the country
Paragraph Content	Includes at least two reasons per category with accurate supporting data from chapter and Activity Cards	Includes one reason per category with some accurate supporting data	Includes one reason per category without supporting data
Paragraph Organization	Includes a clear persuasive topic sentence and an effective concluding sentence that adds to the topic sentence	Includes a mostly clear and persuasive topic sentence and a concluding sentence that repeats the topic sentence	Includes an unclear or unconvincing topic sentence and a concluding sentence that does not refer back to the topic sentence

Name _____ Class _____ Date _____

myWorld Chapter Activity Support   **Country Crests**

National Crest Contest

Directions Write the name of your assigned North African nation at the top of the page. Then design and draw four colorful pictures in a crest for your country. Each picture should represent the category labeled above it.

Country _____

HISTORY

GOVERNMENT

ECONOMY

GEOGRAPHY

North Africa

- Introduce the Essential Question so that students will be able to understand the big ideas of this chapter (see earlier page, Connect to the Essential Question).

- Help students prepare to learn about North Africa by looking at the chapter's maps, charts, and photos.

- Have students make and record chapter predictions with the *Essential Question Preview* in the **Student Journal.**

- Ask them to analyze maps on this page.

GUIDE ON THE SIDE

Explore the Essential Question . . .

Have students complete the Essential Question Writer's Workshop in their **Student Journal** to demonstrate in-depth understanding of the question in the context of this chapter.

Analyze Maps Point out the political map.

- Which country is the largest? (Algeria) Which country controls the most coastline? (Morocco)

- What is this region's only river called? (Nile River)

- Why do you think most of the cities are near the coast? (These places have access to the sea for trade.)

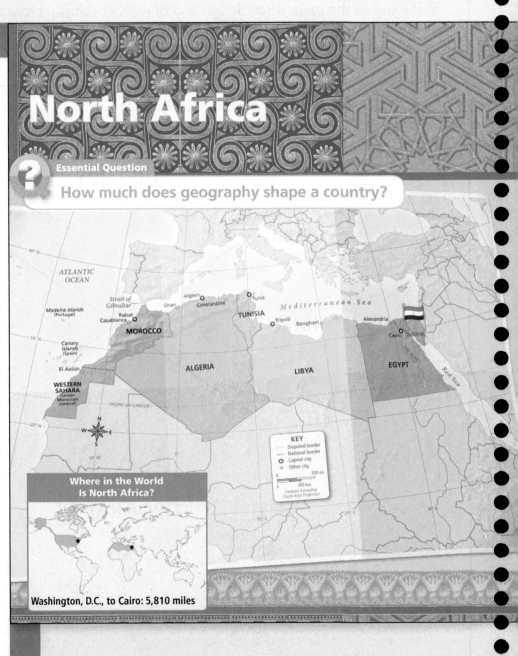

North Africa

? Essential Question

How much does geography shape a country?

Where in the World Is North Africa?

Washington, D.C., to Cairo: 5,810 miles

KEY
- - - Disputed border
—— National border
◉ Capital city
○ Other city

INTRODUCE my Story

Get students excited to learn about North Africa by first experiencing the region through the eyes of Shaimaa, a young woman living in Egypt's busy city of Cairo.

- Read myStory and watch the myStory Video about Shaimaa's life.

- Have students complete *Shaimaa's Neighborhood* in the **Student Journal** to prepare to learn about the region's growing cities.

my Story
SHAIMAA'S NEIGHBORHOOD

In this section, you'll read about Shaimaa, a young Egyptian woman who lives in Cairo. *What does Shaimaa's story tell you about life in North Africa today?*

Story by Oliver Wilkins for myWorld Geography Online

Sitting on the top of Cairo's medieval city wall, 18-year-old Shaimaa is focused on her sketchbook. Pencil in hand, she traces the domes and towers that make up the skyline of Darb al-Ahmar, the neighborhood where she was born and raised. Her spot overlooks a large park, and the sound of birds fills the air. For Shaimaa, it seems a million miles away from the hustle and bustle of the crowded neighborhood below where she lives with her family.

"I have four sisters. We all sleep in the same room. My older sister Asmaa got married. They had to leave the area because they couldn't afford an apartment."

Shaimaa's parents, like many in the neighborhood, moved here from the countryside. They originally came from a village in southern Egypt. They moved to Cairo to find a new life.

Shaimaa's apartment is located in one of the hundreds of small alleys that make up Darb al-Ahmar. The neighborhood lies in the shadow of the citadel, or fortress. The citadel was once home to Cairo's rulers and its wealthiest families lived in Darb al-Ahmar.

Explore the Essential Question
- at **my worldgeography.com**
- using the **myWorld Chapter Activity**
- with the **Student Journal**

GUIDE ON THE SIDE

my Story

Shaimaa's Neighborhood

- **Identify Details** Where is Shaimaa's family from originally? (a village in Southern Egypt)

- **Cause and Effect** Why did Shaimaa's family come to Cairo? (to find a new life)

- **Summarize** What is life like in the family's neighborhood and apartment? (crowded)

On Assignment

Have students go to www. myworldgeography.com to learn more about going On Assignment to collect and analyze images and data from north africa

NOTES

COMMON MISCONCEPTIONS

Education for Girls Some students may assume that girls in Arab-Muslim countries don't go to school very much. Explain that customs vary from country to country. In Egypt, where Shaimaa lives, almost as many girls as boys attend high school. But more boys than girls attend university. Only about half as many girls as boys continue to this level in Egypt.

GUIDE ON THE SIDE

- **Compare and Contrast** How has Shaimaa's neighborhood changed since it was built? (It used to be very wealthy. Now it is struggling.)
- **Summarize** What are the two main parts of Shaimaa's day? (She goes to school and she volunteers at a community center.)

Shaimaa at a market

Laundry drying in Darb al-Ahmar

The neighborhood was very prosperous. Its wealthy residents built beautiful mosques.

But later, the area fell on hard times. For many years the beautiful buildings crumbled. As the population mushroomed, the area became overcrowded. Like many parts of Cairo today, Shaimaa's neighborhood is struggling to support a growing population.

Every weekday Shaimaa leaves her house at 9 A.M. and makes her way through the bustling market to catch a bus to school in downtown Cairo. She is studying computer science and hopes to continue at a university at the end of the year.

However, Shaimaa's real passion is to help restore her neighborhood. Most days after school she volunteers at a community center to do her part.

With hammer in hand, Shaimaa nails together a wooden backdrop, painted with the minarets and domes of Darb al-Ahmar's distinctive skyline. Today she is helping a group of children

Two puppets and a backdrop showing the skyline of Darb al-Ahmar

NOTES

CULTURE

Puppet Theater Egyptian puppet theater takes two common forms: al-aragoz, which uses hand-held puppets, and khayal al-dhill, which uses puppets out of view to create shadows for viewers to see. Puppetry came to Egypt thousands of years ago from Persia (now Iran) and Southwest Asia. Mustafa Othman worked for 40 years as a puppeteer, or aragoz. He loved puppet shows as

a boy in Cairo, and later learned to perform them. Like Shaimaa, Othman sees what puppetry can do for children. "An aragoz performer can and does talk directly to the audience. . . . Some of my happiest moments as a performer are when I can address a child individually."

— "Theatre of Shadows" by Amira El-Noshokaty from *Al-Ahram Weekly*

The puppet show

Shaimaa on the city wall

to prepare a puppet show on the history of their neighborhood. Puppet shows are a traditional form of entertainment. Shaimaa hopes that by bringing these old stories to life, she may be able to encourage a sense of pride in the neighborhood.

"We are trying to tell the people about this neighborhood through the program. We are trying to make people proud of Darb al-Ahmar by reminding them about their history, trying to revive the heritage and the folklore of the neighborhood."

In the courtyard of the school, the children rehearse the puppet show. In two weeks they will be performing it in the park by the city wall. It's hard to believe now, but the park was a garbage dump until a few years ago. After centuries of people throwing their trash over the wall, the dump grew into a hill, Shaima recalls.

"I remember before it was a park, it was a dusty

hill. We were frightened to go in there because the wild dogs would chase us."

Sketching on the top of the wall, Shaimaa gazes down on her neighborhood. She points out the buildings that are undergoing restoration.

"Here, each house is like a piece of art from the past. After being restored, each house regains its sense of history."

Shaimaa is optimistic about the future of her neighborhood. "I hope that I'll have more chances to represent the habits and traditions of my neighborhood and to let other people know more about Darb al-Ahmar."

 myStory Video

Join Shaimaa as she shows you more about her life in North Africa.

Meet the Journalist

Name Oliver Wilkins
Favorite Moment Watching Shaimaa teach her mother to write.

- **Identify Details** What does Shaimaa do at the community center? (She helps children prepare puppet shows about their neighborhood's history.)
- **Infer** How does Shaimaa feel about her neighborhood and its history? How do you know? (She is proud of it. She wants to teach children to share that pride.)
- **Compare and Contrast** How is Shaimaa's neighborhood changing? (It is being restored.)
- **Draw Conclusions** What do you think is helping Shaimaa's neighborhood to change? (Many people like Shaimaa are working to change it.)

myStory Video

Have students watch the video at myworldgeography.com about Shaimaa's life in Cairo. Tell students to use their trackers to take notes on ways Shaimaa is working to improve her life.

SECTION 1 LESSON PLAN

Chapter Atlas

OBJECTIVES

Students will know

- physical and human geography of the region, and population distribution.
- positive and negative results of human–environment interaction in the region.

Students will be able to

- label an outline map of North Africa.
- analyze effects of urbanization in North Africa.

SET EXPECTATIONS

In this section, students will

- read Chapter Atlas.
- act out the process of urbanization in Tunisia.
- go On Assignment in North Africa and explore an ancient temple.

CORE CONCEPTS

You may wish to teach or reteach the following lessons from the Core Concepts Handbook:

- Types of Climate, pp. 40–41
- People's Impact on the Environment, pp. 52–53
- Urbanization, pp. 80–81

KEY

Differentiated Instruction
L1 Special Needs **L2** Extra Support
L3 On-Level **L4** Challenge

English Language Instruction
ELL Beginner **ELL** Early Intermediate **ELL** Intermediate
ELL Early Advanced **ELL** Advanced

1 Connect
Make learning meaningful

Make Connections Ask students to name where in your community, region, or state most people live. Discuss why—students might say that people live near activities, events, housing, or jobs. Ask students to brainstorm challenges that arise when many people live in a small space. Discuss how similar reasons and challenges might affect North Africa, a region where population is unevenly spread.

L2 Extra Support Show an overhead map of your community's physical features. Then overlay population density. Link specific features to areas of current and prior settlement.

Activate Prior Knowledge Remind students that in the previous chapter, they learned about uneven water supplies in Southern and Eastern Africa. Ask students to predict how this unevenness might affect North Africa.

ELL Beginner/Early Intermediate Use visuals of Southern and Eastern Africa to recall the image of areas without access to regular water supplies.

Prepare Follow the steps in the section **Preview.** Preteach the Key Terms. Then have students complete *Word Wise* in their journals using in-text clues and the glossary for help.

2 Experience
Teach knowledge and skills

Read Use **Background** notes and **Guide on the Side** questions to model active reading. Have students use *Take Notes* in their **Student Journal** to record important places to know in North Africa on an outline map. Students should use the maps in the Chapter Atlas and the Active Atlas at myworldgeography.com for assistance. As needed, refer students to the **Online Student Edition.**

L1 Special Needs Have students match a Key Idea to each bold red subheading. After reading the text, have students state the Key Idea and a detail relating to that idea.

ELL Intermediate Review English adjectives used to describe physical geography, such as *dry, wet, hot, warm, cool, cold, mountainous, flat, high, low*, etc.

L3 On-Level Have students read *Enrichment: Where Is the Water?* to compare precipitation levels in different parts of the region.

Practice: myWorld Activity Students will act out migration and overcrowding in urban areas, and then compare experiences and draw conclusions on the effects of urbanization. **Step-by-Step Instructions** and **More Activities** follow on pp. T66–T67. Have students complete **21st Century Online Tutor** *Draw Conclusions* and apply this skill to the activity.

SECTION 1 RESOURCE GUIDE

FOR THE STUDENT

worldgeography.com Student Center
- Active Atlas
- Culture Close-up

Student Edition (print and online)
- Chapter Atlas

Student Journal (print and online)
- Section 1 Word Wise
- Section 1 Take Notes

21st Century Learning Online Tutor
- Draw Conclusions
- Use Parts of a Map

FOR THE TEACHER

worldgeography.com Teacher Center
- Online Lesson Planner
- Presentations for Projection
- SuccessTracker

ProGuide: Africa
- Lesson Plan, pp. T64–T65
- myWorld Activity Step-by-Step Instructions, p. T66
- Activity Support: Reflection, p. T67
- myWorld Geography Enrichment, p. T68
- Section Quiz, p. T69

Accelerating the Progress of ELLs
- Reading Support Strategies, p. 42

3 Understand
Assess understanding

Review Review *Word Wise* and *Take Notes* in the **Student Journals.**

Assess Knowledge and Skills Use the Section Assessment and Section Quiz to check students' progress.

Assess Understanding Review students' responses to the Section Assessment Essential Question prompt.

Remediate Use these strategies to review and remediate.

If students struggle to . . .	Try these strategies.
Describe the region's physical geography	Show a video of North African geography, pausing frequenty for students to describe what they see.
Label an outline map	Have students start with the Sahara desert and Nile River.
Locate natural resources	Link each image in the key to an example on the map.

ELL Support

ELL Objective Students will be able to use English to categorize people who live in different environments.

Cultural Connections To reinforce the important link between water and daily life in North Africa, invite students to use their home language to describe two ways that they used water today.

ELL Intermediate Content Tip Post the term *urbanization* and circle the root *urban*. Define it as "having to do with a city." Then define the suffix -*ation* as "process of becoming." Ask students what *urbanization* means.

ELL Activity Provide word banks for conditions facing city-dwellers, rural farmers, and nomads, such as *crowded* and *need water for* City-Dweller. Have students make index cards for each term, with definitions or visual reminders. Then have partners prompt each other with categories and anwer with descriptions. Model this with a volunteer. **(Visual/Verbal)**

myWorld Activity   **Step-by-Step Instructions**   ⏱ 20 min

On the Move

OBJECTIVES

Students will

• experience migration and overcrowding in urban areas.

• compare experiences and draw conclusions about the effects of urbanization.

LEARNING STYLE

• Kinesthetic
• Interpersonal

21st Century Learning

• Draw Conclusions

MATERIALS

• Activity Support: Reflection, p. T67
• Tape or rope
• Paper cups

Activity Steps

1. Tell students that they will act out recent population shifts in Tunisia. They will then express their views on Tunisian population trends and interview others to compare experiences and draw conclusions.

2. Assign roles from 1950s Tunisia to each student: 32% are city-dwellers; and 68% are rural residents or nomads.

   ELL Beginning/Early Intermediate Show three video clips of city-dwellers, rural residents, and nomads. State the titles and have students repeat.

3. Clear desks and use tape or rope to make a small urban area. Have city-dwellers enter and remain in the urban area. Rural residents scatter in the room. Nomads wander through the rural areas.

   L1 Special Needs Model what each role does.

4. Preview the information listed on *Activity Support: Reflection*. Clarify that for the activity, students will

reflect the increase in city population by moving from rural areas. Then direct rural residents or nomads to relocate as you read each change.

   L2 Extra Support Help students calculate how many students should move in each shift.

   L4 Challenge Give city-dwellers cups half full of water and all others empty cups. After each population shift, those in the urban area must share water equally.

5. Allow students five minutes to write about their role and five minutes to interview those in other roles.

6. Have students complete *Activity Support: Reflection* and then share conclusions about the future effect of urbanization on Tunisia.

   ELL Intermediate Instruct students to use words from ELL Activity in interviews and discussion.

More Activities From myWorld Teachers

Local Connections Ask students to identify ways people in your community have changed the environment, such as with dams or canals. Have students draw cause-and-effect charts to show positive and negative effects of the changes. **(Logical/Visual)**

Tunes for the Open Road Invite students to make and perform a song or rap about nomadic life. The lyrics should capture advantages and disadvantages of

the nomad's lifestyle. Let students perform their songs while walking around the room. **(Kinesthetic)**

Eco-Friendly Community Have groups consider the climate and resources of North Africa and then write a planning proposal for a community that takes advantage of the region's physical geography while limiting negative effects. Proposals should include a sketch or drawing. **(Visual)**

my worldgeography.com **Teacher Center** ➡ Find additional resources in the online Teacher Center.

Name _____ Class _____ Date _____

myWorld Activity Support   **Reflection**

On the Move

Directions Study the information about Tunisia listed below. After completing the role-play activity, answer the questions that relate to the role you played. Then interview classmates who played the other two roles. Finally, draw a conclusion to prepare for discussion.

In 1950, 68% of Tunisians were rural residents; 32% were city-dwellers.

1950s *Post-World War II manufacturing created jobs; 5% more lived in cities.*

1960s *Government forced nomads to settle in villages and cities; 6% more lived in cities.*

1970s *Better farm machines reduced jobs for farm workers; 7% more lived in cities.*

1980s *Tourism offered jobs in cities; 7% more lived in cities.*

1990s *Better farm machines again reduced jobs for farm workers; 6% more lived in cities.*

2000s *Tourism from Europe brought more jobs to cities; 4% more lived in cities.*

City-dweller

1) How did you feel when rural Tunisians moved to your city?

2) How did it affect your living conditions?

3) How did it affect the resources available to you?

Rural resident

1) Did you move to the city or stay in a rural area?

2) If you moved, what problems did you have entering city life?

3) If you could choose, which path would you prefer? Explain.

Nomad

1) If you went to the city, how did the city change?

2) How did these changes affect your quality of life?

On a separate piece of paper, summarize population changes in Tunisia from 1950 to 2000. What conclusion can you draw about new challenges Tunisia will face in the 2000s? Share your conclusions in a class discussion.

Name _____ Class _____ Date _____

Enrichment: Where Is the Water?

Directions Study the table. Then answer the questions that follow and complete the activity.

Precipitation (inches)	Tunis, Tunisia	Casablanca, Morocco	Cairo, Egypt
January	2.3	1.6	0.2
February	2.2	0.0	0.1
March	1.9	0.0	0.1
April	1.5	1.7	0.0
May	0.9	0.6	0.0
June	0.4	0.0	0.0
July	0.1	0.0	0.0
August	0.3	0.0	Trace
September	1.3	0.4	Trace
October	2.6	2.7	0.0
November	2.2	0.7	0.1
December	2.6	4.2	0.2
Annual	18.3	11.8	1.0

1. Which city gets the least annual rainfall? Which city gets the most? Use the North Africa: Physical Map in the Chapter Atlas to explain the differences in precipitation amounts.

_____

_____

2. In which month does each city get the most rainfall? In which month does each city get the least rainfall?

_____

_____

3. Activity Find a city in the United States that gets a similar amount of rainfall to one of these North African cities. Make a packing list for a trip to either the U.S. or the African city.

Name _____ Class _____ Date _____

Section Quiz

Directions Answer the following questions using what you learned
in Section 1.

1. _____ What feature of North Africa is
large, triangle-shaped, and packed with
cities and towns?
a. the Nile River delta
b. the Sahara
c. the Mediterranean Sea
d. the Atlas Mountains

2. _____ Why does life in the Sahara cluster
around oases?
a. Oases have good roads.
b. It rains less at oases.
c. People can find water at oases.
d. An oasis causes big lakes to form.

3. _____ What is the definition of nomads?
a. people who have moved to cities to find
better jobs and schools
b. people who raise cows on farms for
their milk and meat
c. people who grow crops to make their
living
d. people who move from place to place
without a permanent home

4. _____ Urbanization is the way in which
a. annual rivers flood to enrich the
surrounding soil.
b. cities grow as people move from the
countryside.
c. land loses its soil and becomes a desert.
d. people pipe water to cities from distant
sources.

5. _____ What change was brought about by
the Suez Canal?
a. Oil was developed.
b. People irrigated more land.
c. Goods moved more quickly.
d. Deserts expanded due to overgrazing.

6. Complete the table below to show the effects of limited water
on population distribution and the environment in North Africa.

Limited Water →	Population Distribution	
	Environment	

Chapter Atlas

- Model preparing to read by previewing the Key Ideas, Key Terms, headings, visuals, and captions. Have students make predictions about what they will learn. For ELL support, post the prompt, "I predict I will read about . . ."

- Preview and practice using parts of a map by looking at the Natural Resources map. Help students identify the elements of the map's key.

- Preteach this section's high-use Academic Vocabulary and Key Terms using the table on the next page and in-text definitions. Have students practice Key Terms by completing the *Word Wise* page in their journals.

GUIDE ON THE SIDE

Physical Features

- **Identify Details** What body of water do all the countries of North Africa lie along? (Mediterranean Sea)

- What geographic feature covers much of North Africa? (the Sahara)

- **Summarize** Describe this geographic feature and its effect on climate. (It is the world's largest hot desert. Conditions are dry with sand storms and very high daytime temperatures.)

Reading Skill

Label an Outline Map While they read, have students identify the Places to Know! on the outline map of the region in the **Student Journal.**

Section 1

Chapter Atlas

Key Ideas
- North Africa is very dry, especially in the vast desert called the Sahara.
- People settle where rivers or rainfall provide water.
- More and more North Africans are moving to cities.
- People in the region have altered their environment with both positive and negative consequences.

Key Terms • oasis • delta • nomad • urbanization

→ Visual Glossary

Reading Skill: Label an Outline Map Take notes using the outline map in your journal.

▲ The Atlas Mountains in Morocco

◀ A Tunisian woman

Physical Features

The five countries of North Africa lie along the Mediterranean coast from Morocco in the west to Egypt, Shaimaa's home, in the east. The region is very dry. In fact, most of North Africa is desert.

The world's largest hot desert, the Sahara, covers much of North Africa. Conditions in the Sahara are harsh. In some places it does not rain for years at a time. Sandstorms are common. Temperatures can be extremely high during the day but cool or even cold at night. Life in the Sahara centers around oases. An **oasis**

ACADEMIC VOCABULARY

High-Use Word	Definition and Sample Sentence
percent	*n.* one part out of one hundred *Beth answered every question correctly to earn 100 percent on her quiz.*
available	*adj.* present, ready to be used *I am available to help you any time after 7:00 P.M.*
reverse	*v.* turn back, turn in the opposite direction *Unfortunately, it is impossible to reverse time.*

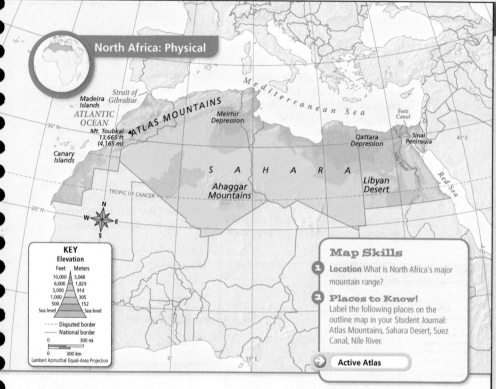

North Africa: Physical

Map Skills

1 **Location** What is North Africa's major mountain range?

2 **Places to Know!**
Label the following places on the outline map in your Student Journal: Atlas Mountains, Sahara Desert, Suez Canal, Nile River.

Active Atlas

is a place in the desert where water can be found.

The Atlas Mountains run through Morocco, Algeria, and Tunisia. They sit between the desert and the sea. Clouds move in from the west and drop their rain as they rise over the mountains. That gives more rainfall to the slopes of the mountains facing the coast and to areas north of the mountains.

The country of Egypt gets almost no rain. It is about 96 <u>percent</u> desert. But the remaining land is green and lush thanks to the Nile River. The Nile travels through its valley north from eastern Africa and

Sudan to the Mediterranean Sea, splitting Egypt in two. It brings water to a strip of land along its banks and to its triangle-shaped delta. A **delta** is a flat plain formed on the seabed where a river deposits material over many years. Until a dam was built on the Nile, the river flooded every year, coating its banks in rich soil.

One part of this region, Egypt's Sinai Peninsula, sits between Asia and Africa. The peninsula is a mountainous desert separated from Africa by the Suez Canal.

Reading Check What is an oasis, and why would people live near one?

percent, *n.,* one part out of one hundred

READING CHECK An oasis is a place in the desert where there is water. People live near oases because life is impossible without water.

MAP SKILLS **1.** Atlas Mountains **2.** Students should correctly locate and label each place on the outline map in their Student Journals.

GUIDE ON THE SIDE

- **Identify Details** What geographic feature separates the sea from the inland desert in western North Africa? (Atlas Mountains)
- **Categorize** Which parts of North Africa get more rainfall than others? (Areas on the coast and on north-facing mountain slopes get more rainfall than areas south of the mountains.)
- **Cause and Effect** Why is about 4 percent of Egypt lush and green? (Water from the Nile River and delta helps vegetation grow.)
- **Predict** How might a dam that controls Nile River flooding change the land? (Land below the dam might get less water, so nearby land might not be as green.)

Map Skills Discuss the map.

- Where are the lowest places in North Africa? (the Melrhir and Qattara Depressions)

 Active Atlas

Point out the map of North Africa's physical geography.

- Have students go to myworldgeography.com to learn more about the physical geography of North Africa.

GEOGRAPHY

Nile River Delta The name *delta* comes from the Greek letter delta, which looks like a triangle. River deltas form because the river water loses speed. As this happens, bits of sediment settle, much as they do in a glass of water left standing. Today,

the Nile delta is changing. It is sinking because less soil and sediment are coming from upriver. As a result, waves from the Mediterranean are slowly wearing away the delta.

Living in a Dry Place

- **Identify Evidence** Support the statement: People in North Africa have always settled where water is available. (Almost all Egyptians live near the Nile River and almost one half of all North Africans are Egyptians.)

- **Build Cultural Awareness** How do nomads live? (They move from place to place without a permanent home.)

- **Ask Questions** List questions you would ask a nomad to learn about pros and cons of the nomadic lifestyle. (Sample: What is difficult about moving all the time?)

Map Skills Have students examine the map and photograph and then locate the area of the photograph on the map.

- Estimate the distance between the Nile River and the desert. (Almost none; the desert extends nearly to the River.)

 Active Atlas

Point out the map of North Africa's ecosystems.
- Have students go to myworldgeography.com to learn more about the ecosystems of North Africa.

Living in a Dry Place

North Africa's population is increasing rapidly. Cities are large and expanding. But people still live in areas where water is <u>available</u>, mostly along the coasts or near rivers. Away from these areas, the land is too dry to support more than a handful of people.

Settlement Patterns Almost all Egyptians live near the Nile River, where water makes agriculture possible. Few live in the deserts that make up the rest of the country. Egypt has the largest population

available, *adj.,* present, ready to be used

in the region. In fact, almost half of all North Africans are Egyptians.

Most people in western North Africa live near the coast or in the mountains. Rain supports farming in these areas.

A small population lives in the Sahara. Many of these people live and farm in oases. Others are **nomads,** people who move from place to place without a permanent home. Away from oases it is too dry for agriculture, so people who live in the desert make a living by herding animals such as sheep and goats.

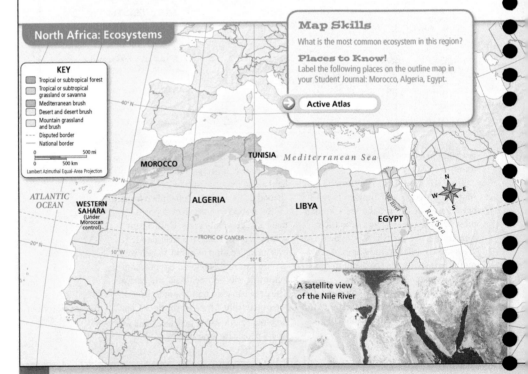

Map Skills
What is the most common ecosystem in this region?

Places to Know!
Label the following places on the outline map in your Student Journal: Morocco, Algeria, Egypt.

 Active Atlas

North Africa: Ecosystems

KEY
- Tropical or subtropical forest
- Tropical or subtropical grassland or savanna
- Mediterranean brush
- Desert and desert brush
- Mountain grassland and brush
- Disputed border
- National border

0 500 mi
0 500 km
Lambert Azimuthal Equal-Area Projection

A satellite view of the Nile River

MAP SKILLS 1. desert **2.** Students should correctly locate and label places on the outline map in their **Student Journal.**

CULTURE

Nomadic Life One group of nomads in North Africa is the Bedouins. These Arab-speaking, mostly Muslim people once populated most of North Africa and are ethnically similar to other people in the region. The Bedouin travel with their animals on a seasonal basis, usually to regular grazing areas. In those areas, the Bedouin live in tents made from animal hair. The use of land is organized among families clustered in groups and led by a sheikh. The way of life is governed by values such as courage, hospitality, and loyalty. More and more Bedouin are settling permanently in order to access social services such as schools and healthcare.

Cities Slightly more than half of all North Africans live in cities. Over the past century, farmers across the region have left their villages and migrated to urban areas in search of jobs and a higher standard of living. North Africa is experiencing urbanization. **Urbanization** happens when people in an area move into cities and those cities grow larger.

Cairo, the capital of Egypt, is the largest city in Africa and home to more than one in five Egyptians. It is Egypt's economic, political, and educational center. That makes it a magnet for poor people from the countryside, like Shaimaa's parents, who have moved there in large numbers.

The trend of urbanization is even stronger in the western part of the region. More than half of all Moroccans, Tunisians, and Algerians live in cities, as do more than three quarters of Libyans.

Rapidly growing urban populations can cause problems. Cities have trouble providing services like drinking water to so many people. Many cities are severely overcrowded. Still, people keep moving to the cities to find new opportunities.

Reading Check Why do people in North Africa move to cities?

myWorld Activity
On the Move

The Nile River, Egypt. Many of Egypt's people live in rural areas near the Nile.

Marrakech, Morocco. Urban North Africans visit cafes and souqs, or markets.

READING CHECK People move to the cities for jobs, educational opportunities, and a higher standard of living.

ECONOMICS

Fishing Industry Chemical fertilizer from upstream is not the only problem for Mediterranean fishermen. The other problem is lack of natural fertilizer. Without those nutrients, fish have no food. In the early years following the construction of the Aswan High Dam, the sardine catch in the Mediterranean fell from 18,000 tons each year to 525 tons. Shrimp catches fell from 8,300 tons to 1,128 tons. Since a low point in 1975, catches are improving and are now nearly as large as they were before the dam was built. Scientists are not really sure why, but the fishing economy is on the rebound.

GUIDE ON THE SIDE

North Africa's Environment

- **Identify Details** What is the Aswan High Dam? (a large dam across the Nile River)

- **Categorize** What are some advantages and disadvantages of the Aswan High Dam? (Advantages include efficient water use, irrigation, increased crop production, limits on floods, and more electricity. Disadvantages include displacement of people to build the dam, disease from mosquitoes in the lake, and pollution from chemical fertilizers.)

↪ **Culture Close-up**

Point out the feature about Abu Simbel. Have students go to myworldgeography.com to learn more about the temple.

THE FLOODING OF LAKE NASSER

Culture Close-up

The Aswan High Dam helped Egypt but the large lake it created flooded many ancient monuments (above).

The ancient Egyptian temples at Abu Simbel (below) were cut into pieces and moved to a location away from the new lake. They are now a tourist attraction.

The temples at Abu Simbel were cut into **20**-ton blocks and moved **213** feet up and **820** feet back.

North Africa's Environment

Human beings have changed the environment of North Africa. These changes have made life easier, but they sometimes have had negative side effects.

In 1964, the Egyptian government built a dam across the Nile River called the Aswan High Dam. Building the dam allowed people to use water more efficiently, irrigate more land, and grow more crops. It also stopped dangerous flooding, and it produces electricity.

Unfortunately, the dam has also had negative effects on Egypt's environment and people. Before the dam was built, Egyptian farmers relied on annual floods to bring fertile soil to their fields. Since the river no longer floods, farmers must use chemical fertilizers to keep their land productive. These fertilizers eventually wash back into the river and through it into the sea. That pollutes water, killing fish and hurting people who fish for a living. Fortunately, fish stocks have recovered in recent years to near what they were before the dam was built.

As water collected behind the dam, it formed a giant lake called Lake Nasser. It is now a habitat for malaria-carrying mosquitoes. The creation of Lake Nasser forced 100,000 people out of their homes.

Like Egypt, Libya has also made serious changes to its environment. As you have read, Libya gets very little rain. However, there are large underground reserves of water deep in the Sahara. The Libyan government has built pipelines to carry water to the coast. The water is used to irrigate farmland and support growing

CORE CONCEPTS: PEOPLE'S IMPACT ON THE ENVIRONMENT

Review Core Concept 4.3 before discussing desertification in North Africa. Recall causes of desertification, such as cutting down trees. Have students explain the process to check their comprehension. Then ask them to predict how grazing animals could lead to the same result as clear-cutting.

GUIDE ON THE SIDE

coastal cities, where four out of every five Libyans now live.

Across this region and other parts of Africa, desertification is a major environmental problem. You learned already that this can happen when people cut down forests. It can also happen in regions such as North Africa that have few forests to begin with.

One way desertification happens is through overgrazing. Herders allow their goats to eat the grass in an area down to the roots. Without those roots, there is nothing left to hold the soil in place. Wind then blows top away, leaving barren desert behind. So much of North Africa is desert already that the region cannot afford to create more.

However, desertification can be slowed or even <u>reversed</u>. When land that is at risk is set aside and herds of sheep or goats are kept away from it, desertification can be reversed and plant life can return. People can also prevent the spread of deserts by planting a "green wall." This is a belt of trees and other vegetation planted along the edges of the desert. The trees and other plants hold soil in place and protect the land.

Algeria pioneered this technique in the 1970s. Since then, belts of forest have been planted along the edges of deserts in other parts of Africa and in different countries around the world.

Reading Check What are two environmental issues in North Africa?

reverse, *v.,* turn back, turn in the opposite direction

- **Compare and Contrast** How are Libya's changes to the environment similar to Egypt's? (Both countries tried to control access to water.)

- **Predict** What problems might result from desertification? (As soil blows away, less can grow on the land. This leaves people with less land on which to grow food and fewer trees under which to find shade. This may displace people and communities.)

- **Problem Solve** What can people do to reduce desertification? (People can limit the animal grazing so that grass can grow back. They can also plant "green walls" along the edges of the expanding desert.)

A landscape in Morocco that shows the effects of desertification. Overgrazing can cause desertification.

READING CHECK any two of the following: pollution from chemical fertilizers in the Nile valley, malaria around Lake Nasser, or desertification

ANSWERS

QUICK FACTS

The Nile The Nile River is the world's longest river at 4,160 miles (6,695 kilometers). It flows northward from a source near the Equator, draining water from about 1,100,000 sq miles (2,850,000 sq km). In addition to the countries listed in the Chapter Atlas, the Nile also drains water from the nations of Eritrea, Kenya, Rwanda, Burundi, Tanzania, and Congo. In Egypt alone, the Nile irrigates 6 million acres (2.4 million hectares).

GUIDE ON THE SIDE

Resources and Trade

- **Infer** Why is water such an important resource in North Africa? (It is scarce.)
- **Draw Conclusions** What political tensions might exist between Egypt and its neighbors? (They must agree on how much water each will use from the Nile River.)
- **Identify Details** Where is most of the oil in North Africa? (inland)
- **Problem Solve** What have governments done to solve this problem? (They have built pipelines to get oil and gas to the coast for shipment.)

Map Skills Have students locate and identify natural resources on the map.

- How are the resources of North Africa distributed? (More are on the coast than inland. Inland resources are mineral or fossil fuel. Coastal resources include crops.)

21st Century Learning

Use Parts of a Map Have students develop this skill with the online tutorial and activities. Students will learn how to read parts of a map and apply the skill to new situations.

Resources and Trade

Water and oil are the most important natural resources in North Africa. The Nile River flows through several countries before it reaches Egypt. As you read in Southern and Eastern Africa, deciding who gets to use that water is a difficult issue. If other countries take too much water, Egypt could face shortages.

The Nile River in Egypt, and rainfall in the western part of the region, allow farming. Cotton, olives, citrus fruits, and other crops are important exports.

Oil Although North Africa does not produce as much oil as parts of Southwest Asia, every nation in the region has enough to satisfy its own needs and to export, or sell abroad. Algeria and Libya have the largest reserves by far.

Most of North Africa's oil and natural gas reserves are found inland, in the heart of the Sahara. Governments and international companies have built pipelines. They transport oil and gas to the coast, where they are shipped around the world.

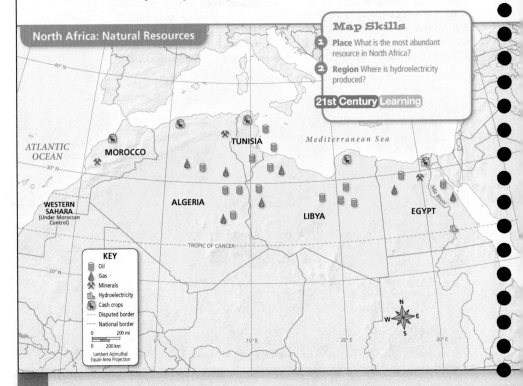

North Africa: Natural Resources

Map Skills
1. **Place** What is the most abundant resource in North Africa?
2. **Region** Where is hydroelectricity produced?

21st Century Learning

KEY
- Oil
- Gas
- Minerals
- Hydroelectricity
- Cash crops
- - - Disputed border
- — National border

0   200 mi
0   200 km
Lambert Azimuthal Equal-Area Projection

MAP SKILLS 1. oil 2. on the Nile River

READING CHECK Algeria, Libya

READING CHECK The majority religion and language came to North Africa from Southeast Asia.

SECTION 1 ASSESSMENT 1. Sample: Nomads in the Sahara move often and have no permanent homes. They often stay near desert oases, where water can be found. 2. Deltas are formed when rivers deposit material on the seabed for many years. 3. Urbanization is when cities grow larger because many people move to them.

GOVERNMENT

Suez Revenue The Suez Canal is an important part of the Egyptian economy. Fees charged to boats that use the canal produced $414 million dollars in 2008, down from a record $3.6 billion in 2006. Those fees form the third-largest source of government funds for Egypt. Only tourism and money sent home by Egyptians working abroad bring in more money than the canal. As a result, lowered canal income means challenges for the Egyptian government in paying for the country's needs.

The Suez Canal The canal was built in Egypt in 1869. It allows large ships to pass from the Mediterranean to the Red Sea. The canal makes traveling by sea between Asia and Europe shorter by thousands of miles. Ships do not have to go around the entire continent of Africa. That makes the cost of transportation cheaper. Businesses can pass the money they save on transportation on to consumers in the form of lower prices.

One of the most important goods that passes through the Suez Canal today is oil. More than 3,000 oil tankers use the canal every year.

Because of its role in world trade, the Suez Canal affects people around the world. The canal is good for Egypt, too, since it collects a fee from each ship that passes through.

Reading Check Which two North African countries have the largest oil reserves?

Crossroads of Continents

North Africa's closeness to Europe, Asia, and Africa south of the Sahara has helped shape life there for thousands of years.

The Sahara made travel between North Africa and other parts of Africa difficult in the past. However, it was not an impassable barrier. People, ideas, and goods have long moved across it.

North Africa and Southern Europe have had connections across the Mediterranean for thousands of years. Today European languages, especially French, are often spoken as second languages in parts of the region. Millions of North African immigrants also live in Europe.

The country of Israel, in Southwest Asia, shares a land border with Egypt. North Africa's majority religion and language both came from Southwest Asia.

Reading Check How did Southwest Asia change North Africa?

my **World**
IN NUMBERS

In 2007, **20,384** ships passed through the Suez Canal. They carried **710** million tons of cargo.

GUIDE ON THE SIDE

Cause and Effect

- How does the Suez Canal change travel for ships? (It allows them to get directly from the Mediterranean Sea to the Red Sea.)

- Why is this important for trade in the region? (It makes transportation cost less.) For Egypt? (Egypt earns money from fees ships pay to use the canal.)

Crossroads of Continents

- **Identify Details** In what ways is North Africa connected to Europe? (It shares languages and sends immigrants to Southern Europe.)

- **Predict** How would you expect the cultures of North Africa to be connected to the other regions around it? (They are probably influenced by all of them.)

Section 1 Assessment

? Essential Question

Key Terms
1. Use the following words to describe life in the Sahara: nomad, oasis.
2. How are deltas formed?
3. What is urbanization?

Key Ideas
4. What single factor most affects where people in North Africa live?
5. What have been the positive and negative changes caused by the Aswan High Dam?
6. How has urbanization affected North Africa?
7. How does the Suez Canal affect world trade?

Think Critically
8. **Compare and Contrast** Compare the Egyptian desert to the Nile River Valley. Which of these areas occupies more space? Which is home to more Egyptians?
9. **Identify Main Ideas** What do you think is the most important environmental problem facing North Africa?

How much does geography shape a country?
10. How does water shape human settlement patterns in North Africa? Go to your student journal to record your answers.

---

4. Access to water most determines where North Africans live. **5.** Positive: It controls Nile River flooding, generates electricity, and expands agriculture. Negative: People had to move, and it led to disease and pollution. **6.** It has created crowded cities that struggle to provide services. **7.** It makes world trade faster and less expensive. **8.** The desert occupies more space than the Nile Valley, but the river valley is home to more people. **9.** Sample: Balancing water consumption with protecting water sources is a big environmental problem. **10.** Much of North Africa is desert that cannot support human settlement, so settlement clusters near water.

ANSWERS

SECTION 2 LESSON PLAN

History of North Africa

OBJECTIVES

Students will know

- contributions of ancient Egypt to North African and world civilization.
- effects of Arab invasion and European influence on the region.

Students will be able to

- analyze cause-and-effect relationships in regional history.
- present ideas about agriculture's advantages for ancient Egypt.

SET EXPECTATIONS

In this section, students will

- read History of North Africa.
- make and present a print campaign advertising benefits of agriculture to ancient Egyptians.
- go On Assignment in North Africa and analyze historical maps.

CORE CONCEPTS

You may wish to teach or reteach the following lessons from the Core Concepts Handbook:

- Economic Process, pp. 60–61
- Cultural Diffusion and Change, pp. 96–97
- Political Systems, pp. 106–107

KEY

Differentiated Instruction	English Language Instruction
L1 Special Needs **L2** Extra Support	**ELL** Beginner **ELL** Early Intermediate **ELL** Intermediate
L3 On-Level **L4** Challenge	**ELL** Early Advanced **ELL** Advanced

---

1 Connect
Make learning meaningful

Make Connections Ask students to share traditions, inventions, or ideas that your community has recently adopted, such as Facebook. Discuss current and possible future influences of each idea shared. Ask students to predict how changes in other cultures and societies might affect the people living during or after the changes.

L2 Extra Support Discuss examples, such as the Internet or cellphones. Help students list effects, such as online shopping.

Activate Prior Knowledge Allow students to list information they know about the ancient Egyptians from museums or previous classes. Also remind students that in the previous chapter they learned about European colonization and Arab trade in southern and eastern Africa. Ask, How might these factors affect North Africa?

ELL Early Intermediate Review English cardinal directions and descriptors: *southern, eastern, western,* and *northern*. Show geographic proximity to southern and eastern Africa to stress shared influences.

Prepare Follow the steps in the section **Preview.** Preteach the Key Terms. Then have students complete *Word Wise* in their journals using in-text clues and the glossary for help.

2 Experience
Teach knowledge and skills

Read Use **Background** notes and **Guide on the Side** questions to model active reading. Have students use *Take Notes* in their **Student Journal** to analyze causes and effects in the history of North Africa. Have students complete **21st Century Online Tutor** *Analyze Cause and Effect* and apply this skill to reading the section. As needed, refer students to the **Online Student Edition.**

L2 Extra Support On a blank outline or projected map, draw shipping routes before and after the building of the Suez Canal. Have students use the visual to explain why the canal was built.

ELL Intermediate/Early Advanced Preteach pronunciation for the Key Terms *pharaoh* and *hieroglyphics*, noting that the spellings of these words come to English from Greek and have different pronunciation rules.

L4 Challenge Have students read *Enrichment: Pyramids and Mummies* to learn more about the achievements of ancient Egypt.

Practice: myWorld Activity Students will identify benefits of agriculture to ancient Egyptians and then develop ad campaigns to promote these benefits to citizens of that time. **Step-by-Step Instructions** and **More Activities** follow on pp. T72–T73.

SECTION 2 RESOURCE GUIDE

FOR THE STUDENT

my worldgeography.com Student Center
- Active Atlas

Student Edition (print and online)
- History of North Africa

Student Journal (print and online)
- Section 2 Word Wise
- Section 2 Take Notes

21st Century Learning Online Tutor
- Analyze Cause and Effect
- Give Effective Presentations

FOR THE TEACHER

my worldgeography.com Teacher Center
- Online Lesson Planner
- Presentations for Projection
- SuccessTracker

ProGuide: Africa
- Lesson Plan, pp. T70–T71
- myWorld Activity Step-by-Step Instructions, p. T72
- Activity Support: Presentation Planner, p. T73
- myWorld Geography Enrichment, p. T74
- Section Quiz, p. T75

Accelerating the Progress of ELLs
- Vocabulary Strategies, p. 45

3 Understand
Assess understanding

Review Review *Word Wise* and *Take Notes* in the **Student Journal.**

Assess Knowledge and Skills Use the Section Assessment and Section Quiz to check students' progress.

Assess Understanding Review students' responses to the Section Assessment Essential Question prompt.

Remediate Use these strategies to review and remediate.

If students struggle to . . .	Try these strategies.
Analyze cause-and-effect relationships in regional history	Show major events on flowcharts. Add Post-it notes to show causal relationships.
Describe ancient Egyptian culture	Review cultural categories, i.e. religion, fashion, architecture, art. Have students describe one category at a time.
Trace Egyptian, Arab, and European influences on the region	Have pairs present one cultural influence to the whole class.

ELL Support

ELL Objective Students will be able to write a persuasive text in English.

Cultural Connections To connect students to the spread of Arabic in North Africa, discuss the origin and current use of their home languages.

ELL Intermediate Content Tip Clarify that government change is different from cultural change. North Africa has had many different governments over time but many aspects of its cultures have continued despite the changes.

 **ELL Activity** Help students write a letter to convince you to take the class on a field trip. Post an outline: state the request, describe its benefits, note possible problems, repeat benefits. List and define common persuasive phrases: *I believe, we must, the best, better, improve, great, excellent, benefits*. Students can refer to the list and outline as they complete *Activity Support: Presentation Planner*. **(Verbal/Visual)**

myWorld Activity   **Step-by-Step Instructions**

 30 min

The Farmer's Pitch

OBJECTIVES

Students will

- understand the effects of improved agricultural techniques on a civilization.
- develop and present an ad campaign promoting the benefits of agriculture to ancient Egyptians.

LEARNING STYLE

- Visual
- Verbal

21st Century Learning

- Give Effective Presentations

MATERIALS

- Activity Support: Presentation Planner, p. T73

Activity Steps

1. Tell students that they will be asked to identify benefits of agriculture to ancient Egyptian society. Students will use the text to research benefits and then generate slogans to promote those benefits in an ad campaign. Students will produce an oral presentation of the campaign.

2. Review the concept of "civilization": societies in which different members have roles beyond those needed for survival. Use Closer Look: Agriculture and Civilization to recall and discuss benefits that agriculture brings to a society and its culture.

   ELL **Intermediate** Have students use bilingual dictionaries to write their own list of important words related to farming.

3. Distribute copies of *Activity Support: Presentation Planner* and review directions and headings. Allow 10 minutes for students to review the section text and generate ideas about benefits.

   L2 **Extra Support** Assign benefits to individual students, and then pair students to exchange information and generate presentation ideas.

4. Give students 15 minutes to list ideas based on one or more benefit and then to list a visual idea.

   L1 **Special Needs** Invite students to present their ideas visually instead of orally by sketching an ad by hand or on the computer. Urge them to use visual imagery, color, words, and various fonts in their work.

5. Have students present their campaign and explain their reasons for introducing new farming techniques to you while you pretend to be a pharaoh.

   L4 **Challenge** Invite students to make a speech imagining the pharaoh or queen's response.

 More Activities From myWorld Teachers

Local Connections Have students research a community tradition around the dead, such as cemeteries, commemorative buildings or statues, Day of the Dead, and Halloween, and present their findings to the class. **(Verbal/Interpersonal)**

Language Diffusion Identify non-English languages spoken in the class. Have students find news articles online in those languages and search them for words taken from or influenced by English. Do the words share a category (technology or pop culture)? What does this suggest about the most influential aspects of Anglo-American culture? **(Verbal/Logical)**

Debate Have students debate this statement: *Only Muslim Arabs should live in Algeria. French settlers should leave.* Students should consider challenges and benefits of a culturally diverse society. **(Verbal)**

my worldgeography.com   **Teacher Center**   →   Find additional resources in the online Teacher Center.

Name ______________________ Class ______________ Date __________

myWorld Activity Support **Presentation Planner**

The Farmer's Pitch

Directions Refer back to the text about the benefits of agriculture for ancient Egyptians. List three benefits. Write advertising slogans to promote agriculture to ancient Egyptians. Use your slogans to make a presentation about one or more benefits. Brainstorm one ad idea for online, TV, or a newspaper.

Benefits of Farming	Advertising Slogans
1.	
2.	
3.	

Visual Ad Brainstorm

____

____

____

____

____

____

____

Name _____ Class _____ Date _____

Enrichment: Pyramids and Mummies

Directions Read the selection below. Then answer the questions
that follow and complete the activity.

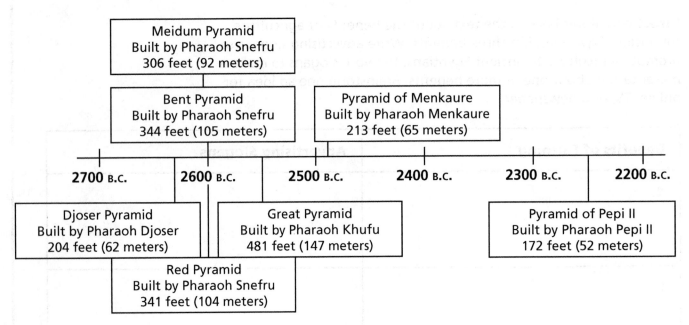

Mummies

Bodies placed in the pyramids were mummified. The process
took 70 days and was completed by special priests. The priests
prepared the body physically and then performed prayers and
other rituals. They dried the body inside and out with a special
salt called natron. Priests wanted the mummy to look as life-
like as possible, so they used false eyes and stuffing to hold the
body's shape. They then wrapped each mummy in hundreds of
sheets of linen, into which small good-luck charms were often
placed. Finally, they sealed the wrappings with warm resin, a
sap-like material from plants.

1. Which pharaoh built the most pyramids? _____

2. Which pharaoh built the largest pyramid? _____

3. What skills did priests need in order to complete mummification?

_____

_____

4. Activity Write a museum guide's script to explain why ancient
Egyptians worked so hard at pyramid building and mummification.

Name _____ Class _____ Date _____

Section Quiz

Directions Answer the following questions using what you learned
in Section 2.

1. _____ A theocracy is a government based
   on
   a. democracy.
   b. communism.
   c. religion.
   d. agriculture.

2. _____ Which achievements came from
   ancient Egypt?
   a. gold-salt trade and mosques
   b. Suez Canal and access to Sinai
   c. spread of Islam and Arabic
   d. pyramids and hieroglyphics

3. _____ What do supporters of Pan-Arabism
   believe?
   a. Arabs will travel to an afterlife.
   b. Arabic-speaking countries should unite.
   c. Arabic should be Morocco's language.
   d. Berbers should live in Western Sahara.

4. _____ Which culture was led by pharaohs?
   a. ancient Egyptian
   b. Arab Muslim
   c. French Algerian
   d. Berber

5. _____ What was the purpose of a mummy?
   a. to bring ideas to new cultures
   b. to house the bodies of dead kings
   c. to preserve dead bodies for the afterlife
   d. to communicate ideas in writing

6. Complete the table below to describe the effects of each culture
   on North Africa.

Ancient Egyptian	Independent Egyptian
Arab	**European**

History of North Africa

- Model preparing to read by previewing the Key Ideas, Key Terms, headings, visuals, and captions. Have students make predictions about what they will learn. For ELL support, post the prompt, "I predict I will read about . . ."

- Preview and practice analyzing cause and effect by using examples from the oldest history of your community.

- Preteach this section's high-use Academic Vocabulary and Key Terms using the table on the next page and in-text definitions. Have students practice Key Terms by completing the *Word Wise* page in their journals.

GUIDE ON THE SIDE

- **Analyze Text** A hearth is a fireplace, the center of a family's life and the heart of its home. What does it mean to say that ancient Egypt is a "cultural hearth"? (It means that ancient Egypt is one of the centers of world civilization.)

Ancient Egypt

- **Cause and Effect** How did the Nile River affect Egyptian civilization? (It made civilization possible by providing water and fertile soil.)

- **Compare and Contrast** How were farming societies different from earlier societies? (Farming societies had extra food. Populations grew and towns and cities formed.)

- **Summarize** What did ancient Egyptians share? (language, culture, and religious beliefs)

 Reading Skill

Analyze Cause and Effect
While they read, have students practice this skill by completing the *Take Notes* graphic organizer in the **Student Journal.**

Section 2

History of North Africa

Key Ideas
- Ancient Egypt was among the world's first complex civilizations.
- The Arab-Islamic conquest made lasting changes to the region's culture.
- Europeans colonized North Africa in the 1800s, but its nations achieved independence in the 1900s.

Key Terms
- pharaoh
- mummy
- theocracy
- Berbers
- hieroglyphics
- Pan-Arabism

→ **Visual Glossary**

Reading Skill: Analyze Cause and Effect Take notes using the graphic organizer in your journal.

The Great Sphinx in Egypt ▼

North Africa produced one of the world's first civilizations. The ancient Egyptians took advantage of their country's fertile river valley and built a wealthy and sophisticated society. Ancient Egypt's achievements influenced other cultures. In fact, ancient Egypt is considered a cultural hearth, or one of the places where human civilization began.

Ancient Egypt

About 5,000 years ago the civilization of ancient Egypt developed in the Nile River Valley. It endured for almost 3,000 years.

Ancient Egypt Develops An ancient Greek writer called Egypt "the gift of the river." The Nile River made Egyptian civilization possible. The river was like an oasis surrounded by desert. Every summer it brought great floods. They left behind deposits of silt, a rich soil, along the river's banks. Plants and animals thrived in this environment. In ancient times, nomads lived around the river. They survived by hunting, gathering, and fishing.

Fertile soil made the river valley a perfect place for agriculture, which spread into Egypt from Southwest Asia. Societies that farm are different from fishing and hunting-gathering societies. Farming produces more food than hunting and gathering or fishing. It allows the population to expand. Small villages grow into towns and then cities.

By about 3,000 B.C., as many as one million people may have lived along the Nile. They shared a language, a culture, and religious beliefs.

ACADEMIC VOCABULARY

High-Use Word	Definition and Sample Sentence
transform	*v.* change into a new form or appearance *Baking transforms flour and water into bread.*
majority	*n.* a group with more than half of a population *The majority of our team is boys, but we have two girl players.*

Early on, Egypt developed a powerful government ruled by a **pharaoh,** or king of ancient Egypt. The Nile River and the need to use it for irrigation encouraged powerful central government in Egypt. A single ruler could direct the people's labor to build irrigation canals. Canals changed Egypt's environment. They brought water to fields far from the river. They also helped control floods. Pharaohs taxed the people to pay for building the canals or forced people to work part of the year for no pay. Pharaohs also used these methods to build temples and tombs.

The pharaoh was not just a political leader. Egyptians also believed he was like a god and worshipped him after his death. That belief made Egypt a **theocracy,** a government based on religion.

Egypt's strong central government made it different from ancient civilizations in Iraq and India. They were often politically divided. Egypt was more like China, which unified at an early date.

Egyptian Culture The Egyptians were among the first people to study mathematics, astronomy, engineering, and other scientific fields. They built trade networks into Eastern Africa and other regions. Egyptian culture influenced other parts of the world.

The Egyptians invented **hieroglyphics,** a system of writing using pictures and other symbols. Hieroglyphics were used to help the government keep records and to write about history and religion. Egyptians also invented papyrus, the first paper, which they made from reeds that grew along the banks of the Nile River.

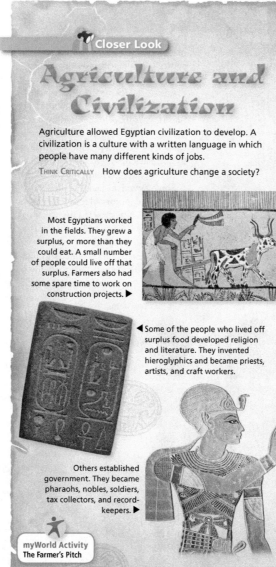

Closer Look

Agriculture and Civilization

Agriculture allowed Egyptian civilization to develop. A civilization is a culture with a written language in which people have many different kinds of jobs.

THINK CRITICALLY How does agriculture change a society?

Most Egyptians worked in the fields. They grew a surplus, or more than they could eat. A small number of people could live off that surplus. Farmers also had some spare time to work on construction projects. ▶

◀ Some of the people who lived off surplus food developed religion and literature. They invented hieroglyphics and became priests, artists, and craft workers.

Others established government. They became pharaohs, nobles, soldiers, tax collectors, and record-keepers. ▶

myWorld Activity
The Farmer's Pitch

THINK CRITICALLY Agriculture allows a society to become more complex.

HISTORY

Pyramid Construction Historians have developed many theories about how the ancient Egyptians built the pyramids without any modern machines or even iron tools. One idea is that huge blocks of limestone were cut with copper chisels and saws. Some of these blocks were floated down the Nile from a quarry to the pyramid site. It took many men to move the blocks into position.

For the higher levels, the Egyptians used ramps made of brick or earth to get the blocks into position. Each new level required a longer ramp. All of these efforts were directed by architects that used ropes to check the position of each stone. The Pyramids at Giza probably took about 80 years to build and used the labor of 20,000 to 30,000 workers.

- **Identify Details** What did Egyptians believe about death? (that an afterlife followed death)

- **Build Cultural Awareness** How did Egyptian beliefs about death affect traditions when a person died? (Wealthy and powerful people were buried with objects to use in the afterlife. Some had their bodies preserved as mummies.)

- **Infer** What went into the tombs that pharaoh's built? (the mummy of the pharaoh's body and the pharaoh's possessions)

- **Sequence** In what order did Persians, Greeks, and pharaohs rule Egypt? (pharaohs, Persians, Greeks)

Egyptian Religion Ancient Egyptians believed in hundreds of gods that controlled all places and things. They also believed in an afterlife, life after death. Pharaohs and the very rich were buried with valuables, favorite pets, food, and even boats to take them to the afterlife.

Many pharaohs built elaborate tombs. In fact, the famous pyramids of Giza are tombs. Each has rooms on the inside to hold the pharaoh's body and possessions.

Some Egyptians had their bodies mummified, or turned into mummies after death. A **mummy** is a body that has been preserved so it will not decompose. The corpse's internal organs were removed and the brain pulled through the nose with a hook. Then the body was

◀ An ancient Egyptian mummy

dried and wrapped in sheets of linen to preserve it. Much of what we know about ancient Egypt comes from its tombs.

Greek and Roman North Africa After more than 2,000 years of rule by pharaohs, Egypt was conquered by Persians and then Greeks. Greeks ruled Egypt for 302 years. The famous Queen Cleopatra VII was the last Greek ruler of Egypt. Around 800 B.C, Phoenicians from modern-day Lebanon built the powerful city of Carthage in what is now Tunisia. Eventually the whole region fell under Roman rule. By the A.D. 400s most North Africans had converted to Christianity.

Reading Check Why was Ancient Egypt called the "gift of the Nile"?

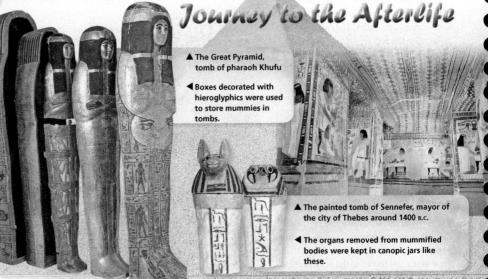

Journey to the Afterlife

▲ The Great Pyramid, tomb of pharaoh Khufu

◀ Boxes decorated with hieroglyphics were used to store mummies in tombs.

▲ The painted tomb of Sennefer, mayor of the city of Thebes around 1400 B.C.

◀ The organs removed from mummified bodies were kept in canopic jars like these.

READING CHECK Ancient Egypt was called the "gift of the Nile" because the Nile River made the civilization possible.

GEOGRAPHY

Trans-Saharan Trade The Arab trading caravans that crossed the Sahara were carefully prepared to survive the harsh geography. First, traders used local people from the deserts as guides. For example, Berbers had been crossing the desert since the A.D. 400s so many knew the routes well. Second, they used camels to carry the trading goods, an approach also begun by the Berbers. Camels can go a long way without water and are strong enough to carry heavy loads of cargo. Third, traders planned a route from oasis to oasis. This allowed them to refill their water supply, which they carried in animal-skin bags.

Arab North Africa

With the arrival of Arab Muslims from Southwest Asia, North Africa's religion, language, and culture were <u>transformed</u>.

The Arab Conquest In the A.D. 600s, the religion of Islam was first preached in Arabia. Followers of Islam are called Muslims. The first Muslims were Arabs. Arab Muslim armies built an empire that stretched from Spain to Iran. North Africa was part of this empire.

Religious leaders and merchants followed the army, building trading centers and mosques, or Islamic houses of worship. Then many Arab migrants came. They spread Islam to Egyptians and **Berbers,** the indigenous people of western North Africa. These migrants also helped spread the Arabic language throughout the region. Most North Africans converted to Islam, although many Jews and Christians continued to live in the region.

North Africa became one of the most culturally productive parts of the Islamic world. Arab rulers founded cities such as Kairouan in Tunisia and Cairo in Egypt. Both grew into major centers of religion and learning. Cairo became one of the largest cities in the world. Art and literature flourished under Arab rule.

Trade in Arab North Africa While earlier conquerors saw the Sahara as a barrier, the Arabs saw it as an opportunity. They quickly came to control the trans-Saharan caravan routes that linked Africa south of the Sahara with North Africa. Merchants spread Arabic and Islam to peoples they traded with in the Sahara and beyond.

Reading Check How did the Arabs change North Africa?

transform, *v.,* change into a new form or appearance

Painted tiles are often used to make decorative geometric shapes in Arab architecture. ▼

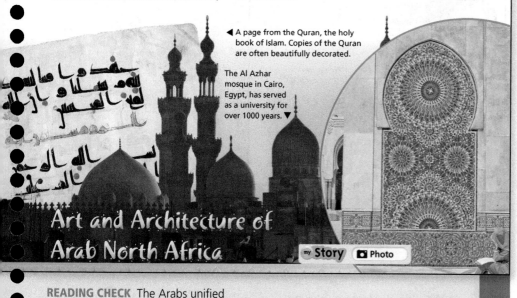

◄ A page from the Quran, the holy book of Islam. Copies of the Quran are often beautifully decorated.

The Al Azhar mosque in Cairo, Egypt, has served as a university for over 1000 years. ▼

Art and Architecture of Arab North Africa

my **Story**   📷 **Photo**

READING CHECK The Arabs unified North Africa by bringing a common religion, culture, and language to the region.

Arab North Africa

- **Identify Main Ideas** What did Arab invaders bring to North Africa? (the religion of Islam, the Arabic language)
- **Categorize** What groups of Arabs came to North Africa, and in what sequence? (Armies came first, then religious leaders and merchants, and finally Arab migrants.)
- **Cause and Effect** How did these groups change North Africa? (They all brought their language and religion to the region. Religious leaders built mosques. Merchants founded trading centers. Migrants shared their religion and language with those they met while traveling.)
- **Analyze Text** What does the text mean by "Arabs saw it [the Sahara] as an opportunity"? (It means that the Arabs knew how to successfully cross the desert and trade with people who lived south of it, while other people did not.)

CULTURE

Battle of Algiers In 1966, the new independent government of Algeria commissioned a film about its struggle to break free from France. The film traces that struggle between the Algerian National Liberation Front and French police. It is widely admired as an honest, but bleak, look at war. Both sides are shown to behave badly, for example by killing civilians. *Battle of Algiers* received multiple Academy Awards, including Best Foreign Language Film and Best Director.

GUIDE ON THE SIDE

European Rule and Independence

- **Cause and Effect** Why did European powers want to rule North Africa? (to control resources and trade routes; to collect debts)

- **Categorize** How did North Africans feel about European rule? Explain. (Many resented it, feeling they had no say in their own government.)

Map Skills Have students locate the boundaries of French North Africa on the map.

- What areas did Spain control? (northern Morocco, Western Sahara)

Active Atlas

Point out the map of French North Africa.
- Have students go to myworldgeography.com to learn more about French colonialism in North Africa.

European Rule and Independence

The united Arab empire did not last long. Various states gained and lost power in the region over time.

European Colonization During the 1800s, European powers came to rule North Africa. They wanted to control the region's resources, to guard important trade routes, or to force local rulers to pay debts they owed to European lenders. Britain took control of Egypt, while France ruled most of western North Africa. Spain and Italy governed other parts of this region.

majority, *n.,* a group with more than half of a population

The Struggle for Independence Resistance to European rule began immediately and grew into nationalism. North Africans resented that they did not get a say in their own government. Many protested European rule. Most of the region gained independence in the 1950s.

Algeria had a longer road to travel. Around one million Europeans had settled in Algeria. Many argued that Algeria was a part of France. Some Algerians agreed and wanted to be more like the French. But the majority disagreed. They argued that Algeria had a different culture, language, and religion from France. According to a nationalist,

The leader of France visits Algiers in 1958. At this time around 15 percent of the city's people were Europeans. ▶

French North Africa

Mediterranean Sea

Tangier · Algiers · Tunis
Rabat ·

ATLANTIC OCEAN
30°N

MOROCCO

TUNISIA
Tripoli ·

WESTERN SAHARA (Under Moroccan Control)

ALGERIA

LIBYA

TROPIC OF CANCER

20°N

0   300 mi
0   300 km
Lambert Azimuthal Equal-Area Projection
10°W

KEY
French possession
Italian possession
Spanish possession
— 1914 border
--- Present-day border

Map Skills

1 **Region** Which three modern countries were controlled by France?

2 **Place** Who ruled Libya?

Active Atlas

MAP SKILLS 1. Morocco, Tunisia, Algeria **2.** Italy

READING CHECK In 1967, Israel took the Sinai. In 1979, Egypt regained it.

SECTION 2 ASSESSMENT 1. Ancient Egyptian society was a theocracy, ruled by a pharaoh believed to be a god. The dead were made into mummies to preserve them in the afterlife. Egyptians used hieroglyphics to write about their religion and history. **2.** The Berbers are an indigenous people of North Africa. **3.** They

ANSWERS

QUICK FACTS

Building the Suez Canal It took about ten years to build the Suez Canal. It was just 230 feet wide (70 meters), but has since been widened to 741 feet (226 meters). At 624,180 feet (190.250 km), the canal is the longest canal in the world that has no locks to raise and lower ships.

66 Islam is our religion, Arabic our language, Algeria our fatherland. 99

—Ben Badis

It took eight years of bloody war for the country to win independence. In 1962, French troops left. Most Europeans in Algeria fled the country.

Egypt Since Independence Egypt gained its formal independence in 1922, but Britain continued to quietly control the country for many years. In 1952, a group of military officers led by Gamal Abdel Nasser overthrew the government and seized control of Egypt. Nasser ruled like a dictator.

Nasser tried to modernize and strengthen Egypt. In 1956, he seized control of the Suez Canal from its British and French owners. Britain, France, and Israel responded by attacking Egypt, but the United States and the United Nations forced them to withdraw. As a result, Egypt gained control of the canal.

This event, the Suez Crisis, was seen as a major success of Nasser's rule. Arabs in other countries admired him for standing up to European powers and for building the Aswan High Dam. He was a leader of the Pan-Arab movement. **Pan-Arabism** is the idea that all Arabic-speaking peoples should unite into one country.

In another area, Nasser was less successful. He opposed the existence of the country of Israel and tried to fight it. In 1967, Israel defeated Egypt and its allies Jordan and Syria. Israel took the Sinai Peninsula from Egypt. Nasser's successor, Anwar Sadat, failed to take the Sinai back when he went to war with Israel in 1973. Egypt only regained the Sinai when it signed a peace agreement with Israel in 1979.

Reading Check What happened to the Sinai Peninsula in 1967 and 1979?

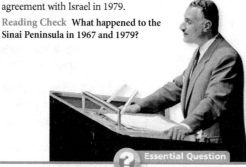

Gamal Abdel Nasser, Egypt's president from 1956 to 1970 ▼

Section 2 Assessment

Key Terms

1. Use the following words to describe ancient Egyptian religion and government: pharaoh, theocracy, mummy, hieroglyphics.
2. Who are the Berbers?
3. What do people who support Pan-Arabism believe?

Key Ideas

4. How did the Arab-Islamic conquest of North Africa change the region?
5. What were two of Gamal Abdel Nasser's major achievements?

Think Critically

6. **Analyze Cause and Effect** Why was the development of agriculture important for ancient Egypt? What did agriculture allow?
7. **Compare and Contrast** How were independence struggles in Algeria and Egypt different?

Essential Question

How much does geography shape a country?

8. How did physical geography shape the development of ancient Egypt? Go to your student journal to record your answers.

GUIDE ON THE SIDE

- **Analyze Text** What do you think the quotation means? (It means that Algerians are shaped and unified by their common religion and language, so they should not have loyalty to France.)
- **Identify Details** Who controlled Egypt in 1922? (Britain)
- **Sequence** How did this change in 1952? (The Egyptian military, led by Nasser, took power in a coup.)

Categorize

- What type of leader was Abdel Nasser? (He was like a dictator.)
- Identify one success and one failure of Gamal Abdel Nasser. (Successes: modernizing and strengthening Egypt, controlling the Suez Canal, building the Aswan High Dam, and standing up to European powers. Failures: military loss to Israel in 1967 or possibly opposition of Israel.)

believe Arabic-speaking countries should unite. **4.** The Arab-Islamic conquest gave North Africa a new religion, language, and culture. **5.** Nasser took the Suez Canal and built the Aswan High Dam. **6.** Agriculture was important because it allowed ancient Egyptians to grow extra food. This freed people to build culture. **7.** Unlike Egypt, Algeria fought a long war with its colonial power. **8.** Yearly floods made the Nile Valley a perfect place for agriculture. Agriculture made Egyptian civilization possible. The need to irrigate land led to the creation of a strong central government.

ANSWERS

Ancient Egyptian Culture

OBJECTIVES

Students will

- describe key aspects of Ancient Egyptian culture.
- **21st Century Learning** summarize achievements of ancient Egyptian religion, art, and literature.
- **ELL** write descriptively in English.

SET EXPECTATIONS

In this case study, students will

- read Ancient Egyptian Culture.
- make museum exhibit cards describing elements of ancient Egyptian religion, art, and literature.

1 Connect

Poll students on whether they agree with this statement: *Art reflects a community's beliefs.* Ask for volunteers to make an argument for or against the statement. Prompt further discussion by inviting volunteers to describe favorite examples of art. The art can be advertising, popular music, clothing styles, literature, jewelry, and so on.

Discuss what, if anything, students think that each example presented reflects about American culture. Tell students that historians often use art to draw conclusions about cultures from earlier times.

L1 Special Needs Bring examples of pop art into class and have students describe them. Ask, What do you think the artist's message is?

2 Experience

Preview Read the Key Ideas aloud and then have students preview the pictures and headings. Ask if they agree with the Key Ideas, and tell them they will return to them after reading.

Read While students read Ancient Egyptian Culture, ask questions found on the **Guide on the Side** to build understanding of Key Ideas and objectives.

myWorld Activity: Ancient Egypt Museum Give students the *Activity Support: Exhibit Cards* and read the directions with them. Ask pairs to make exhibit cards for specific achievements discussed in the text. Then have students pool their cards and make a classroom exhibit showing the

30 min

art, religion, and literature of ancient Egypt. Invite other students to visit the exhibit and assign students to act as tour guides. **(Visual/Kinesthetic)**

ELL Early Advanced Use the chapter text to make a word bank of descriptive language related to each category. Provide this word bank for students to use in writing captions only.

L4 Challenge Have students find additional images for the exhibit cards on the Internet and make an interactive online version of the exhibit.

3 Understand

Review Review the Key Ideas and discuss students' contributions to the myWorld Activity, probing for students' understanding of content and main ideas.

Assess Have students write their responses to the Assessment questions in their notebooks. Check answers in their notebooks. Invite students to say if their reaction to the Key Ideas has changed.

Remediate If students struggle to understand the Key Ideas, review the Core Concepts Lesson "What Is Culture?" on pp. 86–87. Then walk through the myWorld Activity exhibit to show examples of each aspect of culture.

Name _____ Class _____ Date _____

myWorld Activity Support   **Exhibit Cards**

Ancient Egypt Museum

Directions For each category below, choose an achievement of ancient Egyptian culture. Write a short description of that achievement. On separate paper, paste or draw a picture to show it. Write a caption for your picture. Cut out your descriptions and captions to post with the pictures in a class exhibit on ancient Egypt.

Religion   **Caption**

Art   **Caption**

Literature   **Caption**

CORE CONCEPTS: RELIGION

Review Core Concepts 7.4 before discussing with your students the essential idea of ancient Egyptian religion. Review the characteristics of Judaism, Christianity, and Islam. Ask students to identify the main way that these religions are similar: they are all monotheistic. If students do not know the meanings of the terms *monotheism* and *polytheism*, review meanings of the Greek roots and prefixes. Ask them to identify other religions they have learned about that are not monotheistic (such as Greek or Roman religion). Discuss how these religions are structured and what their believers worship.

GUIDE ON THE SIDE

Egyptian Religion

- **Identify Main Ideas** What did ancient Egyptians believe about gods? (They believed there were many gods, who controlled different parts of nature and human life.)

- **Categorize** What did each Egyptian god control? Give three examples. (Sample: Ra controlled the sun and the other gods; Osiris controlled the world of the dead; Isis controlled nature and fertility.)

- **Identify Details** How was the symbol for each god chosen? (Symbols could reflect the god's personality or area of control and often used animals to stand for qualities such as majesty.)

Case Study

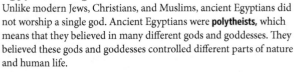

Ancient Egyptian Culture

Key Ideas	• Ancient Egypt produced a rich culture including religion, art, and literature.	• Religion was an important theme in ancient Egyptian art and literature.

Key Terms • polytheist • pictogram • scribe • Book of the Dead

In the previous section, you read about the development of ancient Egypt and its pharaohs. In addition to creating a government, the ancient Egyptians produced one of the longest-lasting and richest cultures in world history. Their religion, and especially their belief in the afterlife, influenced many aspects of their culture. Most of what we know today about ancient Egypt comes from surviving tombs and the paintings, objects, and documents they contain.

Egyptian Religion

Unlike modern Jews, Christians, and Muslims, ancient Egyptians did not worship a single god. Ancient Egyptians were **polytheists,** which means that they believed in many different gods and goddesses. They believed these gods and goddesses controlled different parts of nature and human life.

Gods and Goddesses Ra was one of the most important Egyptian gods. He was god of the sun, as well as the chief of all the other gods. Isis was a goddess of nature and fertility, while Horus ruled the sky.

Each god had familiar symbols. Sometimes these were animals reflecting the god's personality, such as Horus' high-flying falcon. Sometimes symbols related to the god's area of influence. Osiris often appeared with a Pharaoh's crown and mummy wrappings, showing that he was king of the dead. Gods and goddesses were often represented as having the heads of animals or as animals themselves. The goddess Bastet appeared as a cat while Isis was often shown as a cow.

The Egyptians worshipped their gods and goddesses in temples. An image of the god was kept in a temple and treated like royalty. It was dressed, fed, and praised. Egyptians believed it was important to keep the gods happy. If they did, the gods would reward them.

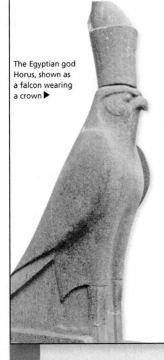

The Egyptian god Horus, shown as a falcon wearing a crown ▶

QUICK FACTS

Egyptian Gods The ancient Egyptians worshipped about 2,000 different gods. Some had enormous power, such as Thoth. He was a scribe for the other gods, so like scribes on Earth he had great power. Some of the pharaohs had personal gods. This means they took a god's name and made a symbol for that god. For example, one pharaoh took the name of the god Akhenaten. Only the pharaoh and his family worshipped this god, and the god died with the pharaoh.

For example, a god might provide a good harvest or keep disease away. The priests and priestesses who tended to the gods were wealthy and powerful landowners. Common people were not allowed into the temples.

Isis, Osiris, and Set Like other ancient cultures, the Egyptians had many stories about their gods. One story was the myth of Isis, Osiris, and Set. Osiris and his wife Isis ruled Egypt until Osiris' brother Set grew jealous. Set planned to trick Osiris and steal his throne. Set hired craftsmen to build a beautiful box. It was designed so that only Osiris would fit inside it. The sneaky Set offered the box to the person it fit best. Of course, that person was Osiris. As soon as Osiris got into the box,

Set shut him in. He threw the box, with Osiris inside, into the Nile River. The box became Osiris' coffin.

Isis searched the world for her husband. Eventually she found Osiris' body and brought it back to Egypt. Set tried to take the body from her and they fought, but Isis won. She wrapped Osiris in bandages, like a mummy, and brought him back to life. She and Osiris went to live in the underworld where Osiris became god of the dead.

Egyptians believed that after death, they would travel through the underworld to Osiris. He would judge who could pass to live among the gods.

Reading Check **According to ancient Egyptian religion, who were Ra and Horus?**

- **Summarize** What happens in the myth of Osiris? (Set tries to steal Osiris's throne by killing Osiris. Isis defeats Set and saves Osiris. Isis and Osiris move to the underworld.)
- **Draw Conclusions** Based on the myth of Osiris, what values or beliefs do you think ancient Egyptians had? Explain. (They believed that trickery and sneakiness were bad and that stealing was bad. Set is described as evil in the myth and he loses. They believed that love was powerful. Isis is described as loving and devoted, and she wins.)

ISIS AND OSIRIS

Isis and her husband Osiris

Osiris judges the dead.

READING CHECK Ra was god of the sun and chief of the other gods. Horus was god of the sky.

PRIMARY SOURCE

Tutankhamen Diary British archaeologist Howard Carter spent more than six years looking for the tomb of the Pharaoh Tutankhamen, which he believed was under the Valley of the Kings. He finally found the entry room to it on November 26, 1922. His diary reads, "Feverishly we cleared away the remaining last scraps of rubbish on the floor of the passage before the doorway. . . . It was some time before one could see . . . Our sensations and astonishment are difficult to describe as the better light revealed to us the marvelous collection of treasures . . . [Nowhere] could we see any traces of a mummy or mummies. . . . [T]he mystery gradually dawned upon us. We were but in the anterior portion of the tomb. Behind that closed doorway was the tomb-chamber, and . . . [Tutankhamen] probably lay there in all his magnificent . . . death."

GUIDE ON THE SIDE

Art in Ancient Egypt

- **Synthesize** Why did Pharaohs build tombs? (Tombs were built to house Pharaohs' mummified bodies and precious objects they might need in the afterlife.)

- **Connect** How do the tombs and their artwork reflect Egyptian beliefs? (The tombs show the Egyptian belief that a person travels to an afterlife where precious objects might be needed. The paintings show what Egyptians believed might happen to that person in the afterlife.)

Writing and Literature

- **Identify Details** What is Egyptian writing called? (hieroglyphics)

- **Compare and Contrast** What did hieroglyphics use instead of letters? (picture symbols)

◄ Jewelry from the tomb of Tutankhamen

▲ A statue of Queen Nefertiti

◄ The funeral mask of Pharaoh Tutankhamen, found in his tomb with many other beautiful objects

A page from the Book of the Dead ▼

Art in Ancient Egypt

The Egyptians' beliefs and myths affected the art they created and the buildings they built. Ancient Egyptians worked hard to prepare for the afterlife. Pharaohs and other wealthy Egyptians built tombs with many rooms, stocking them with precious objects and useful goods. Thieves robbed most of these tombs in ancient times, but they missed the tomb of Pharaoh Tutankhamen. This tomb was discovered by archaeologists in 1922.

The walls of tombs were often richly painted. These paintings sometimes showed scenes from the life of the person buried in the tomb, such as hunting trips, military expeditions, or religious festivals. The paintings could also depict scenes from mythological stories.

Reading Check **What did Egyptians paint on the walls of their tombs?**

Writing and Literature

As you read, ancient Egyptians invented their own system of writing called hieroglyphics. Different forms of hieroglyphics were invented elsewhere in the world, but Egyptian hieroglyphics were used only in Egypt.

Egyptian hieroglyphics included three kinds of symbols. The first kind was called a **pictogram,** or picture symbol. A picture of a cow meant "cow." Next, there were sound symbols, or phonograms. These were similar to our letters. Last, there were guide symbols. These told readers what topic or idea a nearby symbol referred to. For example, an eye symbol might appear after a symbol with

READING CHECK They painted scenes from the life of the buried person or scenes from myths.

READING CHECK Picture symbols (pictograms), sound symbols (phonograms), and guide symbols

COMMON MISCONCEPTIONS

Education and Literacy Although most Egyptians could not read or write, it is not true that they were uneducated or that they didn't value education. Young boys were taught by their fathers and young girls by their mothers. In both cases, children learned moral values, proper behavior,

and also knowledge of elaborate Egyptian religious beliefs. Fathers often referred to the Books of Instruction for verses they spoke to their sons. One example: You should only talk when you are sure you know your subject.

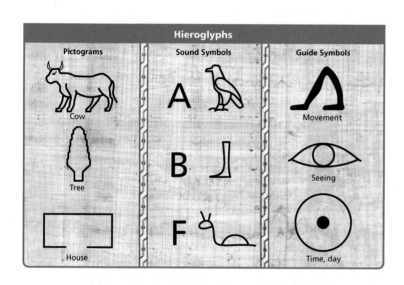

many meanings, one of which was connected to seeing. The Egyptians used about six thousand symbols. Hieroglyphics were written by **scribes,** people trained to write. Most Egyptians, even many pharaohs, could not read or write. Those who could gained a great deal of power.

Scribes wrote about many different subjects. They recorded the events of their time, described the lives of important people, and wrote poetry. But most

Egyptian writing was related to religion. One important example of Egyptian literature was the **Book of the Dead.** This was a collection of prayers and other writings that was meant to help the dead find their way on the difficult journey to the afterlife. Priests recited these prayers at funerals. They were written on tomb walls and on scrolls left in tombs.

Reading Check What are the three types of Egyptian hieroglyphics?

- **Identify Details** Who used hieroglyphics? (scribes)
- **Identify Main Ideas** Why did the ability to write make a person powerful in ancient Egypt? (Not many ancient Egyptians could read or write.)
- **Connect** How are writers in ancient Egypt similar to people today that speak many languages? (Both are able to communicate ideas to many different people in ways that those without those skills cannot.)
- **Identify Details** Give an example of ancient Egyptian literature. (the Book of the Dead)
- **Summarize** How did the Book of the Dead help ancient Egyptians? (It gave guidance for behavior on the journey to the afterlife.)

Analyze Visuals Point out and discuss the table.
- What might the symbol for "time" show? (sample: the sun)

Assessment

1. What do polytheists believe?
2. What animals are Horus and Bastet associated with?
3. Why is pharaoh Tutankhamen's tomb special?
4. How was the Book of the Dead used?
5. What role did religion play in Egyptian art and literature?

ASSESSMENT 1. Polytheists believe in many gods. **2.** Horus is associated with a falcon and Bastet with a cat. **3.** Tutankhamen's tomb is special because it was discovered undisturbed. **4.** The Book of the Dead was used to help the dead find their way to the afterlife. **5.** Religion was the topic of most art and Egyptian literature.

North Africa Today

OBJECTIVES

Students will know

- how Islam and Arabic unify North Africa.
- obstacles to regional economic development, and current religious and political conflicts in the region.

Students will be able to

- identify main ideas and supporting details about contemporary North Africa.
- use a bar graph to evaluate economic progress in North Africa.

SET EXPECTATIONS

In this section, students will

- read North Africa Today.
- compare and rank countries of North Africa, using a living bar graph.
- go On Assignment in North Africa, and analyze data.

CORE CONCEPTS

You may wish to teach or reteach the following lessons from the Core Concepts Handbook:

- Economic Process, pp. 60–61
- What Is Culture?, pp. 86–87
- Religion, pp. 92–93
- Political Systems, pp. 106–107

KEY

Differentiated Instruction

- **L1** Special Needs
- **L2** Extra Support
- **L3** On-Level
- **L4** Challenge

English Language Instruction

- **ELL** Beginner
- **ELL** Early Intermediate
- **ELL** Intermediate
- **ELL** Early Advanced
- **ELL** Advanced

1 Connect
Make learning meaningful

Make Connections Introduce categories such as in school, at a job, in a community, in relationships, or through spiritual matters. Then ask students to think about obstacles that sometimes get in the way of success in each of these areas. Link these obstacles to the efforts of nations or regions to succeed. Ask students what problems nations or regions might encounter in each category.

L2 Extra Support Share a problem you have had in reaching a goal. Discuss ways that the problem made your efforts more difficult.

Activate Prior Knowledge Remind students that in the previous section they learned about ways that Islam and the Arabic language unified the region. Ask them to predict how the presence of these dominant ideas might both solve and cause problems for modern nations in North Africa.

ELL Early Advanced Review and clarify the labels *Islam, Muslim,* and *Arabic. Islam* is the name of a religion. Its followers are called *Muslims. Arabic* is a language spoken by Arabs and others.

Prepare Follow the steps in the section **Preview.** Preteach the Key Terms. Then have students complete *Word Wise* in their journals using in-text clues and the glossary for help.

2 Experience
Teach knowledge and skills

Read Use **Background** notes and **Guide on the Side** questions to model active reading. Have students use *Take Notes* in their **Student Journal** to identify main ideas and details about cultures, governments, and economies in North Africa. Have students complete **21st Century Online Tutor** *Identify Main Ideas and Details* and apply this skill to reading the section.

L1 Special Needs Help students chart ideas and goods leaving and entering the region. Students can record information as they listen to the audio **Online Student Edition.**

ELL Early Advanced Use numerals or fingers to clarify the quantitative adjectives *primary, secondary, tertiary,* and *quaternary*.

L3 On-Level Read *Enrichment: Rai Music of Algeria* to emphasize how culture and politics interact.

L4 Challenge Note the Muslim Brotherhood's calls for Islamic government and greater democracy. Ask, Are these views contradictory?

Practice: myWorld Activity Students will make a living bar graph to rank economic progress in North African nations. **Step-by-Step Instructions** and **More Activities** follow on pp. T80–T81.

SECTION 3 RESOURCE GUIDE

FOR THE STUDENT

my worldgeography.com Student Center
- Data Discovery

Student Edition (print and online)
- North Africa Today

Student Journal (print and online)
- Section 3 Word Wise
- Section 3 Take Notes

21st Century Learning Online Tutor
- Identify Main Idea and Details
- Use Charts and Graphs

FOR THE TEACHER

my worldgeography.com Teacher Center
- Online Lesson Planner
- Presentations for Projection
- SuccessTracker

ProGuide: Africa
- Lesson Plan, pp. T78–T79
- myWorld Activity Step-by-Step Instructions, p. T80
- Activity Support: Background, p. T81
- myWorld Geography Enrichment, p. T82
- Section Quiz, p. T83

Accelerating the Progress of ELLs
- Peer Learning Strategies, p. 46

---

3 Understand
Assess understanding

Review Review *Word Wise* and *Take Notes* in the **Student Journal.**

Assess Knowledge and Skills Use the Section Assessment and Section Quiz to check students' progress.

Assess Understanding Review students' responses to the Section Assessment Essential Question prompt.

Remediate Use these strategies to review and remediate.

If students struggle to . . .	Try these strategies.
Identify main ideas and details	Have students use Key Terms to restate main ideas.
Understand measures of economic progress	Draw circle graphs to demonstrate percentages in the text.
Describe the regional role of Islam and Arabic	Have students list the main religion and language for each country and ethnic group in the region.

ELL Support

ELL Objective Students will be able to use English quantitative adjectives to analyze measures of economic activity.

Cultural Connections To help students assess governments in the region, review types of government in students' home countries. Compare voting systems, types of leaders, and level of democracy.

ELL Intermediate Content Tip Post the term *GDP per capita and* the Spanish cognate *cabeza.* Explain that *per capita* literally means "per head" but is used to mean "per person." The English and Spanish words come from the Latin word *capita,* or "head."

ELL Activity To prepare for the graph activity, post ordinal numbers *first* through *fifth.* Have students use each to describe their steps in getting ready for school. Then have students complete sentence frames with the literacy rates from *Activity Support: Background* for example _____ is *first* (*second, third* . . .) in literacy in North Africa. **(Logical/Verbal)**

myWorld Activity   **Step-by-Step Instructions**

 20 min

Human Bar Graph

OBJECTIVES

Students will

- rank North African countries according to economic data and graph these rankings.
- analyze meaning and usefulness of different economic measures.

LEARNING STYLE

- Logical
- Kinesthetic

21st Century Learning

- Use Charts and Graphs

MATERIALS

- Activity Support: Background, p. T81

Activity Steps

1. Tell students that they will read about economic conditions in all five North African nations, and then represent one nation in making group bar graphs to show and compare the nations in six categories of economic measurement.

   L2 Extra Support Review how to read a bar graph before introducing the activity.

2. Distribute *Activity Support: Background*. Allow students ten minutes to read the data and rank each nation 1–5 in each of the six categories. Tell them to use 1 for the highest quantity in each category.

   ELL Early Intermediate Review meaning and clarify units of measurement on the Activity Support table.

   L1 Special Needs Note that countries are listed alphabetically, not in ranking order. Model how to enter the rank for one category.

3. Organize groups by nation. Have groups check data and rank their assigned nation in each category.

4. Model how to use height to represent rank in human graphs. Students can sit cross-legged, kneel, stand, stand with raised arms, or stand carefully on a chair. Call out a category. Have groups send one representative to show their nation's rank in that category. Direct the five representatives to position themselves from largest to smallest. Repeat the category name and ask students to state their country, statistic, and rank. Repeat for each category until all students participate in a graph.

   L4 Challenge Have students find out and share where their assigned nation ranks worldwide in the various categories.

5. As a class, discuss the Wrap-up Questions on *Activity Support: Background*.

More Activities From myWorld Teachers

Local Connections Have students make poster-size tables that identify primary, secondary, tertiary, and quaternary industries in your community. **(Logical/Visual)**

Four Country Use paper to label parts of the room by nation. When you call out a feature such as *Islamic, Arabic, Berbers, high standard of living, oil production, dictatorship, Islamism,* or *republic,* students should stand in or move toward the country's label that

best relates to that feature. Have students explain their choices—sometimes more than one country will be relevant. **(Kinesthetic)**

Annotated Map Have students make an illustrated map labeled with an assigned country's statistics on living conditions and illustrated to describe those living conditions. Students can use research to add to information from the text. **(Visual/Logical)**

 my worldgeography.com   **Teacher Center** → Find additional resources in the online Teacher Center.

Name _____ Class _____ Date _____

myWorld Activity Support   **Background**

Human Bar Graph

Directions Read about economic progress in the countries of North Africa. Then use the numbers 1–5 to rank the five countries below in each category. Follow your teacher's directions to translate the rankings into a human bar graph. After the activity, answer the questions at the bottom of the page to reflect on the activity.

Category	Country	Number	Rank
Area (square km)	Algeria	2,381,741	
	Egypt	1,001,450	
	Libya	1,759,540	
	Morocco	446,550	
	Tunisia	163,610	

Category	Country	Number	Rank
GDP per Capita (dollars)	Algeria	6,801	
	Egypt	6,044	
	Libya	14,539	
	Morocco	4,519	
	Tunisia	8,220	

Category	Country	Number	Rank
Population	Algeria	35,322,000	
	Egypt	76,546,000	
	Libya	333,000	
	Morocco	31,879,000	
	Tunisia	10,429,000	

Category	Country	Number	Rank
HDI (human development index)	Algeria	0.748	
	Egypt	0.716	
	Libya	0.840	
	Morocco	0.646	
	Tunisia	0.762	

Category	Country	Number	Rank
GDP ($ billions)	Algeria	240.238	
	Egypt	462.666	
	Libya	92.084	
	Morocco	144.073	
	Tunisia	85.73	

Category	Country	Number	Rank
Literacy (% of people over 15)	Algeria	69.9	
	Egypt	71.4	
	Libya	82.6	
	Morocco	52.3	
	Tunisia	74.3	

Wrap-up Questions Discuss these questions with your class.

1. Why is GDP per capita a better measure of standard of living than GDP?

2. What factors in a society does HDI take into account?

3. Which measure helps most to identify a country's economic situation? Explain.

Name _____ Class _____ Date _____

Enrichment: Raï Music of Algeria

Directions Read the selection below. Then answer the questions that follow and complete the activity.

Raï (rah EE) music began in Algeria in the early 1900s, where it combined traditional folk music with other musical styles popular at that time. Later, raï musicians added Western influences such as electronic instruments. Raï sometimes reminds listeners of American blues and traditional African call-and-response music.

Many popular raï songs are protest songs. Protest reflects the meaning of the word raï, which is "opinion." For example, some raï songs protest the contrast between the easy lives of the wealthy and the struggles of the poor. They call on young people to be brave and come forward as leaders that can change societies. Most of all, they recognize the frustration people feel about problems that are hard to solve, but cannot really be escaped.

In Algeria today, many raï singers protest political conditions. Though the government no longer bans raï, and in fact promotes it as an Algerian art form, many musicians still oppose the government's policies. Some of these musicians record and perform their music in exile, living in other countries due to their political beliefs.

1. What is the meaning of raï? How is this meaning reflected in the music?

_____

_____

2. When and where did raï music begin? What was the most important early influence?

_____

_____

3. **Activity** Locate some sound clips of raï music, for example by Cheb Khaled or Rachid Taha, on the Internet. What is the mood of the music? What styles of music do these songs remind you of?

_____

_____

_____

Name _____ Class _____ Date _____

Section Quiz

Directions Answer the following questions using what you learned
in Section 3.

1. _____ What is the main goal of the
Muslim Brotherhood?
   a. to make the government of Egypt
   follow Islamic law
   b. to unite all Algerians
   c. to give Egyptian Christians equal rights
   d. to promote the use of Arabic instead of
   Tamazight

2. _____ What does the term *gross domestic
product,* or *GDP,* mean?
   a. total value of all goods and services
   produced in a country in a year
   b. total value of goods and service that
   belong to each person
   c. total value of a country's exports
   d. total value of a country's imports

3. _____ What does a high human
development index (HDI) say about a
nation?
   a. It imports more than it exports.
   b. It has a unified religion and culture.
   c. It has a democratic government.
   d. It has a high standard of living.

4. _____ What is the name for the idea that
government should be separate from
religion?
   a. Islamism
   b. secularism
   c. monarchy
   d. polytheism

5. _____ In which nation are Copts an
important minority?
   a. Morocco
   b. Algeria
   c. Egypt
   d. Libya

6. Complete the table below to show the effects of Islam and the
Arabic language on the culture and politics of North Africa.

	Effects of Arabic language . . .	**Effects of Islam . . .**
. . . on the region's culture		
. . . on the region's politics		

North Africa Today

- Model preparing to read by previewing the Key Ideas, Key Terms, headings, visuals, and captions. Have students make predictions about what they will learn. For ELL support, post the prompt, "I predict I will read about . . ."
- Preview and practice identifying main ideas and details, using examples from your local newspaper.

- Preteach this section's high-use Academic Vocabulary and Key Terms using the table on the next page and in-text definitions. Have students practice Key Terms by completing the *Word Wise* page in their journals.

GUIDE ON THE SIDE

North African Culture

- **Identify Details** What religion and language are most common in North Africa? (Islam, Arabic) Where else are this religion and language common? (Southwest Asia)

- **Infer** What might Muslims in North Africa share with Muslims in other regions? (religious practices)

- **Draw Conclusions** Why does the term *Middle East* have different meanings? (Some times it is defined by religion. Other times it is defined by geography.)

- **Build Cultural Awareness** How do common religion and language connect people in different countries? (They can speak easily and are familiar with each other's religious rituals.)

Reading Skill

Identify Main Ideas and Details While they read, have students practice this skill by completing the *Take Notes* graphic organizer in the **Student Journal.**

Section 3
North Africa Today

Key Ideas
- Islam and the Arabic language dominate North Africa, but there are minority groups and significant outside influences.
- North Africa is more developed than other parts of the continent, but its people still struggle to make a living.
- Tensions between Islamism and secularism have complicated the region's politics.

Key Terms • Copts • gross domestic product • gross domestic product per capita • human development Index • secularism • Muslim Brotherhood

Visual Glossary

Reading Skill: Identify Main Idea and Details Take notes using the graphic organizer in your journal.

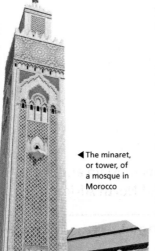
◄ The minaret, or tower, of a mosque in Morocco

North Africa is today the most developed region on the continent. It benefits from large oil deposits and a more peaceful recent history than other regions. North Africa's culture links it closely to Southwest Asia, while trade and migration tie it to Europe.

North African Culture
Most North Africans practice Islam and speak Arabic. These traits tie the region to Southwest Asia and to other parts of the Islamic world.

North Africa and the Middle East Arabic is the most widely spoken language in North Africa and much of Southwest Asia. As in North Africa, most people in Southwest Asia practice Islam. North Africa and Southwest Asia together are often called the Middle East.

The term *Middle East* can have different meanings. It usually includes Egypt but not always other countries in North Africa. It includes Israel, where Islam is not the majority religion. It may also include Iran and Turkey, where Arabic is not generally spoken. It does not include mostly Muslim countries like Indonesia or Nigeria, which are outside of Southwest Asia and North Africa.

People in the Arabic-speaking world from Morocco to Iraq are bound together by their common language and religion. Arabic-speaking countries form a culture region. That means that they share many aspects of their culture with one another.

ACADEMIC VOCABULARY

High-Use Word	Definition and Sample Sentence
stable	*adj.* firm, likely to last, well established *The store is a stable business that has been open for 20 years.*
extract	*v.* get, take out, remove *Sometimes the dentist has to extract a tooth that doesn't fall out on its own.*

Egypt has the largest population of any Arabic-speaking country. It produces many of the most popular books, films, and television shows in Arabic. An Egyptian writer says of Egypt's film industry,

66 With a scale of production unequalled anywhere else in the Arab world, and with its Egyptian-Arab cultural appeal, it became the commercial cinema for all Arab countries. 99

—Samir Farid

Raï (rah EE) music is originally from Algeria, but it appeals to Arabic-speaking people from many different countries. Raï blends traditional and modern styles and deals with current issues.

Minority Groups Ethnic and religious minorities also live in North Africa. The Berbers are the largest ethnic minority. They speak their own language, Tamazight, and live in the western part of the region. Berbers have worked to preserve their culture. Today, Tamazight is an official language in two countries.

The **Copts** are a minority group in Egypt. They practice Christianity. Coptic Christianity has been practiced in Egypt since ancient times. Copts are generally tolerated by the Muslim majority but are sometimes treated as second-class citizens. The Copts are the largest Christian population in the Middle East.

Large Jewish populations lived in the region from ancient times until the 1900s. Most now live in Israel, but small numbers remain, particularly in Morocco.

Reading Check What regions are often considered part of the Middle East?

North African Life

◄ A woman prepares couscous, a common dish in western North Africa. ▶

◄ Berber men in Algeria enjoy a cup of tea.

◄ Algerian raï singer Rachid Taha gives a performance.

- **Analyze Text** Why did Egyptian film become "the commerical cinema for all Arab countries"? (because Egypt produced so many Arabic movies in Arabic and because of its cultural appeal)

- **Identify Details** What are two minority groups in North Africa? (Berbers, Copts)

- **Compare and Contrast** How are the Berbers different from other North Africans? (They do not speak Arabic.)

- **Summarize** What is the relationship between Copts and Muslim Egyptians? (Copts are sometimes treated as second-class citizens.)

READING CHECK North Africa and Southwest Asia

ANSWERS

CULTURE

Copts and Coptic Art The Copts are ethnically similar to other Egyptians. They are descendants of people who did not convert to Islam when Arab invaders arrived in the 600s, but rather kept their Christian faith. They still use the language of ancient Egypt in their religious services, though they speak Arabic. Because Arab-Muslim culture has dominated Egypt, Coptic art developed very little after the 700s. Three key achievements of

Coptic art are colorful linen fabrics, illuminated manuscripts, and wood mosaics made of elaborate patterns of many small pieces. The fabrics reflect the first use of colored thread in Egypt. The illuminated manuscripts include paintings, often in gold and silver, that add details to a text. The woodwork can be seen in geometric designs on doors and furniture. Most Coptic art is religious in subject matter.

GUIDE ON THE SIDE

Economy and Development

- **Compare and Contrast** How does the standard of living in North Africa compare to that of other parts of Africa? (It is higher.)

- How does standard of living in North Africa compare to Europe and North America? (It is lower.)

- **Identify Details** What are two major issues that lower the standard of living in North Africa? (water shortages; urban problems)

- **Compare and Contrast** How do people use GDP to figure out GDP per capita? (They divide GDP by the number of people in a country.)

Chart Skills Direct students to examine the graph of North African GDPs.

- How can the size of a country affect its GDP? (a larger country is likely to have a larger GDP than a smaller country)

 Data Discovery

Point out the chart of GDP in Libya and Algeria.
- Have students go to myworldgeography.com to see more data about GDP of North African countries.

Economy and Development
North Africa is the wealthiest and most developed region in Africa. It benefits from large oil reserves, trade with Europe, good educational systems, and relatively <u>stable</u> governments.

Living Conditions The standard of living in North Africa is generally higher than in other parts of Africa. But, it is not as high as in Europe or North America. Many North Africans live in poverty. Water shortages and urban problems such as overcrowding are serious issues.

stable, *adj.,* firm, likely to last, well established

One way to compare living conditions from place to place is to compare life expectancy, or how long an average person lives. High life expectancy is a sign that a country has a good healthcare system and enough food. Libya has the highest life expectancy in Africa.

You can also compare different countries by their **gross domestic product (GDP).** Gross domestic product is the total value of all goods and services produced in a country over a single year. Bigger countries often have bigger GDPs. For example, Algeria has more people than Libya, and it has a higher GDP.

But GDP does not show how real Algerians or Libyans live. In a big country, all those goods and services are shared among more people. The **gross domestic product (GDP) per capita** gives a better picture of conditions. It is a country's GDP divided by the number of people in the country. Libya has a higher GDP per capita than Algeria. That means that on average, a Libyan

GDP of Libya and Algeria, 2008

Libya
$88.86 billion

Algeria
$235.5 billion

10 billion dollars

SOURCE: CIA World Factbook

Chart Skills
1. What is Algeria's gross domestic product?
2. Does this graph show that, on average, an Algerian earns more than a Libyan? Explain your answer.

Data Discovery

CHART SKILLS 1. 235.5 billion **2.** No. The graph shows GDP, not GDP per capita.

ECONOMICS

HDI by Gender HDI (human development index) is part of the Human Development Report from the United Nations. The Report also includes GDI (gender-related development index), which compares standards of living for women and men in the same country. For example, in Algeria and Tunisia, for every 10 men that can read, only 8 women can read. In Morocco, it is closer to 6 women for every 10 men. Women in these countries, however, generally live longer than men. The United Nations also uses a measurement called the gender empowerment measure, or GEM. It looks at the role women play in government and in top businesses, and at their relative earning power compared to men. Algeria and Morocco rank 104 and 105 out of 108 countries evaluated by the United Nations, suggesting that women's opportunities are very limited in this region.

has a higher income than an Algerian. On average, a Libyan has more purchasing power, meaning he or she can afford more things, than an Algerian. The problem with this measure is that it does not show inequality. Some people earn more than others but the GDP per capita does not reflect this difference.

The **human development index,** or HDI, takes more into account. An HDI is a number that reflects a country's average life expectancy, education, income, and other factors. HDI values are shown as decimals. For example, Egypt's HDI is 0.7. The closer a country's HDI is to one, the higher its standard of living.

Looking at the literacy rate, or the percentage of adults who can read, is also helpful. A high literacy rate suggests that country has a good education system. Tunisia's literacy rate is 74.3 percent. The United States' is 99.9 percent. Educated workers are more productive, so education can improve a country's economy.

North Africa's Economies Oil production is the most important primary industry in North Africa. A primary industry <u>extracts</u> natural resources. Agriculture is also an important primary industry. Secondary industries make finished products from raw materials. Food processing, textile production, and crafts such as making leather goods or jewelry are important secondary industries in North Africa.

Oil, food, and manufactured goods are all exported from North Africa to Europe. In this trade, Europeans buy needed products, and North Africans receive the money they need. Voluntary trade like this can benefit both sides.

Tourism brings a great deal of business into the region. Tourists flock to North Africa for its historic sites and warm winters. Tourists spend money at hotels and restaurants. These services are called tertiary, or third-level, industries. Fourth-level or quaternary industries, such as scientific research, produce knowledge. They are less important in North Africa than in more developed regions.

Despite its advantages, the region still suffers from economic problems. For example, corruption and unemployment are serious issues.

Reading Check What are three factors that the human development index measures?

myWorld Activity
Human Bar Graph

extract, *v.,* to get, take out, remove

A silversmith's shop in a market in Tunisia ▼

READING CHECK average life expectancy, education, income

GUIDE ON THE SIDE

- **Categorize** List ways to compare standard of living. (GDP, GDP per capita, HDI, literacy)
- **Identify Evidence** Explain why GDP per capita may not tell much about how individuals live in a country. (Sample: GPD per capita is an average, but doesn't reveal inequalities such as differences between rich and poor.)

Categorize

- Define the four categories of industry. (primary: natural resources; secondary: finished products; tertiary: services; quaternary: knowledge)
- Name a North African industry and identify its category. (Sample: Oil and agriculture are both primary industries.)
- **Infer** Why might quaternary industries be less important in North Africa than in more developed regions? (Because North Africa is poor and cannot build its education systems.)

 myWorld Activity

Human Bar Graph Find Step-by-Step Instructions and an Activity Support on pp. T80–T81. **(Logical/Kinesthetic)**

BACKGROUND

PRIMARY SOURCE

Muslim Brotherhood Egyptians debate the role of the Muslim Brotherhood in government. Some believe that the Brotherhood's push for democracy is sincere. Others believe it is a trick to gain power for the organization's members, in the hopes of eventually seizing control entirely. Those concerned about the Muslim Brotherhood's intentions cite comments such

as the following from the organization's 2004 Political Platform: "Our mission is to . . . uphold God's law in secular as well as religious matters. . . . to build a Muslim individual, a Muslim family, and an Islamic rule to lead other Islamic states."

Source: "Egypt's Muslim Brotherhood And Political Power: Would Democracy Survive?" by Magdi Khalil

---

GUIDE ON THE SIDE

Different Forms of Government

- **Compare and Contrast** In what ways are all the governments of North Africa different from the government in America? (They have different methods of selecting leaders and making laws.)

Categorize

- Describe Egypt's government. (single-party rule with some voting)

- What is the largest opposition party? (Muslim Brotherhood)

- **Compare Viewpoints** How are the Muslim Brotherhood's views different from the government's? (The Brotherhood wants the government to follow Islamic law while the government wants to keep government separate from religion.)

- **Synthesize** How might Egyptian Copts respond to Muslim Brotherhood ideas? Explain. (Because they are Christian, they probably don't like the opposition's idea of an Islamic government.)

- **Categorize** Describe Algeria's government. (an unstable, corrupt republic)

- **Compare and Contrast** How is Islamism in Algeria different from Islamism in Egypt? (Some Algerian Islamists are more radical and more powerful than Egyptian Islamists.)

Muslim Brotherhood members protest against the Egyptian government.

Different Forms of Government

Each nation in North Africa has its own form of government. All are different from the American system of government, with different methods of selecting leaders and making laws. For example, many political parties compete for office in Morocco, while political parties are banned in Libya.

Egypt: Secularism and Islamism Egypt is not a democracy, but its people have some say in their government. A single party has ruled Egypt since the 1950s. It controls the newspapers, television, and radio. The government of long time president Hosni Mubarak imprisons many of its opponents. Corruption is common, and the police regularly abuse people they arrest. Egyptians elect members of parliament, but the largest

opposition party is not allowed to run for office. The government has not been able to greatly improve Egyptians' standard of living. Rapid population growth makes this problem even more difficult.

Because of these problems, many Egyptians oppose the government. But it is the issue of religion and politics that most divides Egyptians. The government is based on **secularism**, the idea that religion and government should be separate. However, many Egyptians are Islamists. They believe that the government should be run according to Islamic law.

The **Muslim Brotherhood** is an Islamist party. It is the largest group that opposes the Egyptian government. It also opposes the policies of the United States, and the country Israel. In addition to supporting Islamism, the brotherhood pushes for a more democratic Egypt and against corruption. The party generally does not use violence to achieve its goals. However, small groups of Islamic extremists in Egypt have comitted terrorist attacks that target foreign tourists.

Algeria: An Unstable Government As a republic, Algeria has a constitution. However, the country is politically unstable, and elections have been manipulated or rigged.

As in Egypt, Algeria's rulers are secular, and there is a moderate Islamist opposition. However, violent Islamic extremists are more powerful in Algeria than elsewhere in the region. They fought a civil war with the government from 1991 to 2002. Even after the end of the civil war, terrorism remains a problem.

READING CHECK Secularism separates government from religion. Islamists want government to follow Islamic law.

CAPTION In Egypt, power does not change from one party to another.

SECTION 3 ASSESSMENT 1. Egypt's government supports secularism. The opposition Muslim Brotherhood party calls for government by Islamic law. **2.** GDP: value of all goods and services a country produces GDP per capita: value per person of those goods and services **3.** People in a culture region share

ANSWERS

CORE CONCEPTS: POLITICAL SYSTEMS

Review Core Concepts 8.2 with students before discussing Morocco's government. Review the types of states and have students identify those in Egypt and Algeria. Then point out the blue subheading about Morocco's government and ask students to predict how they think that government works. Ask, How is power shared in a constitutional monarchy?

Morocco: A Constitutional Monarchy Morocco is the only nation in North Africa still ruled by a king, Mohammed VI. The king is very powerful but does not completely control the government. A written constitution limits his power. An elected parliament plays a role in government.

In recent years, Morocco has taken steps to increase women's equality. People have more rights than ever before, but the government restricts some civil liberties such as complete freedom of speech.

Morocco has also been criticized for its decades-long occupation of neighboring Western Sahara. This occupation has complicated relations with neighboring countries and with the African Union. Still, Morocco has made greater strides towards full democracy than most other North African nations.

Reading Check **How is secularism different from Islamism?**

Members attend a meeting of the Moroccan parliament. After the 2007 election, control of parliament changed peacefully from one political party to another. An opposition party won the election, and the head of that party became the prime minister. *How does this fact show that Morocco is different from Egypt?*

- **Categorize** How is Morocco's government unique among the nations of North Africa? (It is ruled by a monarch.)

- **Identify Details** What features of democracy exist in Morocco? (a constitution, an elected parliament)

- **Compare and Contrast** How has Morocco's government changed in recent years? (It has increased women's equality and given people more rights.)

Section 3 Assessment

Key Terms

1. Use the following terms to describe Egypt's government and its interaction with religion: secularism, Muslim Brotherhood.

2. How are the gross domestic product and the gross domestic product per capita different?

Key Ideas

3. What is a culture region, and which culture regions is North Africa a part of?

4. What are some ways to measure and describe North Africa's standard of living?

5. What religion do the Copts practice, and where do they live?

Think Critically

6. **Compare and Contrast** How is Morocco's system of government similar to Egypt's? How is it different?

7. **Compare and Contrast** What aspects of culture link North Africa and Southwest Asia? What aspects might divide societies?

Essential Question

How much does geography shape a country?

8. How has oil affected life in North Africa today? How has geography affected standards of living in different North African countries? Go to your Student Journal to record your answers.

many aspects of culture. North Africa is part of Arabic-speaking and Islamic culture regions. **4.** GDP, GDP per capita, HDI, adult literacy **5.** The Copts practice Christianity and live in Egypt. **6.** Both have strong single leaders and some elected government. Morocco has a king, while Egypt has a president but bans opposition candidates. **7.** Islamic faith and the Arabic language link North Africa and Southwest Asia. Ethnic and economic differences could divide societies. **8.** Oil and the oil industry have produced income to develop economies and raise standards of living; Libya has the highest life expectancy, and a higher GDP than Algeria.

PRIMARY SOURCE LESSON PLAN

Reform in Morocco

OBJECTIVES

Students will

- make connections between public statements and political actions of Morocco's King and his opponents.
- **21st Century Learning** identify bias in the views of King Mohammed VI of Morocco about his own government.
- **ELL** understand the terms *democracy, reforms,* and *freedom of the press.*

SET EXPECTATIONS

In this case study, students will

- read and analyze two documents on Morocco's democratic reform process.
- play a game to identify the ways that power affects freedom of press in Morocco.

1 Connect

Start a concept web for the word *democracy.* In one outer circle, write *free elections.* Have students add their own ideas/words. Urge them to consider ways we adapt democracy, such as when a teacher's vote might carry more weight. Clarify also that sometimes elected officials share power with a monarch. Tell students that they will explore how people and leaders in the country of Morocco are defining democracy.

ELL Early Intermediate Have students translate the terms *democracy, reform,* and *freedom* into their home language. Then have them write English definitions they can understand.

2 Learn

Preview Have students preview the two pages of images and documents. Read the Key Idea, glossary terms, and definitions before students begin reading. Clarify the meaning of terms by providing examples. Read the introduction to the documents.

L3 On-Level Slowly pronounce the name Khadija (ka DEE jah) and have students repeat.

Read Slowly read the first excerpt without stopping. Read it again, this time stopping to read the questions at the left and prompt students to analyze the meaning of the words. Have students answer the questions using the location of the letters to provide clues. Repeat for the second excerpt. Discuss and compare the views. Ask, How does King Mohammed define democracy? How does Khadija Riyadi define democracy? How are their views similar or different?

ELL Intermediate Provide simple paraphrases of each text. Read the full text aloud as students listen.

myWorld Activity: Push and Pull
Hand out the *Activity Support: Game Pieces* and review factors and directions. Instruct students to label blank boxes with additional factors and then cut out all the labeled boxes and mix in a pile. Four players then take turns drawing from the pile and telling how the listed factor could affect Morocco's press freedom. Award one point for a logical answer and two points for helping a stumped classmate. After the game, collect slips of paper to poll students on the most powerful factor in Morocco.
(Kinesthetic/Logical)

10 min

3 Understand

Review Draw a new concept web with *Moroccan democracy* now in the center. Fill in the web using information from the documents and shifting perspectives from the United States to Morocco.

Assess Have students complete **Analyze the Documents.** Review their answers to determine if students have met the lesson objectives.

Remediate If students struggle to compare viewpoints, have them draw a Venn diagram. Tell them to place unique ideas from the documents in the outer circles for King's reforms and Riyadi's view, and shared ideas in the overlapping part.

Name _____   Class _____   Date _____

myWorld Activity Support   Game Pieces

Push and Pull

Directions Play a game about press freedom in Morocco.

1) Think of ways that each factor below could affect press freedom.

2) Then think of other factors that might affect press freedom. Label the blank boxes with these factors.

3) Cut out all the labeled boxes and add these slips of paper to those of three classmates seated in a circle with you.

4) Take turns drawing slips from the pile. On your turn, tell a way that the listed factor could affect press freedom. Earn one point if you can answer. Earn two points if you help a classmate that is stuck.

5) After the game, decide which factor you think has the most power over press freedom in Morocco. Vote for that factor by giving a labeled slip to your teacher.

Factors Affecting Press Freedom

Religion and Culture	Courts and Laws
History of Monarchy	Government

_____	_____
_____	_____

CULTURE

Moroccan Media There are 23 daily newspapers published in Morocco, with a combined circulation of 846,000, along with 35 television stations broadcasting to more than three million televisions in 76% of Moroccan homes. Until recently, many Moroccan journalists saw themselves as having greater freedom than colleagues in other countries. However, the government has recently jailed 20 journalists and censored 34 news media outlets. It also posts a list of topics that are off limits to the media, such as articles that criticize the monarch or his family. In 2007, it enforced this restriction by destroying nearly 100,000 copies of two newspapers.

GUIDE ON THE SIDE

Identify Bias Use the lettered prompts to help students analyze the documents and identify bias.

ANSWERS

A Moroccans have chosen it for themselves.

B The King justifies his rule by claiming that it is based on religious, historical, constitutional, and democratic grounds.

C The King implies that the monarchy in Morocco will continue forever.

Primary Source

Reform in Morocco

Key Idea
- Morocco's king believes his government is democratic, but some Moroccans say that recent reforms have not gone far enough.

Morocco is a constitutional monarchy. That means there are written limits to the king's power. Still, Morocco's king is a very powerful figure. Mohammed VI came to office promising great reforms, such as a freer press and more openness for political opposition. Many Moroccans love their leader and appreciate his reforms. But other Moroccans such as Khadija Riyadi argue that human rights are not fully respected. They complain that journalists are mistreated, especially if they say anything negative about the King. Study these selections to learn about Morocco's struggle to define its democracy.

▲ The flag of Morocco

Stop at each letter on the right to think about the text. Then answer the question with the same letter on the left.

A **Summarize** According to the King, who chose the monarchy?

B **Synthesize** How does the King justify his rule?

C **Draw Inferences** If the king has a "permanent symbiosis" with his people, will he ever step down and end the monarchy?

quadruple, *adj.,* having four parts
sovereignty, *n.,* independence, self-government
symbiosis, *n.,* relationship in which both members benefit and cannot live without each other

The King in His Own Words

"This is the truly authentic Moroccan monarchy we have chosen for **A** ourselves, whose effectiveness I have reinforced through the citizens' commitment to development. It is a system based on strong attachment to a <u>quadruple</u> legitimacy: religious, historical, **B** constitutional, and democratic; it is also based on deep respect for the nation's struggle and the sacrifices made for the country's <u>sovereignty</u>, unity, and progress, as well as on **C** the permanent <u>symbiosis</u> between the people and the Throne."
—King Mohammed VI of Morocco, speech marking his 8th year as king, July 30, 2007

King Mohammed

ANALYZE THE DOCUMENTS **1.** Sample: The King wants to continue to rule Morocco. As a result, he probably has a bias in favor of viewing the government positively. **2.** Sample: Dear King Mohammed, It is true that freedom of the press has improved in Morocco under your rule. This is clear in the fact that I can speak openly against my government, at least in a limited way. Still, you should do more. You should further expand freedom of the press so that members of the press in Morocco are never intimidated

21st Century Learning IDENTIFY BIAS

To assist your students in identifying bias, use the scaffolded questions to the left of each excerpt as well as the introduction text. Explain that the most important step in identifying bias is to understand the historical and factual context of a speaker's comments. The next step is to figure out what goals a speaker has that might influence his or her views. Discuss what the king wants from Morocco's people. Have students summarize this desire in a few words, such as "to stay in power." Ask students how the king could achieve his goal. Guide them to see that the king benefits from a certain result in evaluating Moroccan democracy. Once students have a goal summary, direct them to read the excerpts again looking for text that would further this goal. For additional help refer them to the **21st Century Online Tutor** *Identify Bias*.

Stop at each letter on the right to think about the text. Then answer the question with the same letter on the left.

D **Summarize** According to the author, what is the state of freedom of the press in Morocco?

E **Draw Inferences** Why might the government crack down on the news media?

F **Analyze Cause and Effect** What may journalists do if they are punished when they anger the government?

mete, *v.,* distribute, usually justice or punishment

taboos, *n.,* customs that forbid people from doing or talking about certain things

The Other Side

D ❝Freedom of the press is going through a real crisis in Morocco. Moroccan courts are used as a **E** mechanism to clamp down on the press and <u>mete</u> out severe punishment to journalists who are known for their courage in breaking **F** <u>taboos</u>.❞

—Khadija Riyadi, president of the Moroccan Human Rights Association, interview with Al-Jazeera, September 2007

Khadija Riyadi

ANSWERS

D Freedom of press in Morocco is in crisis.

E The government might target the news media to restrict their criticism of the government.

F Journalists might speak out more to bring attention to the government's actions, or they might speak out less in order to avoid being punished by the government.

▼ King Mohammed VI

Analyze the Documents

1. **Identify Bias** Does the king have a bias in evaluating how democratic his government is? Explain.
2. **Writing Task** Write a letter from Khadija Riyadi to King Mohammed explaining your point of view about freedom of the press in Morocco.

or punished for their criticism. Reforms must go futher so that the press is truly and totally free to say what it wishes. Respectully, Khadija Riyadi

KEY TERMS AND IDEAS

1. Ancient Egypt was a theocracy, in which the government was based on religion.

2. Secularism is the belief that government should be separate from religion. Islamism is the belief that government should be run under Islamic law.

3. As clouds rise, they drop their rain on the coastal side of the Atlas Mountains, leaving little rain for the inland side.

4. North Africa and Southwest Asia form a culture region by sharing Islamic culture and Arabic language.

5. Overgrazing is a major cause of desertification in North Africa.

6. Ancient Egypt was more unified politically than other ancient civilizations.

7. Both Berbers and Copts are treated poorly in Egypt, as are minorities in many other countries.

THINK CRITICALLY

8. Badis's statement tells you that Algerian nationalism is linked to religion and language.

9. Limited grazing and "green walls" can slow desertification.

10. The fact that most people in the region practice Islam and speak Arabic are results of the Arab-Muslim conquest.

11. Sample: GDP, GDP per capita, HDI

North Africa

Chapter Assessment

Key Terms and Ideas

1. **Describe** How was ancient Egyptian religion related to government?

2. **Summarize** What is **secularism,** and how is it different from Islamism?

3. **Recall** What effect do the Atlas Mountains have on rainfall?

4. **Categorize** How do North Africa and much of Southwest Asia form a culture region?

5. **Analyze Cause and Effect** What is a major cause of desertification in North Africa?

6. **Summarize** How was ancient Egypt different from other ancient civilizations?

7. **Synthesize** How do countries in North Africa treat minority groups? Compare the situations of the **Berbers** and the **Copts**.

Think Critically

8. **Analyze Primary and Secondary Sources** What does Ben Badis's statement in Section 2 tell you about Algerian nationalism?

9. **Problem Solving** What are some steps that governments can take to slow down or reverse desertification?

10. **Identify Evidence** What aspects of modern North African culture demonstrate that Arab Muslims conquered the region in the A.D. 600s?

11. **Core Concepts: Economic Development** What are three different ways to measure a country's level of economic development?

Places to Know

For each place, write the letter from the map that shows its location.

12. **Algiers**
13. **Rabat**
14. **Nile River**
15. **Sinai Peninsula**
16. **Cairo**
17. **Atlas Mountains**
18. **Estimate** Using the scale, estimate the distance between Cairo and Algiers.

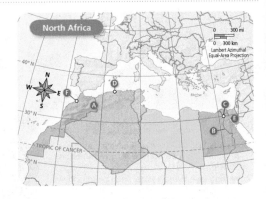

North Africa

PLACES TO KNOW

12. D
13. F
14. B
15. E
16. C
17. A
18. 4,800 km (2,100 miles)

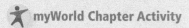

myWorld Chapter Activity

National Crest Contest Find Step-by-Step Instructions, Student Instructions and Rubric, and an Activity Support on pp. T61–T63. **(Visual/Verbal)**

21st Century Learning

Search for Information on the Internet Students' sentences should show a successful search and thoughtful use of information in the sources. If students need help with this skill, direct them to the **21st Century Online Tutor,** *Search for Information on the Internet.*

→ **Online Assessment**

Tailor review and assessment to each student's needs with an array of online assessments.
• Self-Test
• On Assignment Article or Slideshow
• Success Tracker

? Essential Question

myWorld Chapter Activity

National Crest Follow your teacher's instructions to draw a national crest for a North African country that represents its physical geography, history, government, and economy. Consider how the physical geography of your country affects everything else about it.

21st Century Learning

Search for Information on the Internet

Using reliable online sources, research a pharaoh of your choosing. Using at least two sources, find and record the following information:
• name
• dates of reign
• major accomplishments
For each of your sources, write a sentence explaining why you believe it is trustworthy.

WRITING TASK TIP

CONNECT Point out that this Question requires students to make connections to their chapter reading, in addition to viewing Documents A and B. Model how to use the correct answer to question 1 to identify a search term. Then show students how to use chapter headings and subheadings to locate pertinent information about urbanization.

Document-Based Questions

Success ⭐ Tracker™
Online at myworldgeography.com

Use your knowledge of North Africa, as well as Documents A and B, to answer Questions 1–3.

Document A

Egypt's Urban Population

Percentage of Egyptians Living in Cities

60
40
20
0
1950 1970 1990 2015*
Year

SOURCE: UN Common Database
*Estimate

Document B

" In a city where the streets were designed to accommodate half a million cars more than three million daily cross the capital. Cairo is now home to 20 percent of Egypt's population. The streets are packed. . . . Pollution levels have soared."

—Dena Rashed, "To Salvage a City"

1. Which of the following describes the change seen in Document A?
   A corruption
   B desertification
   C urbanization
   D Islamization

2. Which of the following does Document B suggest?
   A Cairo is well governed.
   B Cairo is overcrowded.
   C Cairo is a medium-sized city.
   D Cairo is Egypt's cultural capital.

3. **Writing Task** Why do you think so much of Egypt's population lives in Cairo?

DOCUMENT-BASED QUESTIONS

1. C

2. B

3. Sample: People live in Cairo because it is Egypt's cultural, political, educational, and economic center and offers many different opportunities to people that live there.

QUICK FACTS

World Heritage Sites More than 100 World Heritage Sites are located in Africa. These include cultural sites, natural sites, and mixed sites. The African sites include

- Pyramids in Egypt
- Asante traditional buildings in Ghana
- Mount Kenya National Park and National Forest in Kenya

- Rainforests of the Atsinanana in Madagascar
- Djoudj National Bird Sanctuary in Senegal
- Fossil hominid sites in South Africa
- Serengeti National Park in Tanzania
- Victoria Falls in both Zambia and Zimbabwe
- Great Zimbabwe National Monument in Zimbabwe

GUIDE ON THE SIDE

21st Century Learning

Generate New Ideas Give the class the following definition of *innovate*: "to introduce a new way of doing something, a new idea, or a new device." On the board, create a concept web centered on the word *innovate*. Encourage students to contribute synonyms and examples. Before the class begins the activity, share the following example of an innovation in advertising: In recent years, grocery stores have installed TV screens in the checkout aisles so that commercials can play to customers waiting in line. Tell students that their task is to create a tourism advertising campaign that uses a new approach.

21st Century Learning — Generate New Ideas

Come to Africa
PLAN A TOURISM CAMPAIGN

Your Mission Your group has just been asked to investigate tourism for the African Union. Your job is to increase the number of people who come to the continent, visiting landmarks, going on tours, staying in hotels, and eating in restaurants.

If you had a chance to travel to Africa, what would you do on your trip? Would you want to see the monuments of past civilizations, visit the habitat of wild animals, or explore the vegetation of the rain forest? Would you want to learn about African music and arts? Whatever your interests, you would probably begin by researching places in Africa, reading tour books, or visiting tourism Web sites.

Your impressions of Africa would probably be influenced by tourism books or Web sites. You would find that the best tourism campaign finds a way to combine the uniqueness of a place with the expectations that visitors have for travel there. A trip that is called "the vacation of a lifetime" makes you want to travel! To reach visitors and persuade them to travel, a good tourism campaign should also be innovative. It should generate interest by conveying its message in an exciting and intriguing way.

COME TO AFRICA: PLAN A TOURISM CAMPAIGN RUBRIC

3. Plan uses researched facts about one of the following: the country's geography, economy, history, or culture; doesn't have a tourism focus; and includes two of the following: a target audience, a description of the country, a list of persuasive techniques to be used, and a choice of media.

2. Plan uses researched facts about two of the following: the country's geography, economy, history, or culture; identifies a tourism focus;

CULTURE

Advertising Techniques Even when advertisers find new ways to deliver ads, they usually stick to tried-and-true advertising techniques like the following:

- **The Unfinished Claim** An ad for a printer might claim to be "50 percent sharper" but not finish the comparison by explaining "sharper than what?"

- **Compliment the Consumer** Ads such as "Only sophisticated men use our cologne" try to make people think they will be special if they buy and use the product.

- **The Uniqueness Claim** Advertising often makes claims like "No other bread tastes like ours." The ad doesn't actually say it tastes better, just different.

- **The Endorsement** Advertisers try to get people to buy products by showing famous people using them: "Olympic champions eat Fiber Flakes!"

Go to myWorldGeography.com for help with this activity.

STEP 1
Research Your Country.

Decide with your teacher whether your group will design a tourism campaign for Botswana, Egypt, Ethiopia, Ghana, Kenya, Mali, Republic of the Congo, Uganda, or Tanzania. Research the geography, economy, history, and culture of your country. Study photographs and tourism information to learn what makes these countries appealing to tourists.

STEP 2
Choose Your Specialty.

Based on your country's strengths, determine the special focus of your tourism campaign. You might choose to appeal to people interested in historic sites, ecotourism, wildlife habitats, photo safaris, culture, or sports. Decide what kind of marketing campaign (print or multimedia) will attract the attention of tourists interested in one of those areas.

STEP 3
Plan Your Marketing Campaign.

Develop a proposal for your marketing campaign. Explain who your target audience is, how you will portray the country, and what persuasive techniques you will use. Your campaign may take the form of a Web site, an illustrated brochure, a television commercial, or a video. Write a memo to the head of the tourism ministry that describes your proposal in detail.

and includes three of the following: a target audience, a description of the country, a list of persuasive techniques to be used, and a choice of media.

1. Plan uses researched facts about the geography, economy, history, and culture of the country; accurately identifies the country's tourism focus; and includes a target audience, a description of the country, a list of persuasive techniques to be used, and a choice of media.

GUIDE ON THE SIDE

TIGed
TakingITGlobal for Educators

Have your students go to myworldgeography.com to find solutions to this 21st Century Learning Activity, *Come to Africa: Plan a Tourism Campaign*.

 21c Online Tutor

Using the 21st Century Online Tutor, students can get more tips on how to generate new ideas. Students respond onscreen to successfully practice developing new ideas.

ANSWER KEY

West and Central Africa

See rubric on p. T6.

myWorld Chapter Activity: To Drill or Not to Drill?

73 Harming the Environment Effects: pipelines burst, tankers leak, oils spills pollute. All are negative because they are bad for the environment and cost money to clean up.

74 Bringing in Money Positive effects: Brings in money for oil-rich countries and improves way of life. Negative effects: Oil-dependent countries lose wealth.

75 Fighting Over New Wealth Effects: Oil wealth can cause corruption, violence, pollution, loss of homes, and mistreatment by oil companies. All are negative because they damage a country's economy, society, and its people.

76 University of Qatar Effects: Oil wealth can improve education, infrastructure, and support for the poor and elderly. All are positive because they increase opportunities for citizens.

77 Surviving a One-Resource Economy Positive effects: Countries that rely on exporting oil gain wealth when oil prices rise. Negative effects: Countries face economic problems when prices drop. People's standard of living may decline.

78 Creating Jobs Effects: Oil discovery creates jobs in service and construction. This is positive because an increase in jobs improves the economy.

Conclusion Most students will mark box 3 to conclude that oil development has both good and bad effects on a country.

Report on oil development Students' reports will vary but should reflect the positive and negative effects oil drilling has on a country and support their opinions with evidence from more than one of the Activity Cards.

Section 1
West and Central Africa

myWorld Activity: Compare Climates

	Desert	Sahel	Savanna	Rain-forest
Animal	Scorpion	Senegal gerbil	Gazelle	Bonobo chimp
Plant	Date palm tree	Baobab tree	Grass	Fern

Samples:

1. Desert: Humans can adopt nomadic lifestyles.
2. Sahel: Humans can herd cattle instead of farming.
3. Savanna: Humans can build dwellings that are open in dryer months and covered in rainy months.
4. Rainforest: Humans can gather food from the forest rather than farm.

Enrichment: Rainforests of Central Africa

1. Different kinds of plants and animals live in each layer of rainforest because that layer provides what they need. For example, monkeys and parrots live in the highest layer, or canopy, where they can easily move from tree to tree.
2. Heat and humidity make plant matter break down very quickly, so soil cannot build up. When forests are cleared for crops, the soil wears out quickly.
3. Diagrams should accurately reflect research about various plants and animals that live in each rainforest layer.

Section 1 Quiz

1. b   **2.** b   **3.** c   **4.** a   **5.** d
6.

Climate Zone	Description
Semi-arid	Sahel; short rainy season, high day temperatures, low night temperatures
Tropical wet and dry	Savanna; grasslands with woods and shrubs, less rain, warm temperatures
Tropical wet	Rainforest; heavy rainfall, temperatures warm year-round

Section 2
West and Central Africa

myWorld Activity: The Promise of Independence

Improvements	Challenges
1. Pan-Africanism	1. Borders drawn unfairly by Europeans
2. Democracy	2. Corrupt leaders
3. Ethnic unity	3. Ethnic conflicts, civil war over oil and other resources

Answers regarding teacher's interactions will vary. Sample answer: The teacher reorganized groups. This represented the effects of colonialism on West and Central Africans. This was disruptive and caused confusion. Borders imposed by Europeans made life difficult for West and Central Africans because they were drawn without considering ethnic and language groups. This led to conflict among groups.

Enrichment: Kwame Nkrumah

1. He guided Ghana to independence, freeing the country from colonial rule.

2. He was overthrown because the military was fed up with his oppression and mismanagement.

3. Paragraphs will vary but should reflect an understanding of Nkrumah's desire for freedom from colonial rule.

Section 2 Quiz

1. b   **2.** b   **3.** b   **4.** d   **5.** b

6. Sample answer: Europeans wanted colonies for prestige, for natural resources to produce industrial goods, and as markets for goods made in factories. Getting natural resources was likely the most important reason, because it could increase industry and wealth for European countries.

Case Study: Famous Cities and Kingdoms of West Africa

myWorld Activity: Letter to Home

Students' notes and letters will vary but should accurately describe one of the West African cities from the text and compare and contrast it to their own communities. Students may note similarities and differences in geography, government, customs, and culture. Reasons to visit the city may include works of art and other cultural interests, such as a college or university.

Section 3
West and Central Africa

myWorld Activity: Two Economies

Sample answers: Ghana is having the most economic success. The people in Ghana are better off than the people in the Democratic Republic of the Congo because their country has a growing economy and a stable government. The Democratic Republic of the Congo could improve its economic conditions by working with the African Union and foreign aid agencies that could provide loans for small businesses and help develop a stable infrastructure.

Enrichment: Microcredit and Entrepreneurs

1. Microcredit loans have lower interest rates than traditional loans, which makes it more affordable for poor entrepreneurs to start or expand businesses.

2. A microcredit loan helped Oumy Konte by allowing her to keep most of her profits, expand her business, and save money.

3. Proposals will vary but should detail a plausible business idea, reasons it would succeed, and how much start-up money would be required.

Section 3 Quiz

1. c   **2.** d   **3.** c   **4.** d   **5.** c

6. Sample: Oil development has been bad for Nigeria because oil profits have mostly benefited foreigners and corrupt officials. Some Nigerians resent this and react with violence.

Primary Source: Things Fall Apart

myWorld Activity: Cultural Sampler

Illustrations and samplers will vary but should reflect facts about the Igbo society gleaned from the excerpts.

Answers in order from left to right in each row:

Crime and Punishment Crimes are "male" or "female"; hard to fight when "own brothers" side with "white man"; council ruled villages.

Family Okonkwo could return to clan after seven years; Clan is divided.

Religion Killing a clansman was crime against earth goddess; Europeans and Igbo who converted to Christianity criticize customs; traditional religion had many gods; many Igbo are now Christians.

Land A person who kills a clansman must flee the land; Europeans don't understand "custom about land"; held by clans or related family groups; used for farming and building.

Southern and Eastern Africa

See rubric on p. T34.

myWorld Chapter Activity: Agents of Change

Meet, Greet, Question Sample answer for Nelson Mandela: Everyone else is from the same country; everyone else is against apartheid; F. W. de Klerk was president; no one else spent time in prison; F. W. de Klerk was part of the National Party; no one else was part of the ANC; everyone else is famous worldwide.

Call to Order Nelson Mandela: Apartheid should end. F. W. de Klerk: Apartheid is destroying South Africa. Desmond Tutu: People should oppose apartheid through nonviolent resistance. Miriam Makeba: Singing is a way to promote equal rights for all. Sheena Duncan: Women should work together to fight apartheid in nonviolent ways.

Community Group Name and Slogan Sample answer: Africans Against Apartheid; Together we can change our world!

Wrap-up Comments will vary but should reflect students' understanding of the challenges involved in ending apartheid.

Section 1
Southern and Eastern Africa

myWorld Activity: Cause-and-Effect Pairs

Cards Sample answer: picture of a diamond or diamond ring for cause; picture of a smashed miner's hat for effect

Game Students should be able to identify missing causes and effects when prompted. Sample answer: Cause: drought. Effect: People must irrigate or get food elsewhere.

Enrichment: Victoria Falls

1. Heavy rains; the climate upriver must have periods of intense rain.

2. Being close enough to the falls to feel its spray makes viewing the falls and bungee jumping more exciting. It probably makes transportation more difficult because the road and rail tracks are always wet. Placing the bridge so close to the falls probably meant it had to be taller and wider than if it were lower down or at a narrower point in the river.

3. Students' ideas should be based on logic. Sample: Builders built from gorge edges and worked their way to the middle.

Section 1 Quiz

1. a **2.** c **3.** c **4.** a **5.** b
6.
Students' completed tables should show one example for each cateogry.

Landforms and Bodies of Water Great Rift Valley, Victoria Falls, Mount Kilimanjaro, Mount Kenya. Rivers: Nile, Zambezi, Orange, Limpopo. Lakes: Tanganyika, Victoria, Nyasa; **Ecosystems** savannas (Serengeti Plain), forests or woodlands, mountain peaks with snow, deserts; **Natural Resources** Wildlife such as elephants, lions, or zebras; minerals such as gold, platinum, and diamonds; crops such as coffee, tea, tobacco, and cotton; **Challenges for People** Water shortage and competition; danger from mining; environmental damage from mining; wildlife poaching; disease

Section 2
Southern and Eastern Africa

myWorld Activity: Where I'm From

Table Dates from right to left, top to bottom:
Bantu: A.D. 500; Nubians: 2000 B.C.; Arab Muslims:
after Great Zimbabwe, before Europeans; Boers:
A.D.1800–1900; Mau Mau: A.D.1940s–1960s; Great
Zimbabwe: A.D. 1400s; Portuguese traders: A.D.1400;
European colonists: A.D.1800–1900; Nelson Mandela:
A.D.1960s–1990s; F. W. De Klerk: A.D.1989–1994;
Aksum people: about the same time as Nubians;
Jomo Kenyatta: 1963; African National Congress:
A.D.1960s–1990s; *Homo erectus*: 1–2 million years ago

Identity Cards Students' cards will vary depending
on their assigned person or group, but should reflect
accurate information from the section text. Sample
answer for *Homo erectus*: I am from Eastern Africa.
I lived between 1 and 2 million years ago. I spread
human settlement to other continents. I spread human
settlement to other parts of Southern and Eastern Africa.

Timeline Students should place their cards in the correct
sequence on the timeline.

Enrichment: *Homo Erectus*

1. They use fossils of bones and teeth, plants and
   animals of the same age, and tools, as well
   as the rock in which fossils were found.

2. They agree that *Homo erectus* came from Africa.

3. Maps should label the Beijing finds with "1921–1966"
   and "largest collection," the 1984 Lake Turkana
   find as "most complete," the 1975 Lake Turkana
   find as "oldest African," and the 1891 Java find as
   "first *H. erectus* found." Maps should accurately
   locate the finds in China, Kenya, and Java.

Section 2 Quiz

1. b   **2.** a   **3.** c   **4.** d   **5.** d
6.

Bantu migration	It spread Bantu ways, including iron tools, farming methods, and language, to eastern Africa.
European colonialism	It brought European languages and religions to eastern and southern Africa.
Fall of apartheid	It ended laws of racial separation and gave voting and other rights to all South Africans.

Primary Source: Literature of Southern and Eastern Africa

myWorld Activity: Storytelling Festival

Students' retellings will vary but should accurately
reflect information, ideas, and images present
or suggested by the stories. Sample answers for
Galawdewos: **Ideas** wisdom, beauty, religion **Images**
decorated tower, palace covered with jewels

Section 3
Southern and Eastern Africa

myWorld Activity: Analyze Conflicts

Answers will vary depending on the conflict, but
students should demonstrate their understanding
of facts and opinions that play a role in their chosen
conflict. Not all boxes or circles will be filled. Sample
answers for conflict in Sudan: **Facts** People in the
north are mostly Muslim and Arabic speakers. People
in the south mostly follow indigenous religions or
Christianity. They speak non-Arabic languages.
The two groups have fought for control. **Opinions**
Northerners have acted unfairly in trying to control
southerners. Southerners have acted unwisely in
rebelling violently. **Biases** I am biased toward peaceful
solutions. **Reflection** My opinion about Sudan's civil
war has changed. Before I read about it, I didn't
understand what people were fighting about. Now I
understand, but I still think all Sudanese should share
control.

Enrichment: Culture Spread

1. Sudan, Egypt, Tanzania, Somalia, Eritrea,
   Djibouti, Uganda, Comoros

2. Egypt, Djibouti, Rwanda, Comoros, Mauritius,
   Madagascar, Tanzania, Uganda, Kenya

3. Languages in countries next to each other will likely
   be the same in some way. Languages might differ
   at places where the influence of one colonizer or
   newcomer stopped and another started, such as
   between areas where Arabs traded and Europeans
   colonized. Main languages spoken reflect cultures
   that are well established in the country.

Section 3 Quiz

1. a **2.** c **3.** b **4.** d **5.** b
6.

Country	Conflict
Sudan	Ethnic and religious fighting
Zimbabwe	Political and governmental instability
Rwanda	Ethnic and religious fighting
South Africa	Racial, social, economic inequality
Conclusion	Instability of any kind is an obstacle to development because it keeps society from moving smoothly and takes the time, energy, and money of people and governments.

Case Study: The Effects of Colonialism

myWorld Activity: Colonialism on the Clock

Country Timeline Sample for Tanzania: Portuguese arrive, 1500s; Germans take control, 1884; British take control, after WW I (1919); Tanzania gains independence, 1961. Pictures could show coastal forts, plantation work, tribal group with line for division, or a star for independence. **Three-Part Timeline** Students' timelines should accurately show dates of events from the lesson, and should use color to accurately identify periods of control by different European nations.

North Africa

See rubric on p. T62.

myWorld Chapter Activity: National Crest Contest

Country Crests Sample answer for Morocco: **Government** picture of a group holding a crown, arrow pointing up for improvement; **History** map sketch of Western Sahara with Moroccan flag on it; **Geography** drawing of the coast with mountains beyond; **Economy** drawing of an olive tree

Paragraphs Statements will vary but should include reasons based on specific details. Sample for Morocco: Morocco needs a new crest. My crest shows that the country's government is a partnership between the king and the parliament and that it is getting more democratic.

It shows that Morocco has an obligation to Western Sahara. It also shows the natural beauty of Morocco's coast and mountains. Finally, it shows that Morocco's economy includes important crops such as olives.

Section 1
North Africa

myWorld Activity: On the Move

Sample answers:
City-Dwellers 1. It bothered me. 2. My neighborhood became crowded. 3. I had less water and other resources.

Rural Residents 1. I moved to the city. 2. It was hard to get used to the noise and crowded streets. 3. I would prefer to go back to the countryside because it is peaceful there.

Nomads 1. The city got more crowded. 2. City life was more difficult.

Conclusions Conclusions will vary but should demonstrate an understanding of Tunisia's population patterns. Sample conclusion: As more people move to cities, Tunisia has become more and more urbanized. This creates problems for cities as they try to provide services such as water and education to so many people.

Enrichment: Where Is the Water?

1. Cairo; Tunis; Tunis gets rain as moisture is blown in from the Mediterranean and trapped by the Atlas Mountains.

2. Tunis: December or October, July; Casablanca: December; February–March or June–August; Cairo: December–January; April–July or October

3. Sample cities: Tucson, Phoenix, Los Angeles, San Diego, Albuquerque, and other cities of the desert southwest. Packing List: good hat, cool but long-sleeved shirts, sandals, shorts or lightweight pants

Section 1 Quiz

1. a **2.** c **3.** d **4.** b **5.** c
6. Limited Water →

Population Distribution People live near bodies of water, such as the Nile River, the Mediterranean Sea, and oases, and where rainfall is higher, such as in the Atlas Mountains. Large areas of the region, such as the Sahara, are sparsely populated due to lack of water.

Environment People have built dams to provide water for drinking and irrigation, and to control flooding. Fertilizers cause pollution. Overgrazing limited vegetation has led to desertification.

Section 2
North Africa

myWorld Activity: The Farmer's Pitch

Farming Benefits Sample: 1. Enough food for everyone. 2. Civilization develops as people have time for jobs other than hunting food. 3. Cities develop as people have time to build them.

Slogans Answers will vary but should reflect each benefit's content and use catchy language.

Ad Idea Sample for benefit 3: Image or description of a clock with about 2 hours shaded in and showing food items; the rest of the clock has images of people building or writing.

Presentation Students should refer to specifics of their ad idea or visual as they present their reasons why farming is good for Egypt.

Enrichment: Pyramids and Mummies

1. Snefru

2. Khufu

3. Priests needed detailed knowledge of the human body, knowledge of salt's drying properties, and knowledge of appropriate religious rituals.

4. Scripts should describe ancient Egyptian beliefs about the afterlife and the need to preserve the body for its time there.

Section 2 Quiz

1. c **2.** d **3.** b **4.** a **5.** c
6.

Ancient Egyptian	Independent Egyptian
Agriculture, civilization, pyramids and cities, hieroglyphics, mummification, engineering, astronomy, math, trade	Modernization, Suez Canal, two wars with Israel, loss and regaining of Sinai Peninsula
Arab	**European Rule**
Islam, Arabic, trade that brought these and other ideas through and beyond the region	New political divisions, strife from resistance to outside rule, wars for independence

Case Study: A Closer Look at Ancient Egypt

myWorld Activity: Ancient Egypt Museum

Students' exhibit ideas and drawings will vary but should show understanding of cultural information from the lesson.

Sample answer for Religion: **Description** Very important in ancient Egypt, gods and goddesses controlled everything, pharaoh was a god, there was life after death. **Caption** Isis and Osiris were important gods.

Section 3
North Africa

myWorld Activity: Human Bar Graph

Ordered Rankings 1–5: Area Algeria, Libya, Egypt, Morocco, Tunisia **Population** Egypt, Algeria, Morocco, Tunisia, Libya **GDP** Egypt, Algeria, Morocco, Libya, Tunisia **GDP per capita** Libya, Tunisia, Algeria, Egypt, Morocco **HDI** Libya, Tunisia, Algeria, Egypt, Morocco **Literacy** Libya, Tunisia, Egypt, Algeria, Morocco

Bar Graph Students should use the provided body positions to accurately show their country's place in rankings 1–5 for each category.

Wrap-up 1. GDP per capita tells more about how much wealth individuals have while GDP only tells how much income a nation has. **2.** HDI includes average life expectancy, education, and income. **3.** Sample: Literacy rate is a good measure of a country's economic situation as it reflects the government's ability to invest in education, people's ability to pursue education, and businesses' ability to grow with an educated workforce.

Enrichment: Raï Music of Algeria

1. *Raï* means "opinion." This meaning is reflected in the lyrics of raï songs, many of which are protest songs.

2. Raï began in Algeria in the early 1900s. The most important early influence was traditional folk music.

3. Sample: The mood is excited and probably angry. It reminds me of rap, hip-hop, or possibly of blues or spiritual call-and-response music.

Section 3 Quiz

1. a   **2.** a   **3.** d   **4.** b   **5.** c

6.

Effects of Arabic Language . . .
on the region's culture Most North Africans also speak Arabic, so most can communicate.
on the region's politics In some cases, minority religious or ethnic groups are suppressed by Islamic and Arabic-speaking political majorities.

Effects of Islam . . .
on the region's culture Islam dominates the region, with most North Africans practicing the religion.
on the region's politics Islamist and secularist groups in some countries battle over how much religion should influence government.

Primary Source: Reform in Morocco

myWorld Activity: Push and Pull

Students' ideas about the way each factor could affect Moroccan freedom of the press will vary but should be supportable.

Sample effects:

Religion and Culture Religious and cultural ideas about authority could create pressure on the press to support the king.

Courts and Laws Legislators could pass laws to limit or expand press freedom. Courts have limited freedom by punishing journalists.

History of Monarchy People respect and love the king, so they may discourage the press from criticizing him openly.

Government People could vote for legislators who will make laws that limit or expand press freedom. The government could use its laws and its police force to limit or protect press freedom.

Game Students should provide ideas during their own turn or during the turn of stumped classmates.

Vote Votes will vary. Sample: Courts and laws can have the greatest effect by promoting an accepted understanding of the press's freedoms.

Acknowledgments

The people who made up the **myWorld Geography** team—representing composition services; core design, digital, and multimedia production services; digital product development; editorial; editorial services; materials management; and production management—are listed below.

Leann Davis Alspaugh, Sarah Aubry, Deanna Babikian, Paul Blankman, Alyssa Boehm, Peter Brooks, Susan Brorein, Megan Burnett, Todd Christy, Neville Cole, Bob Craton, Michael Di Maria, Glenn Diedrich, Frederick Fellows, Jorgensen Fernandez, Thomas Ferreira, Patricia Fromkin, Andrea Golden, Mary Ann Gundersen, Christopher Harris, Susan Hersch, Paul Hughes, Judie Jozokos, John Kingston, Kate Koch, Stephanie Krol, Karen Lepri, Ann-Michelle Levangie, Salena LiBritz, Courtney Markham, Constance J. McCarty, Laurie McKenna, Anne McLaughlin, Rich McMahon, Mark O'Malley, Alison Muff, Jen Paley, Gabriela Perez Fiato, Judith Pinkham, Paul Ramos, Charlene Rimsa, Marcy Rose, Rashid Ross, Alexandra Sherman, Owen Shows, Melissa Shustyk, Jewel Simmons, Ted Smykal, Emily Soltanoff, Frank Tangredi, Simon Tuchman, Elizabeth Tustian, Merle Uuesoo, Alwyn Velasquez, Andrew White, Heather Wright

Maps

XNR Productions, Inc.

Illustration

Kerry Cashman, Marcos Chin, Dave Cockburn, Jeremy Mohler

Note: T page numbers below refer to teacher resource pages. Other page numbers refer to Eastern Hemisphere Student Edition pages.

Photography

TABLE OF CONTENTS: Pages vi–vii, All, Pearson Education, Inc.

AFRICA REGIONAL OVERVIEW: Pages 322–327, **Bkgrnd sky**, ImageSource/Getty Images; **Page 323, LT**, Pearson Education, Inc.; **TM**, Pearson Education, Inc.; **RT**, Pearson Education, Inc.; **B**, Stellapictures/JupiterImages; **324, T**, Radius Images/JupiterImages; **B**, Matthew Septimus/Getty Images; **325, T**, Gavin Hellier/Photolibrary; **B**, Roger De La Harpe/Photolibrary; **M**, Eric Isselée/Shutterstock; **326**, Hugh Sitton/zefa/Corbis; **327, R**, Pearson Education, Inc.; **L**, Pearson Education, Inc.; **M**, Pearson Education, Inc.

WEST AND CENTRAL AFRICA: Pages 328–331, All, Pearson Education, Inc.; **T12**, Nigel Bean/Nature Picture Library; **332**, Bruno Morandi/Getty Images; **334**, Bruno Morandi/Getty Images; **335, LM**, Pearson Education, Inc.; **L**, Nigel Bean/naturepl.com; **RM**, Atlantide Phototravel/Corbis; **R**, Bruno Fert/Corbis; **337**, Bruce Dale/National Geographic/Getty Images; **Bkgrnd**, Keira McKee/Alamy; **338**, Martin Dohrn/Photo Researchers, Inc.; **T18**, Bettmann/Corbis **340**, Frans Lemmens/zefa/Corbis; **341, L**, John Webb/The Art Archive; **R**, Joan Pollock/Alamy; **342**, Courtesy of the Wilberforce House Museum, Hull/Dorling Kindersley; **343, T**, National Archives Image Library, UK/Dorling Kindersley; **B**, Popperfoto/Getty Images; **344, L**, Bettmann/Corbis; **R**, AFP/Getty Images; **345**, AP Images; **346, T**, Corbis/Photolibrary; **346, B**, Hugh Sitton/zefa/Corbis; **347, R**, Sebastien Cailleux/Corbis; **348**, Paul Almasy/Corbis; **349, Inset**, Werner Forman/Corbis; **349, Bkgrnd**, iStockphoto.com; **350**, Gideon Mendel/ActionAid/Corbis; **351**, Jacob Silberberg/Getty Images; **352, L**, AFP/Getty Images; **R**, George Osodi/AP Images; **353, Cloth**, Dorling Kindersley; **LT**, Comstock Images/Jupiter Unlimited; **RT**, Paul Almasy/Corbis; **LB**, Studio Patellani/Corbis; **RB**, Philippe Lissac/Godong/Corbis; **355**, Pearson Education, Inc.; **356**, Werner Forman/Art Resource, NY; **357, B**, Newscom; **357, T**, Eye Ubiquitous/Alamy.

SOUTHERN AND EASTERN AFRICA: Pages 360–361, Ksenia Khamkova/iStockphoto.com; **360, B**, Pearson Education, Inc.; **361, T**, Pearson Education, Inc.; **B**, Pearson Education, Inc.; **362–363, All**, Pearson Education, Inc.; **T40**, Getty Images/Jupiter Unlimited; **364, Bkgrnd**, SuperStock; **B**, Steve Outram/Mira.com; **367, L**, Tim Laman/Getty Images, Inc.; **L Inset**, meoita/Fotolia; **M Inset**, Beckman/Dorling Kindersley; **R Inset**, Oleg Znamenskiy/Fotolia; **R**, Image Source/Photolibrary; **368, L**, Ian Murphy/Getty Images; **M**, Charles O'Rear/Corbis; **R**, Kulka/zefa/Corbis; **369, Bkgrnd**, Franco Pizzochero/age Fotostock; **B**, F.A.O. Food and Agriculture Organization of the United Nations; **370, T**, Reza/Webistan/Getty Images; **TM**, Peter Martell/AFP/Getty Images; **BM**, Andrew Holt/Getty Images; **B**, Jenny Matthews/Alamy; **371**, Liba Taylor/Corbis; **372, T**, David Boyer/National Geographic/Getty Images; **B**, Gallo Images/Corbis; **373, B**, Peter Groenendijk/Age Fotostock; **T**, Yadid Levy/age Fotostock; **375, RT**, The Granger Collection, New York; **LT**, The Granger Collection, New York; **B**, Bettmann/Corbis; **376**, Bettmann/Corbis; **377**, David Turnley/Corbis; **378**, The Art Archive/Collection Antonovich/Dagli Orti; **379**, Nicole Duplaix/Corbis; **380**, PCN Photography/PCN/Corbis; **381, T**, Patrick Robert/Sygma/Corbis; **B**, Lindsay Hebberd/Corbis; **382**, Alfred De Montesquiou/AP Images; **384, B**, AFP Photo/HO/US Navy/Jason R. Zalasky/Newscom; **T**, epa/Corbis; **385**, Wolfgang Schmidt/Peter Arnold, Inc.; **386**, Peter Groenendijk/age Fotostock; **387**, Hulton-Deutsch Collection/Corbis; **388, R**, D Barnett/Hulton Archive/Getty Images; **C**, The Stapleton Collection/Art Resource, NY; **389, R**, Peter Horree/Alamy; **L**, David Turnley/Corbis; **Inset**, Keystone/Getty Images.

NORTH AFRICA: Pages 393–395, **All**, Pearson Education, Inc.; **396, Bkgrnd**, Franck Guiziou/Hemis/Corbis; **B**, Hugh Sitton/zefa/Corbis; **398**, Jacques Descloitres, MODIS Land Science Team/NASA; **399, LB**, Tony Craddock/zefa/Corbis; **RB**, Sylvain Grandadam/age Fotostock; **LT**, Aristidis Vafeiadakis/Alamy; **RT**, R. Matina/age Fotostock; **400, B**, Otto Lang/Corbis; **T**, Otto Lang/Corbis; **401**, Cecile Treal and Jean-Michel Ruiz/Dorling Kindersley; **404**, Roger Wood/Corbis; **405, T**, Bojan Brecelj/Corbis; **M**, Peter Hayman/The British Museum/Dorling Kindersley; **B**, The Gallery Collection/Corbis; **Bkgrnd**, Yanta/Shutterstock; **406, LB**, Peter Hayman/The British Museum/Dorling Kindersley; **BM**, John Hepver/The British Museum/Dorling Kindersley; **Bkgrnd**, Hydromet/Shutterstock; **LT**, Peter Hayman/The British Museum/Dorling Kindersley; **RB**, Kazuyoshi Nomachi/Corbis; **RT**, Pearson Education, Inc.; **407, R**, Gavin Hellier/Robert Harding World/Corbis; **L**, The Gallery Collection/Corbis; **M**, Pearson Education, Inc.; **408**, Interpress/Interpress/Kipa/Corbis; **409**, Bettmann/Corbis; **410**, Alistair Duncan/Dorling Kindersley; **411, L**, Roger Wood/Corbis; **R**, The Art Archive/Egyptian Museum Cairo/Gianni Dagli Orti; **412 ML**, JupiterImages/Brand X/Alamy; **LT**, The Print Collector/Alamy; **LB**, British Museum/Dorling Kindersley; **L**, N-a-s-h/Shutterstock; **TM**, Stephanie Pilick/epa/Corbis; **413, M**, N-a-s-h/Shutterstock; **414**, Brakefield Photo/Brand X/Corbis; **415, T**, Claudia Wiens/Das Fotoarchiv/Peter Arnold, Inc.; **B**, Hekimian Julien/Corbis; **417, R**, Olivier Martel/Corbis; **L**, Alan Hills/Dorling Kindersley; **418**, Mona Sharaf/Reuters; **419**, John Chiasson/Liaison/Getty Images; **420, RT**, David Kay/Shutterstock; **RB**, Abdelhak Senna, Pool/AP Images; **421, TR**, Abdelhak Senna/AFP/Getty Images.

AFRICA UNIT CLOSER: Page 424, **RT**, Shutterstock; **B**, iStockphoto.com; **424–425, B**, Pearson Education, Inc.; **425, LM**, Shutterstock; **RM**, Christian Musat/Shutterstock; **RT**, Pearson Education, Inc.; **Bkgrnd**, iStockphoto.com; **LT**, Shutterstock; **M**, Shutterstock.

Text

Grateful acknowledgment is made to the following for copyrighted material:

Page 370 "Thirst for Power" by G. Pascal Zachary from IEEE Spectrum, May 2007. Copyright © IEEE Spectrum.

Page 412 "Tutankhamun: Anatomy of an Excavation" from http://www.griffith.ox.ac.uk/gri/4tut.html. Copyright © Griffith Institute, Oxford.

Note: Every effort has been made to locate the copyright owner of material reproduced in this publication. Omissions brought to our attention will be corrected in subsequent editions.